500 CLEAN JOKES AND HUMOROUS STORIES

and HOW TO TELL THEM

Rusty Wright &
Linda Raney Wright

BARBOUR
PUBLISHING, INC.
Uhrichsville, Ohio

P9-EJH-898

ISBN 1-57748-244-1

Published by Barbour Publishing, Inc., P.O. Box 719, Uhrichsville, Ohio 44683 http://www.barbourbooks.com

Member of the
Evangelical Christian
Publishers Association

Printed in the United States of America.

DEDICATION

*To my parents, Bill and Jean Wright,
and my grandmother, Virginia Bilderback,
who helped me learn the value of humor.*
—R.W.

*To my brother, Bill Raney,
who delights many with his gift of humor.*
—L.R.W.

CONTENTS

FOREWORD

Humor is described in the dictionary as a person's temperament, mood, state of mind, whim, fancy, caprice comicality, and the ability to appreciate or express what is funny, amusing or ludicrous; and a humorist is a person with a well-developed sense of humor. Humor is something which virtually everyone appreciates and enjoys in other people. There is no real substitute for a good laugh which is available to those who have that sense of humor. Dr. Avner Ziv at Tel Aviv University did extensive research and discovered that when humor is used in a presentation, the students not only are more attentive and enjoy the presentation more but will remember what they heard for a longer period of time and recall more of the details.

Humor lightens the burdens of life considerably and enables us to overcome some difficulties in our own lives. Those fortunate enough to have a good sense of humor are less inclined to have ulcers and high blood pressure. Humor relieves tension, breaks the ice, forms common grounds of discussion, brings people closer together, and does a number of other "good things."

Unfortunately, most people are unaware of the fact that a sense of humor can be developed, that a knack for humorous events can be uncovered, that the capacity to relate, reveal, communicate normal events of life in a humorous manner is a skill which can be learned. The exciting thing about *500 Clean Jokes And Humorous Stories* is the fact that it not only has innumerable funny stories and incidents in a variety of settings which will ultimately appeal to every individual, but, more importantly, Rusty and Linda Wright have revealed the proper procedures and techniques for using humor to fit any situation.

Not only does this beautiful book contain a number of stories, jokes and anecdotes, but, far more importantly, it reveals to us exactly how we can adapt humor and tell stories to fit our specific situation. The most beautiful thing Rusty and Linda have done is to emphasize the positive, loving side of humor. There are no negatives, no putdowns, no ethnic jokes of any kind, and, most importantly, the humor is the kind which can be told at the church, school, family picnic, or athletic events. In short, these are stories for everyone to relate to and enjoy. *500 Clean Jokes And Humorous Stories* is one of those rare books which you can pick up for a humorous lift, digest for some serious application, or keep handy for references to fit virtually any kind of speech or presentation situation you're going to encounter.

Even more amazing is that underneath all the fun are some lessons for living that will benefit all. What a delight to know that two fine people such as Rusty and Linda Wright have combined to give us the positive side of humor from the male and female side in such a way that everyone wins because everyone is built up instead of torn down. What a delight, what a pleasure to read, what a lift you'll get from it!

Zig Ziglar

CHAPTER 1

YOU CAN USE HUMOR SUCCESSFULLY!

"BUT I JUST *CAN'T* make people laugh. My humor always bombs. I wish I had the ability to use humor effectively."

Have you ever felt like that? We have heard those statements often lately.

"What do you think of us writing a book about using humor successfully?" we asked many of our friends.

"Another joke book?" some responded.

"No, a book about the importance of humor, as well as how to use it to persuade, entertain, resolve tension, settle arguments and reach other people in a special way. Using the best humorous stories, anecdotes, jokes and illustrations, the book will tell how to put the punch of laughter into your life—in conversations, in relationships, on the job, in social activities, at parties, in public speaking situations and in one-on-one interactions."

"I sure need something like that," they said. "I never can make people laugh. . .or even smile." Others said, "I could use some humor to ease the tensions I'm experiencing." Those who have had success with humor said, "Let me know when it comes out. I'm always looking for new material."

Public speakers, salespersons, pastors, teachers, politicians and executives will benefit from this book, because it is packed with helpful instruction in speaking technique and skill. Adding humor in a talk or conversation may result in a better sale, a more receptive audience or a vote.

Parents also will benefit from this book, as will husbands, wives, teenagers, employees and students who realize the value of humor in their day-to-day lives. Consider these composite situations. (Names have been changed to protect the guilty!)

> Joe and his wife, Mary, quarreled about family finances. Joe was a careful budgeter and conservative spender. Mary frequently bought on impulse. Her favorite item to purchase—and, hence, their greatest point of friction—was her new clothes.
>
> One day in December, Mary received a substantial gift of money from a relative. She told Joe about the gift and asked what he would like for Christmas. "A new TV," he replied.
>
> "Why, Joe, I can't see getting you a new TV. You have one already. To buy a second would be a waste of money."
>
> "All right, how about a new dress?" Joe asked, straight-faced. There was a moment of silence. Then they both laughed.
>
> "Size seven?" she asked, sparring for the funniest line.

Sound familiar? We've all been in situations where humor eased the tension. Perhaps it was in a marriage or dating relationship, or on the job.

Maybe you're like Harry, whose employees seemed to be slackening in their work. They were long on enthusiasm, but short on persistence. As more and more projects missed their deadlines, Harry boiled inside. Those lazy bozos, he thought. *What are they trying to do, rob me?*

Meanwhile, his employees became increasingly frustrated. From their perspective, their boss was a slave driver, loading on the work, but not giving them much direction. The pressure mounted, as neither Harry nor his workers communicated their concerns to each other. Finally, Harry realized he needed to say something. He wanted to address the problem without killing their enthusiasm, so he decided to use humor.

After going over a list of additional responsibilities, Harry added, "and when you finish that, I have some cotton for you to pick and heavy stones for you to haul to the pyramids I'm building." They momentarily looked surprised, then laughed. With the tension eased, Harry could bring up the work problems tactfully.

Humor had helped open the door to communication, so they could begin to work out their differences.

OUCH!

"This is going to hurt you more than it hurts me," the father told his child whom he was about to spank for being disobedient.

"Don't do it, Dad," the child exclaimed. "I don't want you to suffer!"

"That's OK. I'm willing to suffer so that you might learn." He proceeded with the spanking, but this tongue-in-cheek exchange helped the relationship at a crisis point.

Are you a parent? A teacher? Maybe you lead a youth group or head a committee or club. Do you ever experience interpersonal tension? Do you wish you could get someone's attention or clearly communicate a point? Humor can help you. It can break the ice, win respect, improve retention and add fun to the process.

Dr. Nelson Bell, father of Ruth Bell Graham (Mrs. Billy

11

Graham), served as a medical missionary in China for many years before the Communist takeover. Living, working and relating in a foreign culture brought with it many opportunities for misunderstanding and many pressures on his family. Dr. Bell's humor often eased the tensions.

For example, sometimes at dinner, he recited gory medical details of the day, until every family member was laughing at his incredulous lack of propriety. To help keep his family fun-oriented, he built a swimming pool out of bricks and laid out his own golf course, inserting cans into the ground for the holes.

And he had a knack for telling stories. One of his favorites concerned tennis. On a broiling July day, he and an associate were playing a strenuous game of singles. Sweat covered their faces. A Chinese gentleman, hands folded in the sleeves of his gown, watched with amusement and finally asked, "Honorable sirs, could you not hire coolies to hit that ball for you?"[1]

BUT I'M NOT FUNNY

"But I don't have a knack for telling stories! My jokes always bomb. I wish I *could* use humor effectively."

Do you ever feel that way? Then read on! You *can* cultivate and develop a sense of humor. You can *learn* to make people laugh. To begin, practice reading aloud the following quotes. Then read them to your friends.

Many have experienced the confusion that follows a traffic accident and have tried to summarize what happened, in a few words or less, on insurance or accident forms. The following quotes were taken from such forms and eventually were published in a Toronto Sunday newspaper, July 26, 1977:

12

◆ Coming home, I drove into the wrong house and collided with a tree I don't have.

◆ The other car collided with mine without giving warning of its intentions.

◆ I thought my window was down, but found it was up when I put my hand through it.

◆ I collided with a stationary truck coming the other way.

◆ A truck backed through my windshield into my wife's face.

◆ A pedestrian hit me and went under my car.

◆ The guy was all over the road. I had to swerve a number of times before I hit him.

◆ I pulled away from the side of the road, glanced at my mother-in-law, and headed over the embankment.

◆ In my attempt to kill a fly, I drove into a telephone pole.

◆ I had been shopping for plants all day, and was on my way home. As I reached an intersection, a hedge sprang up, obscuring my vision. I did not see the other car.

◆ I had been driving my car for forty years when I fell asleep at the wheel and had an accident.

I was on my way to the doctor's with rear end
trouble when my universal joint gave way,
causing me to have an accident.

To avoid hitting the bumper of the car in front, I
struck the pedestrian.

As I approached the intersection, a stop sign
appeared in a place where no stop sign had
ever appeared before. I was unable to stop in
time to avoid the accident.

My car was legally parked as it backed into the
other vehicle.

An invisible car came out of nowhere, struck my
vehicle, and vanished.

I told the police that I was not injured, but on
removing my hat, I found that I had a skull
fracture.

◆ I was sure the old fellow would never make it to
the other side of the roadway when I struck
him.

◆ The pedestrian had no idea which way to go, so I
ran over him.

◆ The indirect cause of this accident was a little
guy in a small car with a big mouth.

I was thrown from my car as it left the road. I
was later found in a ditch by some stray cows.

- ◆ The telephone pole was approaching fast. I was attempting to swerve out of its path when it struck my front end.

- ◆ I was unable to stop in time, and my car crashed into the other vehicle. The driver and passengers then left immediately for a vacation with injuries.

KEYS TO GOOD HUMOR

Successful humor requires at least four main elements: good material (i.e., the joke, humorous story or situation, funny line, etc.); good delivery; a knowledge of your audience; and, undergirding it all, a healthy self-image. Each of these areas involve skills or traits that you can develop.

Do you doubt that you can cultivate good material? This book will teach you to look for the humorous in everyday life. While you're developing your own style of humor, you can borrow other people's jokes. Does your delivery seem less than clever? You can work on timing, diction, facial expressions, animation and self-confidence.

You may feel that you know little about how people think, why they behave as they do, or what gets them laughing. We'll help you analyze your audience so you can predict which stories will win with which groups. Do you feel uncomfortable as a joke-teller? Perhaps you fear failure. We'll look at that important topic: what to do when your joke or humorous insert bombs. We'll also discuss the barriers to a healthy self-image and how to develop a strong view of yourself, whether you are involved one-on-one or as a public speaker.

We're very familiar with those barriers. For many years, Rusty was shy, quiet and reserved. In his youth, he lacked the self-confidence, charisma, spontaneity, and whatever else he thought it took to be a successful humorist.

In college he learned some principles of communication and self-development that helped him turn the corner. Gradually he became a better conversationalist, able to keep things more positive and lively with dates and other friends. In counseling people, he used humor to help relieve tension. Later, in marriage, he began to learn to use it at the appropriate times to defuse potentially explosive situations. (Still learning!) Now, as a public speaker, he considers humor essential for effective communication.

Linda learned to look on the light side as areas of tension in her life cleared up and her self-confidence grew. (She relates these experiences in her book, *Staying On Top When Things Go Wrong*.) She has found that humor is a valuable tool for handling anger, getting people to listen to what she has to say, diverting people from their problems long enough to see the better side of life, and easing people into needed and helpful conversations.

Today, we speak around the world and train professionals to be more effective communicators. We are privileged to be able to pass on to these folks—and to you—what our mentors shared with us. These principles have worked for us and can work for you, too.

We don't offer a money-back guarantee with this book. (We're not that dumb!) Nor do we promise that you'll soon put Johnny Carson or Bob Hope out of their jobs. (Of course, who knows? You may!)

But you will find plenty of tips on how to use humor. If you are a shy and dubious novice, you'll learn practical ways to get laughs. If you are a seasoned professional jokester, you'll find juicy tidbits to help sharpen your skills. Best of all, you'll find plenty of good stories to tickle your ribs.

A WORD OF CAUTION

One word of caution: there can be weariness in many jokes. Have you ever been at a party or with friends, and a roaring joke session is in progress? You feel like singing, "I could have laughed all night, I could have laughed all night. . .and still have begged for more." Then, for some unknown reason, the laughter begins to dwindle with each successive joke. Perhaps the jokes diminish in quality. Or maybe the audience is simply tired and laughed out. In such a situation, even your million-dollar zingers won't raise a chortle. (A wise humorist recognizes this as a time to stop and save the rest of his or her repertoire for another time, rather than risk boring the audience.)

The same can happen when reading a book of humor. You can laugh through several pages or chapters, then grow numb and lose the enjoyment of subsequent chuckles. Therefore, don't try to read this book in one sitting. If you do, you may become a victim of the "laughter saturation syndrome." A glaze will fall over your eyes. Several minutes—or hours—later you will awaken with a start, amazed that you are on page 110 when your last recollection is of being on page 30. Worst of all (perish the thought), you won't recall any humorous lines from the intervening pages. You may even (heaven forbid!) conclude that pages 30-110 were boring, or that the entire book was boring (how painful it is for us to write these lines). You wouldn't recommend the book to your friends; they wouldn't buy it. They would miss out on all the enjoyment this book offers and (sniff!) it wouldn't become a best-seller.

So shoot for a chapter or two per day. You'll enjoy it a lot more. And as you read, you'll discover the real reason for this book.

THE REAL REASON FOR THIS BOOK

Learning to see the lighter side of everyday life can add sparkle to the routine. It can help you feel better about yourself and open new doors in your relationships with family members, friends, co-workers and acquaintances. Humor can liven up your conversations, allow you to communicate more freely, help illustrate points you want to make. It can help release tension in yourself and others—tension that, if not dissipated, could seriously damage relationships.

But what good humor inevitably communicates is, "I like you. I want you to be happy."

And that's the reason for this book.

CHAPTER 2

~~~~~~~~~~

WHY WE ALL
NEED HUMOR

~~~~~~~~~~

MODERN LIFE IS FULL of tensions, as evidenced by the popularity of psychiatrists, anti-anxiety drugs, exercise spas and meditation techniques. Laughter is one way to deal with pressures. It is not the only way. Nor is it a cure-all. But, properly used, it can provide a release for ourselves and others.

An ancient biblical proverb says, "A joyful heart is good medicine, but a broken spirit dries up the bones."[1] One doctor noted that if you can't take a joke, then you'll have to take medicine.[2] Josh Billings, a famous humorist of the nineteenth century, said, "Anatomically considered, laughing is a sensation of feeling good all over and showing it principally in one spot. If a man cannot laugh, there is a mistake made in putting him together. . . .Genuine laughing is a vent of the soul, the nostrils of the heart, and it is just as necessary for health and happiness as spring water is for a trout."[3]

Humor not only is fun; it also benefits our minds and bodies. . . .all the more reason for us to share humor with others. For anyone interested in communicating effectively, whether with individuals or larger audiences, humor has several advantages:

1. It is one of the most effective forms of emotional communication.

2. It can dissolve tension in people to whom you are relating and can help them relax.

3. It can help you gain and keep your listeners' attention.

4. It can increase your credibility and help you come across as a real person.

5. It can help overcome resistance to points you are trying to make.

6. It can provide needed breaks in a conversation or speech.

7. It can help drive home a point.

Let's consider each of these advantages.

HUMOR IS ONE OF THE MOST EFFECTIVE FORMS OF EMOTIONAL COMMUNICATION

We may think of communication as primarily logical statements with which we send, receive and understand information. Very often, however, successful communication depends not only on the logical content (which is important), but also on the emotional context in which we communicate it.

> One young bridegroom tells of a minor crisis that took place on his honeymoon. His wife was trying to press his trousers with an iron they had received as a wedding gift. The iron

burned a hole, and part of his new trousers went up in smoke. The bride was in tears as she explained to her husband what had happened. "That's OK, sweetheart," he responded. "Let's be thankful that my leg wasn't in those trousers!"[4]

If the groom had said, "That's OK, sweetheart, don't worry about it," that certainly would have helped. But his humorous interjection about the leg in the trousers lightened the mood even more and probably lifted the spirits of his disconsolate bride.

In communication between you and another individual, whether that person is alone or in a crowd, three important factors are at work. The ancient Greeks called these *ethos, logos and pathos.* To communicate successfully, you should understand and develop all three.

Ethos is your ethical appeal. Do you come across as reliable? Before your listener will absorb what you say, he or she wants to know, "Can I trust you?"

Logos refers to your logical appeal, to whether or not what you say makes sense. Your audience wonders, "Do you have anything to say? Can you logically and persuasively make your point?"

Pathos is your emotional appeal. It involves the emotional climate you create while you communicate. Your listener asks, "Do you care about me?" and, "How do I feel when I listen to you?"

Consider how these three factors were at work in the above anecdote. We can assume that sufficient ethos existed, so that the wife believed she could trust her husband. The logos, or logical content, of the husband's response came in the phrase "That's OK, sweetheart." The husband was telling her not to worry, that mistakes happen,

21

that he was not angry. He communicated the pathos, or emotional content, in two ways. He called her "sweetheart," implying that he still loved her, and he used the line about his leg to add emotional warmth, as well as levity.

Humor can enhance pathos. It can communicate that you care enough about people to bring happiness into their lives. It can help open listeners' minds so they will be willing to hear what you say. One reason humor is so effective in this regard is that. . .

HUMOR CAN DISSOLVE TENSION AND HELP RELAX PEOPLE

Dwight D. Eisenhower once observed, "Laughter can relieve tension, soothe the pain of disappointment and strengthen the spirit for the formidable tasks that always lie ahead."[5]

By providing a release from tension and anger, laughter actually can help improve one's health. It is an established scientific fact that "worries, tensions, angers, and fears check the natural flow of digestive juices into the stomach."[6] A doctor at the famous Mayo Clinic related the case of a young man "whose food had digested not one bit in six hours" because of a political dispute in the club of which he was a member.[7] Laughter helps the body by removing or temporarily diverting those impulses that can injure health.

Dr. James J. Walsh, in his book *Laughter and Health*, maintains that laughter provides a much needed massaging of the lungs, heart, liver, pancreas and intestines. He says, "The great majority of people, especially after middle life, do not laugh nearly enough for the good of their hearts."[8]

Everyone needs release from tension. The individuals with whom you converse or the audiences to whom you speak bring with them an assortment of worries, pressures, fears, anxieties and other ailments, psychological and physical. If they remain uptight, they will be less likely to absorb or enjoy what you say.

Here are some stories that can help dissolve tension. The first two will be appreciated especially by married couples.

One husband remarked. . .

> People ask us the secret of our long marriage. It's really quite simple. Two evenings a week we take time to go out to a restaurant. A quiet dinner, soft music, some candlelight, a slow walk home. (Pause) She goes Tuesdays; I go Fridays.[9]

Or, from a wife's viewpoint. . .

> One couple's peaceful marriage was well-known in town for years. When they celebrated their fiftieth wedding anniversary, a newspaper reporter asked the secret of their domestic tranquility.
>
> "Well," the wife explained, "it dates back to our honeymoon when we took a pack mule trip to the bottom of the Grand Canyon. Shortly after we started down, my husband's mule stumbled. Joe took him by the ears, shook him vigorously, and said, 'That's once.' We continued a bit farther and the mule stumbled again. My husband took him by the ears, shook him even more vigorously, and said, 'That's twice.' We had hardly gone half a mile when the mule stumbled a third time. Immediately my husband pulled a revolver from his pocket and shot him. When I began to protest his cruel and

insensitive treatment of the animal, he suddenly grabbed me by the ears, shook me vigorously and said, 'That's once.' "[10]

An exaggeration like this can be well accepted since everyone knows this never really happened. In telling stories like these, though, be careful not to make them seem vindictive (especially considering today's wife abuse problems). Nearly every married couple has had spats that can be spoofed with tongue in check, but when marital discord is pictured as the norm, the stories cease to be uplifting and can become cynical. If used properly, however, stories like these can help release tension, especially the tensions with which many in the audience may be struggling.

Here's one that you might use when you speak about tension. . .or airplanes. . .or planning. . .or a host of other topics.

Pilot: "Pilot to tower. . .pilot to tower. . .we're four hundred miles from land, eight hundred feet high and running out of fuel. . .please instruct. . .over."

Tower: "Tower to pilot. . .tower to pilot. . . repeat after me. . .'Our Father, who art in heaven. . .' "

Yes, humor can help release tension. Perhaps at least partly for that reason. . .

HUMOR CAN HELP YOU GAIN AND KEEP YOUR LISTENERS' ATTENTION

Nothing works like a humorous anecdote at the beginning of a conversation or speech to help you gain attention.

People like to hear stories. In fact, some listeners will tune in only during your stories! A funny opening to a speech not only will help you gain people's ears, but it also will help keep them alert. If they like your anecdote, they may listen carefully to the rest of your speech, for fear they might miss something good. If you are wise, you will reward them with more tidbits along the way.

Let's say you are speaking on a topic about which you know the audience holds a wide variety of opinions, and you expect many to disagree with your point of view. To gain attention and help loosen them up, you might want to open with a story like this:

> A very small, mousy man was hired as a bartender in the Old West. The saloon owner advised him, "If you ever hear that Big John is coming to town, drop everything and run for your life." The bartender worked for six months with no problems.
>
> Then one day a cowboy rushed in shouting, "Big John's a-comin'!" In his hurry to get out, he knocked the small bartender to the floor. Before the bartender could recover, in came a giant of a man with a black, bushy beard. He rode in through the swinging doors on the back of a buffalo, using a rattlesnake for a whip. The man tore the doors off their hinges, knocked over tables, and slung the rattlesnake into the corner. "Gimme a drink," he yelled as he split the bar in half with a pound of his massive fist. The bartender nervously pushed a bottle toward the man. He bit off the top of the glass bottle with his teeth, chugged the contents in one gulp and turned to leave.

Realizing that the man wasn't hurting anyone, the bartender asked if he'd like another
drink. "Ain't got no time," the man roared.
"Big John's a-comin' to town."[11]

You can enhance the effect by adding something like,
"You know, as I drove here tonight, I wondered what kind
of reception my speech would have with you folks. I
suppose I felt a little like that bartender. . .apprehensive
about the situation. But now that I'm here, I see that
you're a likable bunch and I'm sure we'll have a really
good time."

Here's another good icebreaker. You'd probably want
to tell it in a series of several short openers.

The sad, quiet lady with large eyes sat in the
psychiatrist's office while the kind doctor
gently asked her why her family wanted her
behind lock and key.
"Now, tell me," he said, "what is your
trouble?"
"It's just that. . .just that. . .well, doctor,
it's just that I'm so fond of pancakes."
"Oh," the doctor replied, "is that all?
Why, I'm quite fond of pancakes myself."
"Oh, doctor, really?" the lady said excitedly. "Then you must come over to our house.
I have got trunks and trunks full of them."[12]

You also could use this story to point out that things are
not always what they seem to be. Or perhaps to illustrate
that moderation is a virtue, or that "it all depends on your
point of view."

If you ever travel, have traveled or will travel, you

might want to share the following story at a party or in a speech.

> A tourist was vacationing on the sunny and
> hot Mediterranean island of Malta. He was
> appalled by the chaotic traffic. Cars and buses
> were darting every which way with no appar-
> ent order. The tourist asked his hotelkeeper
> why it was so disorderly.
> "Well," the hotelkeeper replied, "in some
> countries they drive on the right side of the
> road; in others they drive on the left. Here, we
> drive in the shade."[13]

Humor helps gain and keep attention, but it also aids communication in another important way:

HUMOR CAN INCREASE YOUR
CREDIBILITY AND HELP YOU
COME ACROSS AS A REAL PERSON

Whether we are listening to a friend, an acquaintance or a speaker who we've never heard before, we all appreciate sincerity. Sincerity relates to ethos (credibility) and helps a listener decide, "Yes, I can trust you." You know that you're sincere, but you may need to convince your audience. Humor can accomplish this by dissolving barriers. It can help you show that you are relaxed and approachable, rather than stuffy; you can have a good time with your listeners. It can help them like you. And, if you can tell a story that pokes a little fun at yourself, you can go a step further in appearing real.

When we speak, write or talk to individuals about love, sex and marriage, we often share the following episode from our personal lives. This simple illustration helps point out the value of unconditional love. . .love that loves regardless of how the other person responds. Here is how Rusty tells the story:

> Shortly after we were married, I learned that Linda, my wife, was allergic to aerosol sprays; they irritated her lungs. I found this out on our honeymoon—on the first night— when she announced, "Your spray deodorant is killing me!" Now, I had used spray deodorant for years, and I wasn't about to switch. So I tried some alternatives.
>
> First, I closed the bathroom door, but do you know what she claimed? She said the fumes came under the door and into the bedroom. Can you believe that? I tried putting a towel under the door, but that didn't help either because I had to open the door to leave.
>
> We travel a lot and stay in motels, and I began to envision what might happen. I could get up very early and tiptoe outside to put on my deodorant while no one was looking! But we travel in the winter, too, and it gets pretty cold outside! I would be embarrassed to be found with my arms frozen in an upward position.
>
> Finally I decided it was better to switch than to fight, so I changed to stick deodorant . . .unconditional love in action!

You also can use humorous stories about others to help open the door for sharing about yourself. Let's say you want to talk about something that aggravated you. You can start with, "Boy, did that (person, event, etc.) ever get me ticked off! In fact, it reminds me of a story I heard. . ."

Two friends, Bill and Tom, were drinking coffee in an all-night café. They got into a discussion about the difference between irritation, aggravation and frustration. At about 1 A.M., Bill said, "Look, Tom, I'll show you an example of irritation." He went to the pay telephone, put in a coin and dialed a number at random. The phone rang and rang and rang. Finally a sleepy voice at the other end answered. "I'd like to speak to Jones," Bill said. "There's no one here named Jones," the disgruntled man replied as he hung up. "That," Bill said to Tom, "is a man who is irritated."

An hour later, at 2 A.M., Bill said, "Now I'll show you a man who is aggravated." Again he went to the phone, dialed the same number and let it ring. Eventually the same sleepy voice answered the phone. Bill asked, "May I please speak with Jones?" "There's no one here named Jones," came the angry reply, this time a bit louder as the man slammed down the receiver onto the hook.

An hour later, at 3 A.M., Bill said, "Now, Tom, I'll show you an example of frustration." He went to the phone, dialed the same number and let it ring. When the sleepy man finally answered, Bill said, "Hi, this is Jones. Have there been any calls for me?"

—supplied by Bill Wright

29

You can follow up this story by referring back to your original gripe and saying, "Well, in my situation, I was not only irritated and aggravated—I was downright frustrated!"

Humor not only helps people open up to you as a person; it also can help them be more open to what you say. . .

HUMOR CAN HELP OVERCOME RESISTANCE TO POINTS YOU TRY TO MAKE

Dr. James F. Engel, a widely respected expert in the field of communications, points out that most people resist new ideas or ideas that differ from their own.[14] In fact, we are so resistant that we limit—consciously or subconsciously—the types of information to which we expose ourselves. We usually read, listen to or watch material that we suspect will support our own beliefs. There are exceptions, of course, but most often we are highly selective in our *attention, perception* and *reception*. We may choose not to give our *attention* to new ideas. If we do give our attention, it may be scant at best, and we may not *perceive* the bulk of the content. Even if we pay close attention and try to perceive most of the content, we still may be unwilling or hesitant to *receive* the message—to accept the new point of view and act on it.

These three filters—selective attention, selective perception and selective reception—each represent barriers to effective communication. They can be shields with which your listeners resist the points you try to make. As previously discussed, humor can help penetrate those shields. It can help you gain the listeners' attention so that they will be interested in perceiving what you say. If they like your humor, maybe they'll like you as a person and be more willing to receive your points. Your points still have to be good, mind you! But your humor can help your listeners become increasingly receptive.

To help your listeners drop their shields and listen to your views, you can share one of these stories about people with differences:

> A minister was not very popular with his congregation. Then one Sunday he announced from the pulpit, "The Lord Jesus has told me He has work for me elsewhere and that I am to pick up and move to another church." The congregation rose spontaneously and sang, "What a friend we have in Jesus. . ."[15]

> A tenant complained to his landlord, "The people in the apartment upstairs sure are annoying. Why, last night they stomped and pounded on the floor until midnight."
> "Did they wake you?" the landlord asked.
> "No," the tenant explained. "Fortunately I was up playing my tuba."[16]

As you are involved in communicating, realize that your listeners need variety. Humor helps in this regard, too, for. . .

HUMOR CAN PROVIDE NEEDED BREAKS IN A CONVERSATION OR SPEECH

Josh McDowell, a respected author, traveling lecturer and television personality, also trains other in communication. He advises speakers to try to interject a humorous line or anecdote into their speeches about every seven minutes. (In conversation, the dialogue provides enough variety to keep both parties alert, so you probably don't need to add humor that often.)

Even the most willing and attentive audience can fade with time. Humor provides a change of pace. The period of laughter allows the listeners to shift in their seats, to get the blood and oxygen circulating again, and to feel refreshed. Like a cool drink on a hot day, it can rejuvenate them and motivate them to stay with you.

Often a brief story—even a one-liner—here or there will do the trick. Here are a few you can try:

Sometimes we speak to dating couples about "How to know if you're really in love." A major question on their minds is "what is love?"

> One philosopher defined love as "a feeling you feel you're going to feel when you have a feeling you feel you haven't felt before!"

Married couples might appreciate the next one. It happens in January. . .

◆ The Super Bowl was over. The frantic fan turned off his TV set with a sigh, looked around the room—and discovered his wife had left him in November.[17]

◆ One workaholic businessman had a sign in his office that read: "Thank God it's Monday."

That last line usually draws laughs from high achievers, who can identify with the workaholic. Once, though, when Rusty delivered that line to a group of Miami

32

Dolphin football players, it drew only blank stares. For a moment, he didn't understand. Certainly these men were high achievers. Then he realized that they do "Thank God it's Monday," for Monday is usually their day off after a game. He told them he understood, and they all had a good laugh as *he* got the point.

◆ A lawyer sent an overdue bill to a client and attached a note that read, "This bill is one year old."

In the return mail, the lawyer received his bill back. To it was clipped another note: "Happy birthday."[18]

◆ A gorilla walked into a drugstore and ordered a $1.50 chocolate sundae. He put a ten dollar bill on the counter to pay for it. The clerk thought, *What can a gorilla know about money?* So he gave the gorilla a single dollar bill in change.

As he did, the clerk said, "You know, we don't get too many gorillas in here."

"No wonder," the gorilla replied, "at nine dollars a sundae."[19]

Often the same humor that provides a break can communicate a lesson, for. . .

HUMOR CAN HELP DRIVE HOME A POINT

One experienced speaker says he tells humorous stories that have a specific point. Then, while people's mouths are open wide with laughter, he pours down large doses of truth.[20]

Here's a good story that can drive home the point that your listeners should be open-minded.

> Perhaps you've heard of the man who thought he was dead, when in reality he was very much alive. His delusion became such a problem that his family finally paid for him to see a psychiatrist. The psychiatrist spent many laborious sessions trying to convince the man he was still alive. Nothing seemed to work.
>
> Finally the doctor tried one last approach. He took out his medical books and proceeded to show the patient that dead men don't bleed. After hours of tedious study, the patient seemed convinced that dead men don't bleed.
>
> "Do you now agree that dead men don't bleed?" the doctor asked.
>
> "Yes, I do," the patient replied.
>
> "Very well, then," the doctor said. He took out a pin and pricked the patient's finger. Out came a trickle of blood. The doctor asked, "What does *that* tell you?"
>
> "Oh my goodness!" the patient exclaimed as he stared incredulously at his finger. "Dead men *do* bleed!!"

If you are speaking on a controversial subject, you might introduce the above story by saying, "Before we begin, I'd like to ask you to please attempt to keep an open mind about this topic. All too often people approach a subject like this with personal assumptions that predetermine their conclusions. Perhaps you've heard of the man who thought he was dead. . . ."

Above all, do not say, "Perhaps you've heard the joke (or the 'one') about the man who thought he was dead. . . ." If you do, you alert your listeners that a joke will follow. This can raise their defenses and spoil the effect. They may think, "I dare you to try to make me laugh." It is better to move into the story more naturally and let the audience enjoy the punch.

You can follow up the story with, "All that is to say that we need to be willing to examine the facts with an open mind." With a brief story and comment, you have illustrated an important point. You also have gained your listeners' attention, entertained them and (hopefully) helped them become open to considering your point of view.

To wrap up this chapter, we'll include one of our favorites that allows us to have a little fun as we make a point. You'll notice that this one also lends itself well to acting out with gestures and pantomime.

When Billy was little, he was a real demon. One day he came home from elementary school and didn't realize that the pastor was inside talking with his parents. Without going into the house, he went around to the back-yard to play. Suddenly, he spotted a big, ugly, hairy rat under a bush.

Billy thought, *Boy, my mom and dad would be so proud of me if I killed that rat!* So he grabbed his baseball bat, tiptoed up behind the rat, raised the bat over his head and . . .*Whap!* He hit the rat with the bat. Then he stepped on it and smashed it with his foot, picked it up and bashed it against a tree, ran it through with his switchblade and killed it.

Little Billy wanted his folks to see what

he had done, so he picked up the bloody rat and raced inside, still not realizing the minister was there. With great excitement he exclaimed, "Mom! Dad! Look at this rat I just killed. You would've been so proud of me. I clubbed it over the head with my baseball bat. Then I stepped on it and smashed it with my foot, picked it up and bashed it against the tree, ran it through with my knife and. . ."

Just then Billy looked up and saw the preacher. With a pious demeanor he held up the rat by its tail and with a solemn voice said, ". . .and then the Lord called him home!"

CHAPTER 3

~~~~~~~~~

SOME KEYS TO NATURAL ONE-ON-ONE HUMOR

~~~~~~~~~

WE PROMISED THAT this book would help not only speakers and entertainers, but also the typical person in everyday situations. Actually, the principles woven throughout each chapter relate to both group and one-on-one situations. Even if you speak primarily to larger audiences, you can benefit from these principles, because to know what makes a group of people laugh, you must understand the individual response.

We don't want anyone to miss the application of these principles to everyday life, so we will focus on two essentials for humor with individuals: cultivating humor in one-on-one or small group situations (addressed in this chapter), and developing spontaneity in humor (covered in chapter 4).

ONE-ON-ONE

Why is one-on-one humor important? For one thing, it helps you appear approachable. People may fear that if they open up to you with a concern, you will judge them. Relating to the lighter sides of certain subjects can help alleviate their fears by communicating that you are tolerant and nonjudgmental.

Individual humor also can help resolve resentment or bitterness. Though not intended as a panacea or an excuse for avoiding necessary confrontation, it can allow two people to get problems off their chests with a minimum of harm.

And one-on-one humor can help people relax about their problems and failures, and gain a fresh perspective on life. Sometimes people feel so overwhelmed that they prefer to be around someone who sees the lighter side.

Of course, one shouldn't try to be funny all the time. Comedian Jonathan Winters says that even he doesn't feel constant pressure to be a barrel of laughs. "It's like a football player," Winters says. "When he comes into a party, he doesn't have to run the length of the room."[1]

At times, humor is inappropriate. A biblical proverb says, "Being happy-go-lucky around a person whose heart is heavy is as bad as stealing his jacket in cold weather, or rubbing salt in his wounds."[2] Another adage says, "Rejoice with those who rejoice, and weep with those who weep."[3]

A German proverb also addresses inappropriate humor: "One shows his character by what he laughs at." People like to be taken seriously, yet they want their mistakes and failures to be taken lightly. Also, many people are insecure about what to laugh at, so the jokester may embarrass, rather than win, the other person.

In deciding when to use humor, consider why you want someone to laugh. Are you trying to encourage and cheer up the person? Or are you doing it to make *you* happier? If you insist that people always laugh, you may even be using humor as an escape, and your listeners probably will feel uncomfortable.

Perhaps the best rule on appropriateness in humor is that love must temper laughter. When you keep that rule, you and your listeners can benefit from your joviality.

PARENT-CHILD

Now consider several categories of situations where one-on-one humor can be appropriate. First, the parent-child relationship.

Parents will do well to integrate humor into family life from early on. Instilling values, building self-esteem, developing abilities in children—these are all important. But having fun with them is an excellent way to maintain rapport and help make the other teachings stick.

The best kind of laughter is built on security and good feelings about ourselves, others and the future. So, in developing humor in any one-on-one relationship, the individual's underlying needs are as important as the well-timed, well-orchestrated joke or story. In family relationships, as parents love and care for their children, laughter can become a natural quality of life.

But first, parents must feel secure, as illustrated by the successful woman described in Proverbs. This careful planner and hard worker not only is secure in her relationship with her loving husband, but we presume that she is secure in the knowledge that her God loves her as well. Therefore, she "smiles at the future."[4]

In homes with secure foundations, parents can use laughter to teach some of life's greatest truths. The key principle: when learning is fun, children do not even realize they are learning. Using humor, parents also can divert a young child or teen from a detrimental decision or action.

Including plenty of fun and laughter around the dinner table helps develop bonds and can lessen the discouragement from a difficult day at school. Also, fights among siblings can be eased when children have been trained, by practice and observation, to see the funny side of situations.

One family had each member share a joke one night per week. The only rule: the joke must be uplifting and not put down anyone. Another family played a game of serendipity at the evening meal. The children were asked to relate the thing that was the most fun of all that had happened to them during the day. Naturally this caused each child to focus on those events, as well as to practice telling them.

One wise father, when confronting a child, began by relating a humorous story from his youth that paralleled his child's situation. By getting the child to laugh with him, he could ease into his admonishment.

Laughing and telling stories to one another can divert children from preoccupation with boredom, difficulties or delay. Therefore, parents should keep on hand good humor books, such as Dr. Seuss, Bugs Bunny, Winnie the Pooh and joke books with quips and funny stories.

Of course, humor is not the answer to everything. To be able to stop joking and get down to serious business is as essential to family unity as the right laugh at the right time. But embellishing a home with plenty of spontaneous laughter is one sure way to enhance one-on-one growth and communication.

MARRIAGE
The same holds true for the marital relationship. Linda likes to tell this story about Rusty and our first winter in the mountains.

> We had just moved to Crestine, California, a small mountain community, and were enjoying our first snow-filled season. Yet, as much as we prized the silent white snow viewed from our warm bedroom, it didn't look quite as good after it surrounded and buried our car.
>
> Rusty borrowed a snow shovel and began to dig it out, but he was ill-prepared. His shoes—light brown hush puppies—were more appropriate for a warmer climate. More than

two hours later, he climbed the steps to our cabin and removed his red feet from his drenched shoes. As he did, he announced in near panic, "I can't move my toes!"

We planned our strategy: lukewarm water and gentle rubbing.

After several minutes, the numbness waned and his feet began to respond.

That night Rusty could have sulked over his calamity, or he could have let his wit and humor win over as usual. As he climbed into bed, he lifted his feet to take a good long look. Then, with a satisfied smile, he said, "Ah, toes. It's so good to have toes!"

In our house, many rough spots have been smoothed, fights terminated and hard days brightened because Rusty and I have *learned* to look on the light side. Fun has become a vital part of our lives.[5]

ON-THE-JOB

In the workplace, a different and perhaps more sophisticated use of humor may achieve the same results of unity, communication and personal fulfillment. One of the greatest contributions a boss can make is a liberal donation of humor. It can grease the wheels of progress, lift the spirits and make dreary work seem to fly by.

One office manager was especially adept at using humor to motivate his workers. His office occupied three stories, and the second floor restroom was at the head of the stairs. If an employee left the door open after leaving the restroom, the first thing people saw as they climbed the stairs to the second floor was a toilet staring them in the face. This could be somewhat awkward for the manager if important visitors were in the building, and all the more indelicate if the toilet lid or seat had been left up.

The manager tried and tried to get his employees to remember to shut the door when leaving the restroom, but to no avail. Finally, in a morning staff meeting he said, "I'd like to comment again on a rather sensitive issue—the matter of the door on the second floor bathroom. Please try to remember to close it when you leave the restroom. Few things are uglier as you climb the stairs than the sight of a toilet yawning in your face."

"Yawning" so appropriately described the scene of the open toilet that the entire staff burst out laughing. The manager made his point; rarely was the door left open after that. And to show their boss how much they appreciated his sense of humor, the employees later presented him with a beautifully framed color photo—a stair climber's view of the yawning toilet!

In sales, a light touch of humor at the appropriate point often can be the key that opens the door to a potential buyer. Sometimes door-to-door book salesmen, after detailing to a prospect the benefits of a certain volume, will add, "And besides that, Mrs. Jones, if you run out of uses for it, this book is so big that you can use it as a doorstop."

In negotiating, humor can be a key to success. At the very least, it can preserve rapport in delicate situations. Jonathan Winters tells of negotiations involving his autobiography. Several publishers he approached about his book wanted to be sure he included details of any scandalous relationships. Winters had decided not to tell all. As he describes it, "Five different publishers asked me, 'What about your affairs?' I said, 'They are in order.' "[6]

One schoolteacher we know, Karen Yerian, wanted to ensure that her tenth-grade students knew that she expected them to show up for a test the next day. She wanted to be firm, but not heavy-handed. So she told them, "Remember that our big test is tomorrow. It's very important that you all be here. The only excuse I'll accept is a note from your mortician."

A San Francisco lawyer, early in his career, found himself defending in the courtroom some accused thieves. "Who's here for these men?" the judge inquired. "I'm representing the bandits, Your Honor," the lawyer yelled out.[7] Far from being miffed, the judge later commented to him about the value of using humor as he had to gain attention and even shared another idea on how to do it effectively in the courtroom.

Humor in individual interaction—it works. The same principles that work for parents, spouses, employers, employees, salespersons, negotiators, teachers, pastors and lawyers also work for doctors, dentists, waiters and waitresses, clerks, neighbors and dating couples.

This book elaborates on principles of humor that can apply to nearly any area of life. Perhaps one of the most important ways we can exercise humor is in relation to ourselves. One pundit said, "Laugh at yourself, before anyone else can." As we learn to perceive the ironies or twists in our own lives—and laugh at them—we can cultivate a spontaneity that will carry over into other relationships. The next chapter provides some glimpses of people laughing at themselves and some tips on cultivating spontaneity in humor.

CHAPTER 4

~~~~~~~~

SPONTANEITY
IN HUMOR

~~~~~~~~

DID YOU ENJOY YOUR TRIP?

> A young man was invited to a party so that
> he could meet some important people.
> Naturally, he was on his best behavior. As he
> entered the room where the guests had gath-
> ered, he caught his toe on the edge of the
> rug. Although he made frantic efforts to
> regain his balance, he landed sprawled on the
> floor in front of everyone. As he picked him-
> self up he said, "I also do card tricks." This
> little joke gained the admiration of all present
> and turned what could have been an embar-
> rassing or awkward social situation into a
> personal victory.[1]

Learning to laugh at ourselves and perceive the humorous twists in our lives can be a great benefit. Though we
don't always do this spontaneously, we often can relate
funny situations later. We enjoy sharing with others our own
embarrassing moments. For Linda, it took place in 1972. As
she relates it. . .

> I was working in Dallas for the press rela-
> tions coordinator of a large conference,

EXPLO '72, which was to bring eighty thousand conferees to Dallas from around the globe. One of my responsibilities was to telephone the speakers to secure biographical information for our printed literature. I had a long list of important speakers to call—professors, theologians, etc.—and when I was unable to reach them, I left messages asking them to return my calls.

At the same time, I developed an acute kidney infection. Since I was new to Dallas, I asked a friend for a reference to a reputable doctor. The doctor could not take my call, so I left a message. Later that day, I received a call.

"Hello, this is Dr. Hook returning your call."

"Oh Dr. Hook," I exclaimed, "I'm so glad you called back. I've had a terrible kidney infection and I don't know what to do." I paused for him to respond, but since he didn't immediately speak, I figured he needed more information.

"You see, it causes pain when I urinate— lots of burning and stinging. . ." I proceeded to relate increasingly private details of my ailment. Then I paused again for his evaluation.

"This is Dr. Hook," the voice said, "Dr. Phil Hook, professor at Dallas Theological Seminary." It was one of the conference speakers, returning my call.

Linda apologized profusely to Dr. Hook, but to this day, we're not sure if he understood what happened. But should such an embarrassing situation ever arise again, Linda can

46

relate the "Dr. Hook" story on the spot, and she and the others involved can have a good laugh. You can do the same.

PARDON ME. . .
IS MY SLIP SHOWING?

Rusty's most embarrassing moment came in 1979 and also can be applied in similar situations. As he tells it. . .

Linda and I were at a national booksellers' convention in St. Louis. We had just published a book about love, sex and marriage, entitled *Dynamic Sex*. It is very discreet, but we still took some good-natured kidding from our friends. Our publisher had invited us to participate in various promotional events, including a reception at a fancy hotel. Many of the leaders of the organization were there along with well-known authors. The reception lasted most of the evening, with booksellers filing through to meet authors and receive complimentary autographed books. After the crowds left, the participants gathered in the same ballroom for some friendly conversation.

For a brief moment, I went to a corner of the room to tend to a matter. When I returned, the group was standing in an informal circle. I walked up behind Linda and began to gently massage her shoulders. It had been a long, tiring day, and I knew she would appreciate my affectionate touch. I was about to put my hands around the front of her waist and pull her close when I looked across the circle and saw. . .Linda! I was about to put my arms around the wrong woman! She was about Linda's height and had the same color of hair and dress. As I blushed in a state of shock, I said to the startled group, "Oh well, what did you expect from somebody who writes a book called *Dynamic Sex*?" Fortunately they—and the kind woman who wondered why I was massaging her shoulders—laughed with me.

SPONTANEOUS HUMOR

Spontaneous humor has all the ingredients of basic humor, yet it possesses the most refreshing twist. It is unplanned, drawing upon only the elements of the moment. As such, it can be the funniest and most tension-releasing of all forms of humor, for it often captures people at their best and delights those who are involved.

Linda's brother Bill is one of the wittiest people we know. His dry, unattached observation of a subject can amuse even the most sour disposition. He catches us all by surprise now and then with the most unexpected statements.

One evening Bill and Linda were eating at a restaurant when several of Bill's friends showed up.

"Hey," one of Bill's friends said. "You two look a lot alike."

"Oh, we're alike in a lot of ways," Linda replied.

"Yeah? Like what?" he asked.

"Well," Linda said, "we have the same personality, the same messiness, same sense of humor, same interests."

At that, Bill sat up straight, turned his head and looked at everyone in a way that commanded their attention. He paused just long enough to cause suspense over what he might say. Then in a slow, deliberate way, he announced,

48

"Same emotional problems!"

Like most humor, spontaneous humor is a developed art. It is not achieved by practicing a certain story or joke, but rather by practicing the elements of humor itself.

One such element of spontaneous humor is exaggeration. Almost any situation can elicit a humorous response if it is exaggerated to the absurd. Erma Bombeck is a great master of this art. Once, while explaining the latest diet fad, she reported that the problem with most people was not that they were too fat but that they were too short. To prove this, she revealed that studies had been conducted with rats.

"Sure enough," she reported. "They found that rats wearing wedgies looked thinner than rats wearing loafers."

This kind of exaggeration can be used on the spur of the moment. One such moment occurred when Linda was trying to explain to some friends of ours how much she excelled Rusty at following directions:

> The other day friends gave me directions to their home. The directions read, "Go west two miles. Turn right for two blocks. Go under a bridge. Bear left at the big oak. Cut a sharp left. Go forty feet. Bear right forty degrees. Cut through the narrow ravine. Climb hill. Turn into the sixth driveway on right. Turn east. Proceed down hill to small lake. Park car. Walk three miles straight left." I arrived in a record six minutes.
>
> Now with Rusty, you must always give him simple, short instructions. Even then, the odds are against his arriving on time. . .or at all! Just last week friends neatly printed directions to their home in our California town. The instructions read, "Go three blocks east

from your driveway. Turn right at the first stop sign. House is third on the left."

Days passed and I didn't hear from Rusty. Finally I got a call from Dallas, 1,200 miles from home. "Could you send me money to get home?" Rusty wanted to know.

Linda actually did two things in relating this story. In a healthy way, she handled her irritation over a small marriage difference, and she entertained her friends.

LET'S DO THE TWIST

Besides exaggeration, another element of spontaneous humor is the twist. One evening we were discussing the subject of who are better, men or women.

"I think I can finally agree that women are as good as men," Rusty said wryly after some discussion of the matter.

"Better," Linda offered.

"Same," Rusty replied.

"Better."

"Same."

"Better."

"Same."

"Better."

"Same."

Rusty then turned to Linda and lightly announced, "Parkay."

Spontaneous humor is not always planned, but may be provided by the unsuspecting in a conversation and camped on by the humorist.

Such was a case of one of our friends. Kathy is very opinionated and seems to tackle every controversial problem that comes across her path, often overcoming her oppo-

50

nent. In so doing, she can arouse fury from her opposition as she demolishes their views.

Kathy told us of a recent experience. She was lunching with a friend who was explaining a personal problem. As she often does, Kathy succinctly related back and clarified the problem for the woman.

The friend, obviously helped by this clearer and briefer communication of her problem, remarked, "Kathy, you have the most interesting way of capsizing things."

The woman meant to say "capsulizing" instead of "capsizing." But in truth, she had hit the nail on the head.

Kathy often uses this spontaneous remark to disarm her opponents. After telling the story she adds, "I don't really mean to capsize things, but maybe by capsulizing efficiently we can come to some better agreements." The story relieves tension by giving her adversaries a glimpse of Kathy's own objectivity about herself.

In their book *The Laughter Prescription,* Dr. Laurence Peter and comedian Bill Dana point out that incongruity is central to humor. Look for the incongruous, they advise, that which "does not fit the generally accepted mold—something out of context, unexpected, illogical, exaggerated, unreasonable, inappropriate."[2] One way to be funny, they suggest, is to rework familiar material—old sayings, television commercials, etc. For instance, one old proverb can become, "A bird in the hand is finger-licking good." Another reworks to "A stitch in time saves—embarrassment." A few other gems from Peter and Dana:

◆ When the boss tells a joke, he who laughs lasts.

◆ Television was better in the old days—before it had pictures and sound.

And one they include from W. C. Fields:

◆ "I am free of all prejudices. I hate everybody
   equally."[3]

One high school teacher relates an incident in which spontaneous humor helped relieve tension in a job setting.

> It was halfway through the school year and
> the principal was lecturing us at a faculty
> meeting. He presented a painful list of all
> our failures, flaws and shortcomings. The
> list of transgressions seemed endless. We all
> felt quite tense. Then he announced that the
> science club was sponsoring a blood drive
> and that, to promote faculty involvement, he
> would donate the first pint of blood.
>   An anxious voice from the rear of the
> room asked, "Whose?" Loud laughter
> ensued.[4]

A new bride used spontaneous humor to communicate an important point to her groom:

> The newlyweds were grocery shopping, she
> with a carefully prepared list and he more
> haphazardly. The bride selected some tomato
> paste; he grabbed pickled watermelon slices.
> She gathered the usual assortment of vegeta-
> bles; he put kumquats into the cart. She chose
> a can of coffee; he took some imported tea.
> With each of his selections, the bride looked
> increasingly dismayed. When she added lun-
> cheon meat and he walked over with several

52

jars of caviar, she knew she had to speak up. Somewhat desperately she inquired, "Are you shopping *with* me or *against* me?"[5]

AN EXPERIMENT

Can you learn to be spontaneous in your humor? For some it comes more naturally than for others, but don't be discouraged if you are one of the others. You can cultivate spontaneity by learning to observe the incongruous in everyday life. Then it is much easier to drop in a humorous word.

Rusty's freshman English professor once said, "Some people have an incredible fear of a blank sheet of paper." So-called writer's block is common and can affect the aspiring jokester as well, but it need not.

Try an experiment. Look for one humorous event or situation each day for two weeks. Maybe it will be an incident at work, or perhaps something a family member does or a story you see in the newspaper. No, reading a joke a day from this book doesn't count, beneficial though that may be. Try to discover something funny yourself. Then share it with someone. Consider beginning a serendipity game at the evening meal, as described in chapter 3.

Like any skill, seeing humor improves with practice. The rest of this book will give you additional tips on cultivating humor—why people laugh, where to find good material, how to adapt it, how to know your listeners, how to relate your stories, even what to do when your story falls flat. But you must start with a desire to pursue humor.

The story is told that during the early days of the American Republic, Benjamin Franklin often spoke about the United States Constitution. After one stirring speech, an uncouth fellow rose and walked toward the platform.

"Aw, those words don't mean nothing at all," the man argued. "Where's all this happiness you say the Constitution guarantees?"

"My friend," Ben replied, "the Constitution only guarantees the American people the right to *pursue* happiness. You have to catch it yourself!"[6]

Interested in pursuing—and catching—some humor and happiness? Read on. . .

CHAPTER 5

~~~~~~~~

WHY FUNNY STORIES
ARE FUNNY

~~~~~~~~

LINDA RECALLS. . .

When I was attending the University of
California at Berkeley, one of the most popular courses was, oddly enough, "A Survey of
the New Testament." It was filled every
semester. The reason it was so popular is that
the professor never gave homework. We
never had to take tests, write papers or read
books. Our entire grade for the course
depended on the final exam, which was
always one question, and it was always the
same: "Discuss the wanderings and missionary journeys of the apostle Paul." We figured
that if we could trace Paul's journeys and
explain what he had done at the various loca-
tions, we could earn an *A* with little trouble.

As you might imagine, most of the var-
sity football squad was enrolled in this course.
A middle linebacker named Meathead used to
sit beside me. Meathead didn't have a whole
lot going for him intellectually, so he asked
me to help him prepare for the final. All
semester we studied Paul's journeys.

On the day of the final exam, I arrived at

the auditorium, which was nearly full, and took a seat in the rear beside Meathead. The bell rang and the professor began to distribute the mimeographed exam questions from the front of the class. I thought, *That's kind of dumb. Everyone knows the question and* he *knows that we know it.* But as the papers were handed out, a moan began to come toward the back of the room. When I received my paper, I realized why: the prof had changed the question. Instead of "Discuss Paul's journeys," the question was, "Criticize the Sermon on the Mount."

Well, I just about folded over and died in a pile right there! I knew very little about the Sermon on the Mount. Students in the front of the class already were taking up their bluebooks (examination booklets), throwing them on the prof's desk, and storming out of the room without writing an answer. In ten minutes, the room was empty with the exception of Meathead and me. I looked at Meathead and couldn't believe what I saw. He was writing furiously, already on the second page.

I took up my empty bluebook and waited in the back of the room. Meathead kept writing. I left and returned halfway through the three-hour exam. There he was—the only student in the room, sweat pouring off of him as he filled up that bluebook with ink. Finally, the bell rang and the prof called for the test. Meathead walked up, checking over his bluebook, laid it on the prof's desk and staggered to the back of the room completely exhausted.

He was so tired, he couldn't even tell me what he'd written.

We waited for the test to be graded and went up to the front to see his mark. On the desk were two stacks of bluebooks. . .one with all *F*'s; then Meathead's. . .and his had an *A+*! Still not believing what I was seeing, I opened it to see what he had written. This was Meathead's answer:

"Who am I to criticize the Sermon on the Mount? What I'd like to do is discuss the wanderings and missionary journeys of the apostle Paul."

This apocryphal story can break the ice in many situations, and it can be adapted to fit alternate backgrounds. For instance, you could call it an American history course with the usual question being "Discuss General Sherman's Civil War march to the sea" and the new question, "Criticize Lincoln's Gettysburg Address."

WHY DO WE LAUGH?

Why is the "Meathead" story funny? One reason is that it builds on a common experience. People who have studied in high school or college can identify with the anxiety and apprehension involved in preparing for and taking a final exam. The fact that the entire grade for the course hinges on the exam provides an element of tension when the surprise question appears. No one has prepared for it. What will they do? What would I, as a listener, do in that situation? (Even years after graduation, a common dream —or nightmare—involves taking a school exam for which the person is unprepared.)

Tension builds as the speaker paints a picture of the room emptying and Meathead writing furiously. *What could he be writing?* we wonder. *And how could he, supposedly a less-than-bright student, write for three hours when no one else even ventured an attempt?* Meathead's walk to the front of the class to deliver his bluebook, his return to the back of the room in exhaustion, and the revelation that he received an *A+* all help bring the audience's tension and curiosity to a peak. As listeners, we eagerly wait for the speaker to open the bluebook to see what Meathead wrote.

A key ingredient for good humor is tension that can be released quickly. Sometimes that tension already exists, so the speaker can throw in an appropriate line and draw a laugh at once. In other situations, he needs to build the tension as he develops his story, as in the "Meathead" joke. The length and imagery of the story serve to bring the listener's inner tension to a point where it needs release.

The release valve is the final line or lines of the story. They provide the *punch* (hence the expression *punch line*). Notice these two key elements, essential to most punch lines: (1) an unexpected twist; (2) the suddenness with which that twist is introduced. The unexpected twist in this punch line hinges on the word "criticize." The professor probably intended it to mean "analyze." In Meathead's answer, however, it meant "to find fault with." He was saying, "Who am I—a lowly student—to find fault with so elegant a speech as the Sermon on the Mount?"

That bit of honest (or tongue-in-cheek) humility opened the door for him to deliver his prepared essay. That Meathead unintentionally used such a clever approach delights us. That he got an *A+* for doing so delights us even more. That we ascertain in an instant what had happened gives us a bit of personal pleasure (i.e., we are proud of ourselves for getting the joke). All this happening so suddenly provides a quick, explosive release of tension. We laugh and enjoy the story.

THE ESSENCE

There, in a nutshell, is the essence of much successful humor: a commonly understood situation, a build-up of tension and a release triggered by a sudden and unexpected twist.

In analyzing a joke, one risks destroying the humorous effect. Indeed, never analyze any joke for your audience. But this is not only a book *of* humor; it is a book *about* humor: why we laugh and how to make people laugh. So as you read, enjoy the joke, have a good laugh, then read the comments and try to think through what makes people laugh. The aim, after all, is for all of us to become more skillful humorists so we can share the fun with others.

A few additional tips about telling "Meathead." If the people in your audience are not familiar with academic settings, examinations, etc., they probably would not understand the apprehension involved. Nor would they likely catch the subtlety of the punch line. (Note: In this book, the term *audience* refers to whoever is listening to your humor. It could be one person, ten people or ten thousand people.)

Once Rusty told "Meathead" to a group of students from an inner city ghetto. All week he had used it with thousands of students in schools around Atlanta and it proved to be a terrific icebreaker. With this inner city audience, though, it bombed. . .*really* bombed. Not a chuckle. Not a smile. Not even a curved lip or twinkle in the eye.

Fortunately, he had the presence of mind to continue with his speech. Then he tried to figure out what had gone wrong. After all, these were high school students. They studied and took tests. He finally decided that they might have taken offense when Meathead was described as lacking intelligence. They may have received criticism for poor grades or felt that kids from their background were stereotyped as dumb. Thus, they anticipated it being a story that poked fun at slow learners and hence, at them (or at what they may have thought—mistakenly—was his stereotype of them). Their defenses went up and the joke was unsuccessful, even though Meathead was a hero in the end. (Of course, another possible reason is they may not have understood the two meanings of "criticize.")

Though he now omits the "Meathead" joke with such audiences, he has added a follow-up line to help dispel possible criticisms from other audiences. You may find it useful, too. As the laughter dies down, he says, "Meathead wasn't so dumb after all, was he?!!"

Think for a moment about the punch line. When you reach that point, timing is crucial. Practice the entire story—especially the punch line—several times before you tell it. If you move through the punch line too quickly, you may spoil the chance to build tension. With proper timing, however, you can use one last opportunity to heighten the listeners' anticipation and increase the laughter. As we've heard various speakers tell the joke, the best approach seems to be as follows: ". . .and this was Meathead's answer. . .(pause two or three seconds). . .Who am I to criticize the Sermon on the Mount?. . .(Pause two to three seconds). . .What I'd like to do is discuss the wanderings and missionary journeys of the apostle Paul!" Often some of the crowd begins to laugh after, "Who am I to criticize the Sermon on the Mount?" With practice, you can time the next line to build on that laughter and get most everyone laughing at the end.

One final comment before we leave Meathead. You'll note that the story is embellished with some details and phrases that could have been omitted or condensed without diminishing the reader's understanding of the situation. As you read it, you may have felt it a bit too lengthy. Remember, though, that when you are *telling* a story verbally, you sometimes need to include details that help the listeners understand and *feel* the situation. They do not have the advantage of rereading concise phrases to clarify their understanding. They either catch them or they don't. The listeners also need time for tension to build.

Of course, too many details can confuse or bore listeners, while the reader can reread them (if he desires) to increase his understanding. The right balance comes with practice. We have tried, within reason, to write the jokes in this book as one might tell them.

Now let's take a closer look at those three factors that form the essence of good humor: (1) a commonly understood situation; (2) a build-up of tension; and (3) an opportunity to release that tension through the introduction of a sudden and unexpected twist. A comprehensive discussion of all the many and varied theories of humor is beyond the scope of this book. Rather than attempt to present a deep and thorough treatment, we hope to give you a brief but helpful look into what we feel are some of the most important elements of good humor.

A COMMONLY UNDERSTOOD SITUATION

Abraham Lincoln once said, "God must have meant us to laugh. Else He would not have made so many mules, parrots, monkeys and human beings."[1] Indeed, many, many, common situations in life evoke laughter. (Chapters 4 and 6 focus on how to see and develop humor in everyday situations.)

For a story to be humorous, it must involve a situation that is commonly understood by both teller and listener. Sometimes the listener's understanding exists before the joke begins. At other times it becomes evident as the story progresses. Sometimes it surfaces only at the punch line. If the necessary understanding—the commonly understood situation—is not present at the appropriate point, the listener rarely laughs.

Most of us have told jokes that bombed because the listener did not understand some element of the story. Maybe it was about a situation at work and required knowledge of people, places, procedures, etc. Perhaps it was a story about life at sea and the listener was a landlubber. Maybe the humor turned on a certain custom in a foreign country or an unfamiliar foreign word.

If the misunderstanding involves the story's basic scene or setting, the tensions may not build. If it involves the punch line, the element of suddenness and surprise is removed. Instead of the tension exploding, it fizzles. The puzzled listener asks, "What in the world is *that* supposed to mean?" or, "Is everybody going to think I'm an imbecile because I don't get this?" At this point, it rarely helps for the story-teller to explain, "You had to be there." It is better to move on to another subject and learn from the situation.

Much of successful humor involves successful communication. This story illustrates the importance of a common understanding:

◆ *Lost in translation.* Members of a trade-union delegation were touring a factory in an Eastern Bloc country. They looked glum when their union-leader hosts explained through an interpreter that their main task was to ensure that the workers achieved the forecast level of output. When asked what would happen if any workers failed to reach the quota, the reply was, "They would be shot."

The subdued mission returned to the hotel to prepare for a farewell dinner. Then a breathless interpreter arrived. "I have been checking my dictionary," he panted. "I meant 'fired,' not 'shot.' "[2]

◆ Phyllis Diller says she once spent seven hours in a beauty parlor—and that was just for an estimate.[3]

Someone who has never heard of or seen Phyllis Diller will not find this line as amusing as someone who has. They may guess that the "estimate" punch line refers to a less-than-attractive person and laugh slightly. How much funnier it is to someone with a mental picture of the famous comedienne who has made a career out of emphasizing her supposed and self-proclaimed "less-than-attractiveness."

This story also illustrates the importance of common understanding:

The captain of a great ocean liner had begun as a cabin boy years earlier and gradually worked up to his high position. He had become one of the most respected men on the high seas. His assistant, who had served with him for years, observed and emulated his every move. But one thing about the captain puzzled him: every morning the skipper went to his cabin, opened the top drawer of his

desk, took out a small slip of paper, read it
with intense concentration, returned the paper
to his desk and locked the drawer.

After many years, the captain retired and
his assistant took command. The first thing he
did was open that drawer to discover what was
on that slip of paper. The paper had but one
sentence on it: "Port is left; starboard is right."[4]

Someone unfamiliar with nautical jargon might not
immediately catch the punch line. Or perhaps they would
be snagged on the meaning of *skipper* and miss the rest of
the details.

A commonly understood situation is essential to good
humor. It helps create the proper mood for the build-up of
tension and the introduction of the humorous twist. Some
have said that, if the correct mood is created, a joke can
be fashioned on nearly any theme, as the following story
illustrates:

British scholar Samuel Johnson often boasted
that he could spontaneously make a joke on
any subject. "The king," a challenger suggested, for who in that day would dare to jest
about royalty? Johnson's quick response:
"The king is not a subject."[5]

A BUILD-UP OF TENSION

Laughter is associated with a sudden release of tension. Often
it has nothing to do with humor. For example, when Rusty
was a child, his family was flying from Denver to Chicago
aboard a commercial airliner. As they neared Chicago, the
pilot announced that he was having difficulty lowering the

landing gear. He had no way of knowing if the wheels were in place, so he instructed the crew to prepare the passengers for a possible crash. The flight attendants collected all sharp and potentially dangerous objects—including Rusty's grand-mother's dentures—and told the passengers to lean forward, grab their ankles and prepare for an impact. Naturally, ten-sion was high among the passengers as the huge plane ap-proached the runway. When the landing came off smoothly and the jet rolled to a stop, the cabin immediately was filled with spontaneous applause, laughter and tears of joy. The tension suddenly was released. Rusty's grandmother was especially happy to get her dentures back safely!

Consider this situation: Growing up in Miami, Rusty became an avid fan of the Miami Dolphins football team. Even through its first four dismal seasons, Rusty and his family were loyal fans. In 1970, Don Shula became head coach and the team started winning. That year they went to the play-offs. The next year they won the AFC champi-onship and went to the Super Bowl (where they lost to Dallas). In 1972, they won all fourteen regular season games. Only three post-season games lay between them and the Super Bowl trophy.

The first game, against the Cleveland Browns, was close. With about ten minutes left in the fourth quarter, Cleveland took the lead on a touchdown pass. The eighty thousand fans wondered if the perfect season had come to an end. Tension peaked as Earl Morrall, the aging quarter-back, called signals from his own twenty-yard line—eighty yards from victory.

The drive was smooth, highlighted by a long bomb and circus catch by ace receiver Paul Warfield. When running back Jim Kiick lumbered over for the winning touchdown, the stadium exploded. People were jumping, yelling, crying . . .and laughing. They had teetered on the edge of the precipice of defeat and now they were safe. Their tension was released.

Sigmund Freud taught that laughter involved release of repressed energy. He felt that "laughter occurs when repressed energy is freed from its static function of keeping something forbidden under repression and away from consciousness."[6] Dr. Horace M. Kallen, widely-known social psychologist, says that we laugh to remove whatever stands in the way of our feeling of freedom. Life is full of anxieties and tensions, so anything that makes fun of the causes of our tensions gives us a sudden sense of freedom, of liberation. As our tensions are released, we laugh.[7]

Two researchers at the Yale School of Medicine, Dr. Frederick C. Redlich and Professor Jacob Levine, found that an inability to appreciate humor can indicate emotional problems. Usually a person with a well-developed sense of humor has a well-developed personality. In contrast, those who rarely see humor in a joke or cartoon often are emotionally maladjusted, the researchers concluded.[8] Their inability to release tension in socially appropriate ways, such as through laughter, could be either a cause of or a result of their emotional disorders.

Laughter involves a release of tension, so the successful humorist seeks to ensure that sufficient tension exists before he inserts a punch line. Sometimes he can use tension that already exists in his audience.

Once a regional director of a large corporation flew in from the home office to speak to his field representatives at a special conference. He knew that they recently had applied for various summer assignments within the organization and, though it was too early for their requests to have been processed, they were curious about where they would be. So, at the beginning of his speech on an entirely different subject, the regional director broke the ice by casually saying,

"By the way, I have your summer assignments with me." The crowd released a sharp blast of semi-nervous laughter. Nothing was particularly funny about the line, but given the circumstances, it drew a laugh. The speaker had worked with an existing tension.

In other situations, the humorist needs to build tension by creatively developing details. He must paint a picture that arouses curiosity, heightens anticipation and builds inner energy to the point where it seeks release. For example, in the "Meathead" story, we wonder what he could possibly be writing. The "port is left; starboard is right" story builds curiosity by describing the revered captain performing his daily ritual. In that same story we also identify with the assistant's desire to succeed. The story could be embellished with even more details, especially when told verbally, to heighten the tension.

As you read or hear jokes that you enjoy, after you finish laughing, go back over the story to discover what contributed to the build-up of tension. Did the jokester play off of an existing tension in his audience? If so, what was it? How could you do the same in a similar situation or with listeners you encounter?

Or did he or she build tension or curiosity by skillfully using details? In your opinion, were there too many or too few? What emotional need did the jokester tap to produce or release tension? What can you learn from this story to help your own storytelling? To be a successful humorist, work hard to learn to build or use the tension of emotional need and curiosity.

THE RELEASE OF TENSION
The third factor in successful humor is the opportunity to release tension through the introduction of a sudden and

unexpected twist. Sometimes this involves the juxtaposing of two incongruous words or ideas.

Science fiction writer Isaac Asimov is also a dedicated jokester and student of humor. In his *Treasury of Humor,* he comments on the place of the sudden and unexpected twist in one form of humor, the paradox:

> It is the quick flip from sense to no-sense. . .that brings the laugh (all the stronger for the feeling of self-admiration at catching the shift). The greater the subtlety of the sense/ no-sense shift and the greater the ease with which it is caught, the better the laugh.[9]

Comedian Woody Allen often draws laughs with stories about his supposed romantic exploits. He skillfully draws a contrast between the Don Juan image he paints of himself and his mousy appearance. The two images seem incongruous, hence he uses them to his advantage to draw laughs.

Don Knotts gained national fame as a comic during Steve Allen's nighttime television comedy show in the late 1950s and early 1960s. One of his standard parts involved an extremely nervous, jittery man. During a popular "Man on the Street" sketch, Steve interviewed Don, who took the surname Morrison. The exchange went as follows:[10]

STEVE: "Good evening, sir. What is your name?"

DON: (trembling violently) "My name is K.B. Morrison."

STEVE: "And what do you do for a living, Mr. Morrison?"

DON: "I'm a munitions and bomb-disposal expert."

STEVE: "I see. By the way, what do the initials
K.B. stand for?"

DON: "Ka-boom!"

The full impact of the humor of this sketch is best caught
by seeing the nervous Knotts. When he says he is a munitions
and bomb-disposal expert, we half-wonder, half-chuckle at
the incongruity, for such work requires careful, controlled
manipulation in dangerous circumstances. The final line
makes us laugh because it exaggerates his fear, which we all
experience or sense. That such a nervous individual would
have such a delicate job is comical. That he, a supposed
expert in (safe) bomb disposal, would have the name "Ka-
boom!" makes us suspect that most of the bombs he attempts
to dispose of are exploded rather than being disarmed. We,
the listeners, catch this all at once, and we laugh.

Some additional stories to illustrate the use of incongruity:

A press agent set up an audition with a famous
television producer for his client, a talking dog.
The skeptical producer warmed up as the dog
started with a couple of jokes, then followed
with an amusing political satire. The press
agent explained that his client's real desire was
to be a singer. After hearing the dog perform
several songs, the producer was convinced he
had found a gold mine. Suddenly, a huge, ugly
dog burst into the audition studio, snatched up
the little dog by the neck and dashed out the
room. The producer was beside himself and
turned to the press agent, who was putting on
his coat to leave.

"What in the world happened?" the producer asked.

"That was his mother," the press agent answered dejectedly. "She wants him to be a doctor."[11]

This story uses several incongruous factors: a talking and singing dog, a mother dog who has a mind of her own, the possibility of a dog being a doctor, and the possibility of a press agent's dream for a dog's future being thwarted by the desires of another dog.

On the wall outside a university library in Tennessee is a row of hooks with a sign that reads, "For Faculty Members Only." A bit of graffiti was penciled in: "May also be used for hats and coats."[12]

The incongruity, of course, is in the image of faculty members hanging on coat hooks. Here are a few more examples for you to enjoy and analyze:

◆ (A person introducing a speaker who is an author)
   "He has just returned from two years in Europe where he finished his first book. (Pause) He's a very slow reader."

◆ Judge: "Twenty days or two hundred dollars."
   Prisoner: "I'll take the money, Your Honor."

◆ Restaurant patron: "Waiter, this food is awful. I won't eat it! You'd better get the manager."
   Waiter: "It won't do any good, mister; he wouldn't eat it either."[13]

◆ Once, in Juarez, Mexico, comedian Steve Martin

70

approached a street vendor and asked the price of a broad-brimmed straw hat. "Four dollars, señor," the man replied. "I'll give you six dollars," Steve said. Out of habit, the vendor shot back, "For you, I make it three." "No, I'll give you eight," Steve said. By now the vendor was confused. "What, señor?" "OK," Steve said, "I'll give you ten dollars or nothing!" The Mexican shrugged and took the money.[14]

◆ One young woman had received an engagement ring the evening before but, alas, none of her friends had noticed it. Finally that afternoon, while her friends were shooting the breeze, she suddenly stood up. "My, but it's hot in here," she said. "I think I'll take off my ring."[15]

◆ News announcer: Flash! Recent government population studies have found that somewhere in the U.S. there is a woman having a baby every eight and a half minutes!. . .I think we ought to find that woman and stop her!

Sometimes the unexpected twist involves a sudden change in point of view. Asimov feels that this is the key ingredient to successful jokes:

The alteration in point of view produces an incongruity which elicits a laugh and a feeling of pleasure. The sharper the incongruity and the more suddenly it can be introduced, the more certain the laugh and the louder and longer it will be.[16]

These stories are examples of sudden changes in point of view:

71

In the Pacific during World War II, a young American pilot landed his fighter plane on an aircraft carrier, ran up to the bridge and, as he pulled his life jacket over his head, related his day's work.

"What a terrific day I had, Skipper!" he said excitedly. "Shot down six Jap planes, sunk a Jap destroyer and left a Jap battleship wounded."

As he finished pulling his life jacket up over his face, he heard, "Velly good, Yank, but you make just one velly bad mistake."[17]

For this story, the change in point of view is obvious. The sudden introduction of this change makes us laugh. It may remind us of unexpected turns in our own life, which may not have seemed funny at the time. Hearing of someone experiencing a similar situation releases tension, reminding us that we are not alone in experiencing difficulty.

A man dressed as Napoleon went to see a psychiatrist at the urging of his wife.

"What's your problem?" the doctor asked.

"I have no problem," the man replied. "I'm one of the most famous people in the world. I have a great army behind me. I have all the money I'll ever need, and I live in great luxury."

"Then why are you here?"

"It's because of my wife," the man said. "She thinks she's Mrs. Levine."[18]

The change in point of view here concerns how we view the man and how he views his wife. The contrast is all

72

the funnier in light of the tendencies of even perfectly sane people to ignore their problems and blame others.

> A farmer from Texas was visiting a farmer in Georgia, who was telling the Texan how big his Georgia farm was. "Our property line starts here," the Georgian said, "goes through those trees in the distance, along the stream on the left, across those hills way over yonder, back along that road on the right and back to this tree stump."
>
> "Well," the Texan said, "that's pretty big. But back home on our farm, we get in the truck at sunrise and start to drive around the perimeter. We drive and drive and drive. Then noon comes and we drive some more and still don't get all around our farm. We drive all afternoon and stop for supper. Then we drive into the night and finally at midnight we get completely around our farm. What do you think of that?"
>
> "Yep," the Georgian replied, "I used to have a truck like that, too!"

In this story, the change is from focusing on the size of the Texan's ranch to the quality of his truck.

Here are some additional stories. After you enjoy each one, try to define its change in point of view. This first one involves Smogarians, a fictitious people tactfully invented by some kind jokester to enable us to enjoy the humor of so-called ethnic jokes without degrading any nationality.

◆ Two Smogarians were arguing about some tracks
   they had found while they were
   hunting.

73

"They're lion tracks!" insisted one.

"No, those are bear tracks!"

As they stood there arguing, the train hit them.[19]

◆ Two hikers were walking through the woods when they suddenly confronted a giant bear. Immediately, one of the men took off his boots, pulled out a pair of track shoes, and began putting them on. "What are you doing?" his companion cried. "We can't out-run that bear, even with jogging shoes."

"Who cares about the bear?" the first hiker replied. "All I have to worry about is outrunning you."[20]

◆ Jim and Mark were hunting pheasant. They approached a farm and decided to ask the farmer for permission to hunt on his land. "You stay here at the gate," Mark told Jim. "I'll go up to the farmhouse and talk with the farmer."

After Mark explained their desire, the farmer replied, "It's fine for you to hunt on our land, but I have one request. See that old gray mare over there? She's sick and dying and needs to be shot, but she's been so good to us all these years that I can't bear to do it. If you'll shoot my horse, you can hunt on our farm."

Mark told the farmer it would be hard for him, too, but he'd do it. As he walked back to meet Jim at the gate, he decided to trick his buddy.

"Well, what did the farmer say?" Jim asked.

"That no-good, lousy farmer," Mark said, obviously angry. "He said no! I'll teach him a lesson. See that mare over there?" Mark took aim with his rifle. Pow! Pow! He pulled the trigger and shot the horse. Then he heard two more shots ring out behind him. Pow! Pow! He turned and saw Jim lowering his own rifle.

"Good job, Mark!" Jim said. "I got two of his cows. Let's get out of here!"

◆ A man was walking along a mountain road and saw an Indian lying with his ear to the ground. As he approached the Indian, he heard him talking.

"Chevy pickup truck. Large tires. Green. Man driving with large German shepherd in passenger seat. Loaded with firewood. California license plate 1-896-PUC."

The observer was astounded. "You mean you can discern all that from listening with your ear to the ground?" he asked.

"Ear to ground, nothin' " the Indian replied. "That truck just ran over me."[21]

◆ A man dashed into a pharmacy and asked the druggist for something to stop hiccups. The druggist filled a glass with water and threw the water into the customer's face.

"Why did you do that?" the man shouted, red-faced and drenched.

"Well, you don't have the hiccups any more, do you?" the druggist asked.

"No!" the man yelled. "But my wife out in the car still does!"[22]

One reason the unexpected twist produces laughter is that we who catch it are pleased with ourselves. We are proud that we have been smart enough to quickly figure out a paradox, so we laugh with joy and self-delight. This perhaps is best seen when people do not catch the point of a joke. Sometimes they feel so badly that when they do figure it out, they are too embarrassed to laugh. Their failure to get it right away may make them slightly disappointed in themselves. They may even become upset with the jokester.

In certain situations, joke-tellers can get laughs by introducing expected, rather than unexpected, twists. Jack Benny was famous for his (supposed) frugality. Often in his sketches or comedy routines, he paused before the punch line and the audience began to laugh. In one radio show, Jack was walking down a dark street. Suddenly a burglar appeared out of the dark, shoved a revolver into Jack's stomach and said, "Your money or your life." The audience started laughing. Jack paused for about thirty seconds, milking the situation for all it was worth, then delivered the punch line: "I'm thinking it over." It brought down the house.

Why did the listeners laugh before the punch line? They already perceived the twist. Normal people would value their money over their life, but they knew Jack's show-biz reputation as a skinflint. Thus, when the straight line came, they immediately caught that Jack might even be more willing to part with his life than his money. They began to laugh about the situation and because of their own self-delight in catching it. Jack's pause further reinforced the humor. His punch line ignited the final charge.

One reason Benny could draw laughs before the punch line was that his audiences knew his stage reputation so well. They knew he was funny. Because of his fame, audiences were conditioned to laugh with Jack, as Steve Allen points out in his excellent analysis on comedians, *More*

Funny People[23] (a sequel to his equally valuable *Funny People*). If you, as an amateur jokester, can work these two factors to your advantage, all the best. But in most cases with most audiences, you will want to bank on the punch line to draw the laughs.

The punch line must not only introduce a twist and, in most cases, make that twist unexpected, but to be successful, the unexpected twist must be introduced *suddenly.*

Remember that laughter is a release of tension, of energy. The more sudden the release, the louder the laugh. If the twist is too long, the tension may dissipate slowly and the laughter will be mild.

In summary, our four keys to successful humor are good material, a knowledge of the audience, good delivery and a healthy self-image. In this chapter, we have said that good material requires three factors: a commonly understood situation, a build-up of tension, and the opportunity to release that tension through the introduction of a sudden and unexpected twist.

The type of humor we prefer—and the type we have included in this book—is not vulgar or vindictive. One can get laughs with such material, but we feel that it degrades human beings. Sometimes we can poke fun at another person in a way that everyone perceives as innocent and friendly, and we have included that type of playful but friendly jest. But even that, if carried to extremes, can be harmful. A knowledge of your audience and of your subject can help provide the right balance.

Now that we have discussed the ingredients of good humorous material, you might wonder, "Where can I find good jokes, anecdotes and stories?" Chapter 6 deals with that question.

CHAPTER 6

~~~~~~~~

FINDING
GOOD MATERIAL

~~~~~~~~

HOW CAN YOU FIND good humorous material? One well-known comedienne has twelve drawers of jokes on three-by-five-inch cards, all carefully catalogued and cross-indexed. Bob Hope has his own joke vault with a combination lock and a heavy steel door. It contains files and files of jokes labeled by date and subject, an accumulation of more than forty years.[1] Many professional comedians employ gag writers.

But how does the ordinary person—who has neither joke vaults nor the funds to pay gag writers—find material? Simply by following the professional's example—by looking for the humorous in life. (How do you think they fill their files?)

In this chapter and the next, we'll explore everyday life situations, speakers, jokesters and friends; television and radio; books; magazines, newspapers and newsletters. As you read, consider how you can use each source.

EVERYDAY LIFE SITUATIONS

Nearly everyone can relate to situations involving family life, romance, the workplace, school, etc. True humorous stories in such settings often have a wide appeal, provided they are not so complex or specific as to limit the humor to those immediately involved.

Remember the three ingredients of successful humorous material: a commonly understood situation, a build-up of tension, and the opportunity to release that tension through the introduction of a sudden and unexpected twist. Look for everyday situations with these ingredients. Maybe it will be a humorous twist in something said or done by a child, co-worker, teacher or employer. Perhaps it will be something that embarrasses you when it happens, but you later feel free to talk about it. Embarrassing moments, tastefully related, can be a great source of lively fun.

Our friend Craig was playing an out-of-town tennis match for his college team. The match was in the town where Craig's brother lived. Though his brother was unable to watch the match due to prior commitments, he arranged for Craig to come by his house afterward to shower and spend the night.

After the match, Craig followed the instructions he had received to get to his brother's house. When he arrived, he could not find the hidden key under the doormat where his brother had told him it would be. So he climbed in through an open window, found the bathroom and took a shower. The shower/bathtub had no curtain, so Craig, who (his wife claims) usually splashes water outside the curtain in a normal shower, soaked the bathroom floor. He then dried off, left the towels on the floor, changed into his street clothes, and left his tennis gear scattered around the home. He stopped by the kitchen and had a bite to eat. After a while he left for dinner.

Later that night, Craig returned to the

house, expecting to find his brother in. He knocked on the door and, much to his surprise, a strange man opened it. Craig asked for his brother.

"There's no one here by that name," the man grumbled.

"Well, I was supposed to spend the night with my brother," Craig said. "This afternoon I couldn't find the key so I climbed in through the window and. . ."

"Are you the blankety blank who messed up my apartment and left his tennis gear all over the place?" the man demanded.

They looked closer at Craig's directions. His brother's house was a few blocks down the road!

Another friend, Lenda Jo, is a beauty. Her business is fashion coordination, and she always displays her cover girl looks with style and grace. Since some people in her audiences might feel intimidated by her poise and beauty, Linda encouraged her to begin her talks by telling this story about herself:

Lenda Jo had a terrific crush on Bill. He was handsome, confident, suave, debonair— exactly what most young women would want in a man. Bill and Lenda Jo dated for some time. Then, alas, Bill seemed to cool in his attention toward Lenda Jo. He stopped calling.

One day, the florist delivered a dozen beautiful red roses to Lenda Jo. The note attached was simply signed "Bill." She could hardly believe it. Her heart raced as she ran to the phone. "Oh Bill, how thoughtful of you," she sighed romantically when she got him on the line. "I just love these beautiful red roses you sent me."

There was a long pause. Then Bill said, "Lenda Jo, I didn't send you any flowers."

It was another Bill who had sent the roses. . .a secret admirer who lived down the street from Lenda Jo; someone for whom she had no romantic interest at all.

Has anything embarrassing ever happened to you? Of course it has! Learn to look at it as a humorous event and it will help you cope with the embarrassment. Learn to retell it as a humorous story and you'll help other people have fun and learn to cope with their foibles.

Steve Allen says, "The best humor, in my opinion, is found in the frequently tragic reality of human experience."[2] He relates the following two stories:

◆ A frightened woman phoned the Los Angeles Police Department one night and in a distracted whisper said, "There's a prowler in my backyard!"

The officer on switchboard duty asked the caller for her address. After a moment's pause, the woman said, "I'd better not tell you; I don't want to get involved."[3]

◆ Then there was the time the late Senator Joseph McCarthy emerged from a congressional committee room in high dudgeon. Reporters asked him to comment on a startling allegation that had just been made. "Why," McCarthy spluttered in all seriousness, "that's the most unheard of thing I've ever heard of."[4]

As Art Linkletter reminds us, *Kids Say the Darndest Things*. In their annual Christmas newsletter, our college friends Mark and Carol Taylor (Mark is now President of Tyndale House publishers) shared the following about two of their children:

◆ Kristen, at five and a half, loves life. She thrives on kindergarten and is busy with ballet lessons, practicing the piano and lots of coloring. She and Jeremy continue to be best friends, playing games of imagination by the hour.

Here is Kristen's recipe for cooking a turkey, exactly as she dictated it:
Go out to the woods and kill a turkey.
Pick up the turkey and bring it home.
Cut it open.
Squeeze out the blood.
Take out the bones.
Clean it out.
Take off the feathers.
Butter the turkey.
Put the turkey in the oven and cook it.
Cook it for 12 minutes.
Take the turkey out of the oven and eat it.

◆ Jeremy (six and a half) is eager to learn new things. He is just beginning to get the idea of simple computer programming on our new Texas Instruments home computer. This essay on Christmas is reproduced exactly as Jeremy wrote it:

> wants-a pan-a-time their livd a man
> named santaclaous. and he had a jabe. his jabe
> wase evre Christmas He went doun to the site
> and gove Everyone a presat.
>
> and new I will tell you about the riel
> stouri of christmas. ther whas a Man named
> Josaf. and a wimin named mary. and mary
> hade a baby named Jesus. and the baby Jesus
> grue up and loved us and hase loved us and
> will love us

Sometimes funny habits of yours or others can be good material. In our family, Linda is famous for mixing her metaphors. Here are some of her better bloopers:

◆ (On a phone call to Rusty at the office, to tell him how well her first book was selling) "They're selling like wildcakes!"

◆ (To a politician friend whose speech she was critiquing) "We'll need to start from scrap."

◆ (Later, concerning the same speech) "If you'd like me to, I'll be glad to fine-comb it."

◆ "Don't put all your marbles in one basket."

◆ (Concerning a questionable idea or venture) "I think you're on shaky ice with that one."

◆ (Concerning an easy task) "That's as easy as duck cake."

◆ "Life is not a bowl of roses."

◆ "The situation just boiled me over."

One of our favorite mixed metaphors came from our boss, Roger Randall, who probably will fire us when he reads this.

> Roger wrote a lengthy paper to outline a plan to expand the work of our fifteen-hundred-person organization by a factor of eight. He carefully detailed all that would need to happen over a twenty-year period. Then he explained that he didn't want to kill our staff in attempting to achieve these ambitious goals. In a dramatic and touching finale, he wrote, "We must never prostitute our staff on the altar of expansion."

Workers of the world, unite!

Here are some additional true stories that show the humor in everyday life:

◆ Kathy, new to California, had just finished her driver's test and was about to have her picture taken for her license.
"Just stand with your toes on the red line," instructed the photographer, who then turned away to handle a brief matter at his desk. When he turned around several seconds later, he was surprised to see Kathy standing with her face flush against the camera lens.
"What in the world are you doing?" he asked.
"Well," Kathy answered, "you told me to stand with my nose on the red light."

◆ While discussing the plight of driver's license examiners, a former motor-vehicle-bureau director told about a woman who was parallel parking. The examiner asked her, "Could you get a little closer?" And she slid over.[5]

TEN REASONS GIVEN FOR NOT TURNING IN HOMEWORK

William R. Jackson, a schoolteacher form West New York, New Jersey, collected "ten best reasons why I don't have my homework."[6]

1. My little sister ate it.

2. My dog (or cat) did his duty on it.

3. We ran out of toilet paper.

4. Our furnace broke down and we had to burn my homework.

5. I had to use it to fill a hole in my shoe.

6. I gave it to a friend and his house burnt down.

7. My mother threw it away by mistake.

8. I got hungry and there was no food to eat.

9. I did it, I swear, but I left it next to my poor sick mother who I was helping and caring for all night.

10. Because I didn't feel like it! (Very often the last words ever spoken by a student.)

THIRTEEN CLEVER PHONY NAMES GIVEN TO A SUBSTITUTE TEACHER

Students in public schools in Chicago gave the following names when reporting to substitute teacher Irene Kozlowski.[7]

1. Anne Chovy
2. Art E. Choke
3. Bud Wiser
4. Frank Furter
5. Chuck Waggon
6. Jim Shou
7. Sandy Beech
8. Polly Gon
9. Ben Gay
10. Liz Onya
11. Ben Dover
12. Eileen Dover
13. Barb De Wyre

THIRTY-THREE EXCUSES GIVEN FOR BREAKING THE SPEED LIMIT

Roger W. Betsill, Jr., who has served as a Georgia State Trooper for nine years, collected the following excuses from people caught speeding.[8]

1. I didn't realize it.

2. I was traveling with the flow of traffic.

3. I was only passing someone.

4. My speedometer must be wrong (or broken).

5. But I had my cruise control set at such and such.

6. Your radar must be wrong.

7. Running late for something.

8. I'm on vacation.

9. I was trying to get to a rest room.

10. Someone else's car.

11. I wasn't paying attention to my driving.

12. Someone sick in vehicle.

13. I didn't know what the speed limit was.

14. I was going downhill.

15. I'm almost out of gas.

16. My accelerator stuck.

17. Someone is dying or just died.

18. I have a fast car and this is a good road.

19. I was just trying to get home.

20. Driver mad at someone.

21. Wife having baby.

22. I was just trying to get away to do someone a favor.

23. I was trying to get away from someone.

24. The kid (or spouse) was fussing.

25. I was trying my car out.

26. I didn't know you were around.

27. I've always driven like this.

28. I was trying to catch someone.

29. I'm just tired and hunting for a place to eat.

30. I did not have my CB on (or it was broken).

31. My fuzz buster wasn't on (or it was broken).

32. I just didn't think I'd ever get stopped.

33. I'm allowed to do that where I come from.

One woman wrote:

> On my birthday, my two children ordered me
> to stay in bed. I lay there looking forward to
> being brought my breakfast, as the inviting
> smell of bacon floated up from the kitchen.
>   At last the children called me downstairs.
> I found them sitting at the table, each with a
> large plate of bacon and eggs. "As a birthday
> surprise," one explained, "we've cooked our
> own breakfast."[9]

A man in New Hampshire relates the following anecdote:

> So many people lined the sidewalks that I
> despaired of ever getting a clear photograph.
> After several unsuccessful tries, I noticed a
> woman focusing her lens directly in front of her.
> I was about to warn her that the shot was impos-
> sible, when she screamed, *"Everybody duck!"*
>   Spectators around and in front of her
> complied, giving her a clear view of the pass-
> ing parade. She then thanked the bewildered
> crowd and walked away with possibly the
> best photo of the day.[10]

SPEAKERS, JOKESTERS AND FRIENDS
You can beef up your joke file by writing down funny stories you hear from speakers, professional humorists or

friends who tell stories at parties. Take care not to sound like a carbon copy of the other person when you retell the joke. Try to deliver the lines in your own style.

To glean pearls from other people, follow this cardinal rule: Listen! Even if you think the joke will be a loser; even if you are sure you have heard it before. . .listen! Not only is it courteous (and perhaps he or she will return the favor some day), there's a chance you may learn something. Maybe you haven't heard it before. Maybe the teller will introduce a new twist or phrase that you can employ.

Listening carefully to other joke-tellers also can give you confidence when you share the same story later, especially if the speaker tells it well and gets a good laugh. Rusty had heard the "Meathead" joke before, but when his friend John Nyquist told it in a fraternity meeting at Emory University in Atlanta and brought down the house, that encouraged Rusty to begin using it often.

Relatives can be a source of humor. Rusty's grandmother, at nearly ninety, loves to collect jokes, which she often passes along to the rest of the family via letters. These are some of her favorites:

◆ Several people were waiting on a street corner for the light to change and a dog was waiting with them. One man asked another, "Does your dog bite?"

"No," the other man said. So the first man reached down to pet the dog, and the dog bit him.

"Ouch!" the wounded pedestrian yelled. "I thought you said your dog doesn't bite!"

The other said, "He's not my dog."

◆ One man told another, "I'm a light eater. The minute it gets light, I start to eat."

◆ Q: How do you get down off an elephant?
   A: You don't. You get down off a duck.

◆ Q: Why is five o'clock in the morning like a pig's
      tail?
   A: It's twirly.

◆ I'm on a seafood diet. Whenever I see food, I eat it.

◆ Height of confidence: Standing up in a hammock.

◆ He's a forthright character: Right about a fourth
   of the time.

◆ Tom: "My wife doesn't understand me. Does
      yours?"
   Bill: "My wife doesn't know you."
                                    —Virginia Bilderback

TELEVISION AND RADIO

Situation comedies, variety shows, talk shows. . .lots of
usable humor comes over the airwaves. Maybe the latest
joke from Bob Hope or Johnny Carson will help keep the
party going. Of course, using television humor has some
drawbacks. If many in your audience watched the same
show you did, your joke may bomb. Also, something may
have been funny in a television or radio program because of
the context (i.e., the situation comedy or humorous sketch).
You may be unable to reproduce the necessary context and
the feelings associated with it for your listeners. But, if you
can overcome such obstacles, television and radio humor
can serve you well.

    Commercials can be good sources of humor. Perhaps

you have seen the television advertisement for *Time* in which the narrator gives a long list of the magazine's features and departments. He recites them without notes and in such rapid succession that viewers are dazzled, tickled and (the ad men hope) influenced by the many features.

Rusty often uses a take-off of this commercial in his talk to university students about "The Dating Game." After touching on ways to help communication in relationships, such as "learn to listen" and "ask creative questions," he says:

"If you still can't think of things to talk about, read *Time* magazine. . .before the date, that is! . . .and ask what your date thinks about national and international events. . .(slight pause, then very rapidly) law, people, religion, science, education, behavior, books, cinema, art, music, medicine, the economy, sports. . .$1.95 at newsstands everywhere."

On a printed page these lines have little humor. But when they are delivered in rapid sequence, with the appropriate facial expressions and counting gestures with hands and fingers, they can get a good laugh. The sudden shift in speed catches the audience off guard. If the lines are delivered smoothly, the listeners delight in a job well done. Ideally, this happens so swiftly that the delight bursts forth in a round of laughter. A skillful communicator often can take advantage of the situation and, with the right timing, take a bow at the end that draws applause and more laughter.

BOOKS

Books can be a great source of jokes. As we stated at the outset, this book is about how to use humor successfully, but we have liberally sprinkled favorite jokes throughout. Other books have jokes carefully categorized, indexed and cross referenced.

Here are a few resources to help you get started:

Bonham, Tal D. *The Treasury of Clean Jokes*. Nashville, Tenn.: Broadman Press, 1981.

Murdock, Clyde. *A Treasury of Humor*. Grand Rapids, Mich.: Zondervan, 1967.

Phillips, Bob. *The World's Greatest Collection of Clean Jokes*. Santa Ana, Calif.: Vision House Publishers, 1974.

____. *More Good Clean Jokes*. Irvine, Calif.: Harvest House, 1974.

____. *The Last of the Good Clean Joke Books*. Eugene, Ore.: Harvest House, 1976.

____. *The All-American Joke Book*. Irvine, Calif.: Harvest House, 1976.

____. *A Humorous Look at Love and Marriage*. Eugene, Ore.: Harvest House, 1981.

____. *The World's Greatest Collection of Heavenly Humor*. Eugene, Ore.: Harvest House, 1982.

Reader's Digest. *Fun Fare*. Pleasantville, N.Y.: The Reader's Digest Association, 1949.

Van Dyke, Dick. *Faith, Hope and Hilarity*. New York: Doubleday, 1970.

Woods, Ralph L. *The Modern Handbook of Humor*. New York: McGraw-Hill, 1967.

As mentioned previously, read joke books slowly, so you do not miss or fail to appreciate many good jokes because you are "all joked out." Also, as you select or eliminate jokes, remember that some are more effective when delivered orally than when read.

Many other books besides joke books have funny snips and stories. Here are two examples from *The Book of Lists 2* which, if presented in the proper context, can draw laughs:

◆ The Longest Kiss on Film (1941)

The longest kiss ever recorded in motion picture history involved Jane Wyman and Regis Toomey in the 1941 production, *You're in the Army Now.* During a scene in this Lewis Seller comedy, Toomey and Wyman held a single kiss for three minutes and five seconds (4 percent of the film's running time.)[11]

◆ The Longest Kiss on Record (1978)

The longest kiss in a "smoochathon" was held between Bobbie Sherlock and Ray Blazina in Pittsburgh, Pennsylvania, between May 1 and 7, 1978. Their record smack lasted 130 hours 2 minutes according to the *Guinness Book of World Records.*[12]

While waiting to have some papers photocopied, Rusty picked up a book of little-known facts. The zaniness of these pieces of legislation from yesteryear and the present provides some good comic relief.

LITTLE-KNOWN LAWS

Have you ever heard of a law in your city or state that you thought was a bit loony? Nearly every state has some old laws on the books that made perfect sense when they were written, but changing times have made them obsolete. Or they have laws that contain bloopers. Here are some of the more interesting and little-known laws:[13]

◆ To take a bath in Boston, you must have a doctor's written prescription.

- Wearing suspenders is illegal in Nogales, Arizona.

- In South Dakota, an eighty-year-old woman cannot stop on the street to talk to a young married man.

- A Louisiana law upholds your right to grow as tall as you like.

- Singing out of tune in North Carolina is against the law.

- An old law in Brainerd, Minnesota, orders that every male must grow a beard.

- In Natoma, Kansas, it is illegal to practice knife-throwing at someone wearing a striped suit.

- Anyone over the age of eighty-eight in Idaho Falls, Idaho, is not permitted to ride a motorcycle.

- During bank holidays in Michigan, the size of wheatcakes is regulated by law.

- It is illegal to set a trap for a mouse in California without a hunting license.

- Idaho law makes it illegal to give your sweetheart a box of candy weighing less than fifty pounds.

◆ You are not permitted to swim on dry land in Santa Ana, California.

◆ It is unlawful to whistle on Sunday in Louisiana.

◆ In Connecticut, the law states that if you are a beaver, you have a legal right to build a dam.

◆ A Belvedere, California, ordinance was written this way: "No dog shall be in public without its master on a leash."

◆ In Marblehead, Massachusetts, it is illegal to cross the street on Sunday unless it is absolutely necessary.

◆ In Idaho, you cannot fish for trout from the back of a giraffe.

◆ In San Francisco, you are forbidden by law to spit on your laundry.

◆ It is illegal to eat peanuts in church in Massachusetts.

◆ In Los Angeles, you cannot use the U.S. mail to complain about cockroaches in your hotel room.

◆ An ordinance of Pocatello, Idaho, makes it illegal to look gloomy.

- ◆ The law in Minneapolis prohibits driving red automobiles.

- ◆ Women may not shine their shoes on Saturday in Marshall, Minnesota.

- ◆ In the Pine Island District of Minnesota, a man must tip his hat when passing a cow.

- ◆ It is illegal to lasso a fish in Knoxville, Tennessee.

- ◆ The legal punishment in Minneapolis for double parking is being put on a chain gang and fed only bread and water.

- ◆ It is unlawful in Portland, Oregon, to wear roller skates in public restrooms.

- ◆ In Minneapolis, it is illegal to install a bathtub in your home unless it has legs.

- ◆ On Market Street in San Francisco, the law requires that elephants must be kept on a leash.

- ◆ In White Cloud, Kansas, it is illegal to break out of jail.

- ◆ In Colorado Springs, Colorado, the law upholds a dog's right to one bite.

◆ Indiana has a law against taking a bath in the winter.

The following chapter contains still more good sources for humor, which are available to most readers.

CHAPTER 7

~~~~~~~~~~

MORE GOOD SOURCES
OF HUMOR

~~~~~~~~~~

MAGAZINES, NEWSPAPERS
AND OTHER SOURCES

The print media provides another useful source of good material. Some newspapers and magazines, such as *Reader's Digest* and *Saturday Evening Post*, run humor columns and fillers. The media also make mistakes in headlines, articles or ads, which make fun fare. Be alert for material that strikes your funny bone. Clip and save—start a file, as the pros do. For instance, Johnny Carson often drew from that day's newspapers for his monologue on "The Tonight Show." The timeliness of the material adds to the humor.

In a barber shop in Delaware, Rusty was flipping through the *Saturday Evening Post* and laughed out loud at a brief article on trivia questions that people might ask one hundred years in the future. Though some of the humor may disappear as time, people and situations pass, the questions provide an amusing reflection of the complexity of current events. We have used these with good success. Here, then, are excerpts from trivia questions that people will ask in one hundred years:[1]

◆ What was the original name of the Russian island off the coast of Florida?

◆ When did New York City become our fifty-first state?

Who was vice-president during the Stassen administration?

When was the national capital moved from Washington, D.C., to Montana?

What was money? When did they discontinue making currency under ten dollars?

When did the prime rate last dip below 45 percent?

In what year did the first-class postage rate go over a dollar?

What are the chances of ratifying the ERA this year?

What is the difference between the Ayatollah from Tehran and the Iacocca from Detroit?

When did members of Congress first begin to make a million dollars a year?

Where was the Panama Canal?

How was Three Mile Canyon formed?

In what year did Arizona become our westernmost state?

Time magazine reported a collection of verbal bloopers uttered by state legislators in Michigan. Newswriters assigned to the capital have covered most of one wall in the Capitol press room with these legislative slips of the lips. Some samples:[2]

- ◆ "Before I give you the benefit of my remarks, I'd like to know what we're talking about."

- ◆ "From now on, I'm watching everything you do with a fine-tooth comb."

- ◆ "Two and two don't make four in my book."

- ◆ "There comes a time to put principle aside and do what's right."

- ◆ "We've got them right where they want us."

- ◆ One statehouse leader proclaimed: "The chair would wish the members would refrain from talking about the intellectual level of other members. That always lead to problems."

Reader's Digest reprinted a few more quotable quotes from the pressroom wall of the Michigan Capitol:[3]

- ◆ "This bill goes to the very heart of the moral fiber of human anatomy."

- ◆ "Some of our friends wanted it in the bill and some of our friends wanted it out, and Jerry and I are going to stick with our friends."

- ◆ "Let's violate the law one more year."

- ◆ "Mr. Speaker, what bill did we just pass?"

Some of the funniest bloopers show up in local news-papers. Here are a few humorous advertisements:

◆ "Wanted—a folding table by a woman with detachable legs."

◆ "Wanted—a boy to take care of horses who can speak German."

◆ "Sale—25 men's wool suits: $15.00—they won't last an hour."

◆ An advertisement in a Pennsylvania paper attracted a great deal of notice, especially as it was headed, "Mother's Day Special." It read: "Don't kill your wife. Let our washing machine do the dirty work."

And this slightly misworded ad. . .

◆ "Why go elsewhere to be cheated? You can trust us to do the job!"[4]

◆ "For Sale—a full-blooded cow, giving three gal-lons milk, 2 tons hay, a lot of chickens and a cookstove."
—Ad in Washington paper

◆ "Wanted: A strong horse to do the work of a country minister."
—Ad in Connecticut paper

◆ "Toaster $3.50. A gift that every member of the family will appreciate. Automatically burns toast."
—Ad in California paper

◆ Piano Moving. If you have a piano to move, take
     advantage of our expert service and careful
     handling. Kindling wood for sale.
                         —Ad in Rome, N.Y., *Daily Sentinel*[5]

Now, a few items from the news and society sections.
These two notices appeared in consecutive order:

◆ "After ten years of marriage, two happy parents,
     Mr. and Mrs. Jay V. Door, announce the birth
     of their first child, a son." "Remember,
     Champaign County want ads bring results."

◆ "It is with real regret that we learn of Mr.
     Wayne's recovery from an automobile
     accident."

◆ "Fifty guests assembled at the Domestic Forum,
     and thirty have been married to the same man
     for more than twenty years."

◆ "At the Ladies' Aid Society Meeting, many inter-
     esting articles were raffled off. Every member
     had brought something they no longer needed.
     Many members brought their husbands."[6]

◆ "Colombia, Tennessee, which calls itself the
     largest outdoor mule market in the world,
     held a mule parade yesterday, headed by the
     governor."
                         —A newspaper report quoted in
                                   Successful Farming

103

◆ "After Governor Baldridge watched the lion perform, he was taken to Main Street and fed twenty-five pounds of raw meat in front of the Fox Theater."

—Idaho paper

◆ "The Tulsa, Oklahoma, 'Daily World' reported: 'Kathleen Winsor has written another book, *Star Money,* that is called a "twentieth-century *Amber,*" and is supposed to outsmell the two million copies of the first book.' "[7]

Often newsletters and other regular mailings are good sources of humor. To help house hunters, *Have a Good Day* newsletter listed handy translations for real estate terms:[8]

◆ *Unobstructed view:* No trees.

◆ *Waiting your imaginative touch:* Complete disrepair.

◆ *Handyman's dream:* Owner's nightmare.

◆ *Pond site:* Swamp, slough or marsh.

◆ *Land alone worth purchase price:* It had better be; the house is worthless.

◆ *House alone worth purchase price:* Small lot next to tavern.

◆ *Central to everything:* A very noisy area.

◆ *Easy commuting:* Remote from everything.

104

◆ *Country kitchen:* no dining room.

◆ *Charm all its own:* Don't lean on the old porch railing.

◆ *All services available:* Nothing hooked up.

◆ *Secluded:* No road in.

◆ *On paved road:* House is ten feet from busy highway.

◆ *Needs finishing touches:* Needs roof.

◆ *Rustic appeal:* Outdoor plumbing.

A church newsletter contained the following new diets, suggested by some adult members as they enjoyed sumptuous food at a Christmas party:

◆ The seven-day diet: eat all you want today because you won't eat for seven days.

◆ The all-desert diet: eat only in the Sahara or Mohave or any other desert of your choice.

◆ The orange-rhyme diet: eat whatever you like as long as it rhymes with *orange*.

◆ The mush diet: you eat while riding in a dogsled.

◆ The eggplant diet: plant an egg and eat whatever comes up.

◆ The garlic diet: eat enormous amounts of garlic and you lose ten pounds and all your friends.

◆ The vaudeville diet: eat only the foods thrown at you.

Another church newsletter included this gem, which especially relates to families:

> One woman was bragging to her next-door neighbor about her son, a college student. "Why, our son is so brilliant, every time we get a letter from him we have to go to the dictionary."
>
> "You're lucky," the neighbor said. "Every time we get a letter from ours, we have to go to the bank."

Yes, you can find humorous material in many sources: everyday life situations; speakers, jokesters and friends; television and radio; books; magazines, newspapers and newsletters. But if all else fails, you can make up something. You may be surprised at how much humor you can devise with your imagination.

DEVELOPING AND ADAPTING MATERIAL

Whatever your source, consider the following questions as you choose material: Did it make you laugh? Did it make others laugh? Does it have broad appeal? When you try it out on friends, what kind of response do you get?

In developing your material, can you make it funnier by changing a few points? Can you make it broader? To perfect the story, write it out and share it with friends. Practice telling it in different ways.

When using humor keep in mind the often distinct differences between effective written English and effective spoken English. Sentences that flow easily when read silently may sound awkward and stilted when spoken aloud. The phrasing may be too complex. The sentences may be too long and have too many subordinate clauses. The words may be too long or complicated. Remember that listeners cannot reread a sentence: they must catch it the first time. If anything seems unnatural, stilted or strained, the listener may focus on that abnormality of delivery and miss the humor. Written communication depends on punctuation; spoken communication depends on voice intonation, facial expression and gestures.

The differences between spoken and written communication are especially pronounced in word plays. Many word plays or spelling bloopers may be detectable only in written form. Consider the following advertisement.

> An ad for insect poison: "One bottle is all you need—Get Rid of Aunts."

Or these news items:

◆ "Mrs. Thompson, President of the Woman's Club, announced that on Wednesday, April 16, the final meeting would be hell."

◆ "Having broken both ankles in a collision, Mrs. Robbins is recovering under the car of her physician."[9]

If rendered verbally the above three lines probably would require explanation, which usually destroys the suddenness and self-delight of successful humor, so the laughs are minimal.

ADAPTING FOR SPECIFIC SITUATIONS

Sometimes you can successfully adapt humorous material to fit specific situations, using the same basic story but altering the details. The more you can tailor your story to a commonly understood situation, the better. If you can relate it directly to the audience's present situation, that is better still.

Consider this time-worn but effective story:

> Joe, my college roommate, was taking a course in ornithology, the study of birds. The night before the biggest test of the term, Joe spent all night studying. He had that textbook nearly memorized. He knew his class notes backward and forward. Joe was ready.
>
> The morning of the test, Joe entered the auditorium and took a seat in the front row. On the table in the front was a row of ten stuffed birds. Each bird had a sack covering its body, and only the legs were showing. When class started, the professor announced that the students were to identify each bird by looking at its legs and give its common name, genus, species, habitat, mating habits, etc.
>
> Joe looked at each of the birds' legs. They all looked the same to him. He started to get angry. He had stayed up all night studying for this test and now he had to identify birds by their legs. The more he thought about the

situation, the angrier he got. Finally he reached his boiling point. He stood up, marched up to the professor's desk, crumpled up his exam paper and threw it on the prof's desk. "What a ridiculous test!" he told the prof. "How could anyone tell the difference between these birds by looking at their legs? This exam is the biggest rip-off I've ever seen!"

With that, Joe turned and stormed toward the exit. The professor was a bit shocked and it took him a moment to regain his composure. Then, just as Joe was about to walk out the door, the prof shouted out, "Wait a minute, young man, what's your name?"

Joe turned around, pulled up his pant legs and hollered, "You tell me, prof! You tell me!"

Now consider this adaption that our friend Karen Yerian uses to introduce some of her speeches on university campuses:

I was an English major in college and I remember one test I took in a poetry class. . . one of those classes where in three and a half months you study two hundred poets, and you're supposed to remember all of their poems. . .you know the type! Well, this was the final test and counted two-thirds of our grade. I stayed up 'til 3 A.M. studying everything from their birthplaces and titles of their poems to iambic pentameter.

It was an 8 A.M. class. I walked in. No, if

I remember correctly, I crawled in at 8:02 with my cup of coffee and NoDoz breath. Well, my teacher handed out the test and at the signal we turned them over. The first thing I heard was a deathly gasp—it was me! There were two lines each from twenty-five poems and we were to write the poet's name beside each pair. I couldn't believe it. I was furious. Finally I got up, walked up to the prof's desk, slammed the test down in front of her, and said, "This is the most ridiculous test I've ever seen!" Then I started to walk out. Just as I got to the door, she said, "Stop. . .What's your name?" There was a blackboard on the back wall so I walked over to it, picked up a piece of chalk, and wrote:

"Two can play this little game.
Here's my poem, you guess my name."

Adaptions like this are possible in many cases. Changing a name or place, or altering details can help the story come alive to your audience. Don't try to tell two similar stories in succession to the same audience, however, as the effect of the second story may be lost.

You can adapt some stories for different audiences by merely changing a name. The story that follows is one such example. In 1972 we were involved in EXPLO '72, a conference of eighty thousand people, which was divided into more than sixty sub-conferences located around the Dallas-Fort Worth metroplex. Rusty helped run a conference of college students at Arlington, Texas. The morning of the last day, he received a telephone call. The voice on the other end whispered, "Hello, Rusty. This is Josh."

It was Josh McDowell, now an internationally-known

author and lecturer. He had spoken numerous times throughout the area that week and was scheduled to speak at the Arlington conference that morning.

"I've lost my voice. Can you pinch hit for me?" he asked.

Rusty agreed to substitute. That left him two hours to prepare two talks. Since he knew the seven hundred students expected Josh, he would have to come up with a sharp opening to establish rapport and make them want to listen to him. After being introduced by Bob Rountree, the popular emcee for the week, Rusty told this story:

> Last night I dreamt that I died and went to heaven. As I approached the pearly gates, I saw a huge table with an enormous, thick book lying on it. To the side of the table was a ladder that stretched off into the sky, farther than the eye could see.
>
> As I approached the table, St. Peter met me and asked my name. Then he thumbed through the huge book until he found it. "Ah, yes, Mr. Wright. Won't you come this way," he said as he walked over to the ladder. "Mr. Wright, you have one small thing to do before we can admit you to heaven. Here is a piece of chalk. I will count out from this book the number of sins you've committed and for each sin, you must place a chalkmark on a successive rung of the ladder. When you've done that for all your sins, we'll let you in."
>
> *This will be a snap!* I thought to myself. *I'll be done in nothing flat!* As St. Peter began counting, I began making my chalk marks, climbing the ladder as I went. "One, two,

111

three, four. . ." he counted. ". . .593, 594, 595
. . . 2,967, 2,968. . ." By now I was so high I
could barely see St. Peter and make out his
voice. "How many more?" I yelled down to
him. "Only three more" came the faint reply.

I reached my left hand up to grab the next
rung. All of a sudden I felt an incredible
crunch, an excruciating pain in my left hand. I
looked up and saw a big foot pinning my
hand to the rung. I looked higher and saw that
it was Bob Rountree, coming down for more
chalk.

Fortunately, the story worked and the crowd was attentive. It's an old story and often used in some circles, but
many audiences have not heard it. You can insert the name
of any well-known local figure in the punch line.

A final comment about developing your material: Work
hard to choose the best words. Mark Twain is reported to
have said, "The difference between the right word and the
nearly right word is the difference between the lightning
and the lightning bug."[10]

Choose words that paint a vivid picture and help the listener identify emotionally with the characters and their situations. In the previous story about chalk, words such as
huge and *enormous* create a stronger image than would *big*
or *large*. "Incredible crunch" and "excruciating pain" help
listeners feel the hurt. No doubt the story could be polished
even more.

Careful wording is essential throughout the story and
especially at the punch line. Remember the three elements of
successful humorous material: a commonly understood situation; a buildup of tension; and an opportunity to release that
tension through the introduction of a sudden and unexpected

twist. Careful wording can enhance each element. Poor wording can distract or confuse the listeners and cause them to miss the point. If their attention is drawn to an inappropriate word, they may miss details that help build tension. And if the punch line is cumbersome, they may not comprehend the twist with the suddenness that is essential for the greatest laugh.

A FORMULA

Suppose you want to fashion a humorous story from a true situation. How do you do it? Word choice is crucial. Based on the principles we have discussed, here are some practical steps:

1. *Identify the incongruity.* This is what ultimately will trigger the laughter, so have it clear in your mind from the start. Is it a situation? A relationship? A twist? An odd phrase? An exaggeration? Define it specifically.

2. *Determine the feasibility.* Do you think it will be feasible to communicate the situation to others so they will understand? Some stories are extremely funny to those experiencing them, but require too much detail to prepare the uninvolved listener. The humor is lost in confusion.

3. *Paint the picture.* Describe the situation that the audience needs to understand to eventually comprehend the punch line. Pay careful attention to colorful details and descriptive words. Ask yourself if your words will grab and hold the listeners' attention.

113

4. *Build the tension.* Can you include details that will arouse curiousity? Anticipation? Excitement? Can you use a bit of drama? Do it! Remember, the greater the build-up of tension, the louder the laughter as the tension is released.

5. *Fashion the punch line.* Make it short, powerful and easy to say, listen to and understand.

Work hard at developing material. Write your story using the words you would use to tell it aloud. That will force you to think through the impact of each word and phrase. Try out your story on friends and ask their advice afterward. When you have honed the story satisfactorily, practice so you can deliver it effortlessly. Make it seem natural. Mark Twain also said, "It takes three weeks to prepare a good ad-lib speech."[11] Effective communication takes work, but the effort spent on polishing your material will be well-spent.

The successful humorist's four tasks are: finding good material, knowing the audience, polishing the delivery and developing a healthy self-concept. In chapters 6 and 7 we have looked at what good material is, where to find it and, briefly, how to develop and adapt it. But an essential factor in finding and developing good material is knowing the audience, for humor is ineffective in a vacuum. It must be heard and appreciated by an audience of individuals, each with his or her background, presuppositions, biases, relationships and state of mind.

How can you target your stories to what your listeners are thinking? This is the subject of chapter 8, "Knowing Your Audience."

CHAPTER 8

~~~~~~~~~~

KNOWING
YOUR AUDIENCE

~~~~~~~~~~

A FRIEND OF OURS was lecturing in Latin
America. He was going to use a translator, but
to identify with his audience, he wanted to
begin his talk by saying in Spanish, "Good
evening, ladies and gentlemen." He arrived at
the auditorium a little early and realized he
did not know the Spanish words for *ladies*
and *gentlemen*. Being rather resourceful, he
went to the part of the building where the
restrooms were, looked at the signs on the two
doors, and memorized those two words.

When the audience arrived and he was
introduced, he stood up and said in Spanish,
"Good evening, ladies and gentlemen." The
audience was shocked. The people seemed
stunned. He didn't know whether he had
offended them or if perhaps they hadn't heard
him or understood him. So he decided to
repeat it. Again in Spanish he said, "Good
evening, ladies and gentlemen."

One person in the audience began to
snicker. Pretty soon the entire audience was
roaring in laughter. Finally, someone told him
that he had said, "Good evening, bathrooms
and broom closets!"

Our friend wanted to identify with his listeners, but was missing one essential ingredient: the ability to speak their language.

Why is an understanding of the audience so important for the humorist? Because humor is a form of communication and, to be effective, it needs to reach people where they are. The humorist must tailor his humor to his listeners' needs, attitudes and backgrounds. He or she must, in effect, speak their language.

When you speak someone else's language, it is not enough for your message to be clear, logical and intelligible to you. It must be clear, logical and intelligible to the listener. Stories that make sense or are humorous to one audience may not have the desired effect on another.

> Mrs. Wheeler put her roast in the oven and she and her husband went off to church. She was sure that the pastor would finish on time and that she would return home before the roast had overcooked. But, on arriving at church, she learned that this was a special Sunday and a famous guest speaker would preach. She sat in the last pew and her husband sat in the front row, right under the pulpit.
>
> The speaker went on and on, and Mrs. Wheeler became concerned about her roast. Finally she wrote a note to her husband and asked the usher to take it up to him. The usher misunderstood and handed it to the speaker, who read it, stopped his sermon immediately and sat down. After the service, the pastor asked his guest why he had ended so abruptly.
>
> "I got a hate letter from a member of

your congregation," the speaker replied.

"Oh, really? What did it say?"

"Go home and shut off the gas."[1]

Right message, wrong audience.

Similarly, the message of humor should be aimed at the right audience. The listener's background, knowledge, mood and current interests must all be taken into account. A funny story about something that happened at the office may not make sense to those unfamiliar with your boss's idiosyncrasies. Or, as Jack Benny explained, "If everyone in the room is arguing about the Cleveland Indians' chances against the Yankees, it's the wrong time for a talking-dog story. If you must tell it right then, at least try to make it a dog who can play shortstop."[2]

One reason humorists are successful is that they identify with their audience and the audience identifies with them. For instance, Woody Allen often portrays himself as a great lover or great adventurer (or at least as someone who is trying to be). As the viewer or listener pictures the rather plain and even mousy Allen in such roles, he or she may think of his or her own Walter Mitty fantasies. Rodney Dangerfield has made a mint telling how he "don't get no respect." Listeners who suffer the daily insults of life (and who doesn't?) relate and enjoy. When Bill Cosby tells of his childhood exploits with Fat Albert and Junior Barnes, and his fear of monsters under the bed, listeners remember their own youth and laugh with him.

By allowing the audience to identify with him, the comedian can help listeners have fun and perhaps even take themselves less seriously. They may laugh at themselves in a healthy, cathartic way. The experience is enjoyable and the comedian is successful.

Billy Graham was to address a student audience at a

prestigious British university, The London School of Economics. Many at the university were skeptical about the American clergyman and what he stood for, so his visit caused quite a stir. When he arrived, the auditorium was packed. The atmosphere was electric. Some booed when Graham stood. Shortly after he began to speak, one young man heckled him by acting like an ape. The student made a monkey of himself using gestures, scratching, etc., all to the delight of the crowd. Graham's response to this situation would greatly affect how attentive the audience would be to his lecture. He handled it with grace and charm. . .and just the right amount of wit.

After a hearty, genuine laugh of his own, Graham said to the audience, "He reminds me of my ancestors." The crowd laughed at the seemingly obvious allusion to the controversial subject of human origins. Then he added, ". . .of course, all my ancestors came from Britain." The audience roared. The joke was on them, but it was handled in such a way that few, if any, could be offended. Graham's lecture was off to a fine start and the crowd listened in total silence.[3]

A sharp mind is essential for the successful humorist. Billy Graham had to think carefully—and quickly—about his audience and the situation to pull off that humorous coup. Professional comedians and gag writers think a good deal about the human condition and how to make it seem funny. And thinking often pays off, as these two stories illustrate:

◆ A village beggar was reputed to lack complete mental capacity. Whenever he was offered a choice between a dime and a nickel, he always chose the nickel. After this had gone on for some time, one kind chap explained to him that a dime was worth twice as much as a nickel and that from now on, he should always choose the dime.

"Oh, I know that a dime is worth more," the beggar replied. "But if I ever chose the dime, people would stop offering."[4]

◆ An elderly gentleman now lives in comfortable retirement on a small fortune amassed in a creative but perfectly legal way. An astute student of the psychology of American people, he simply inserted the following ad in a string of local newspapers:

LAST DAY TO SEND IN YOUR DOLLAR!
                                    John Jones
                                    P.O. Box 184
The dollars rolled in.[5]

ANALYZING YOUR AUDIENCE

In analyzing your audience, you must consider many factors. We will examine: intellectual level, psychological make-up, felt needs, religious convictions, current issues, and local heroes and personalities.

INTELLECTUAL LEVEL

Are the listeners well-educated? Are they very intelligent? Or, more importantly, do they see themselves as being intelligent? If so, a story about academia, a famous poet or a fine point of history may be on target. With a less-educated group, it might bomb. In Rusty's university lecture on "The Resurrection of Jesus Christ: Fact or Fiction?" he refers to a string of learned and respected people who believed in the resurrection. When he mentions Isaac Newton, he says, "Sir Isaac Newton, the famous mathematician and physicist. . .he invented calculus. . . blame him if you don't like it!" With a group of college students, many of whom have struggled with calculus, the line usually draws a laugh. To a less-educated group who do not know what calculus is, it surely would die. For the less intellectual, stick to stories about people, relationships, the workplace, or perhaps sports or neighborhood life.

Suppose you are eager to try a story, but you feel you have to explain some background information. You may be inviting disaster. No one likes to be talked down to. The less intellectual may be embarrassed by your implication and the more intellectual may be indignant at your presumption. This applies to everything from historical details to word choice. It is better to focus on your listeners where they are.

PSYCHOLOGICAL MAKE-UP

Where are your listeners psychologically? Are they self-centered? Materialistic? Self-indulgent? A story about a snob might amuse them (if told tactfully). Are they workaholics, married to their jobs? Tell them about the businessman we mentioned earlier who had a sign in his office that read "Thank God it's Monday."

Are they lazy or apathetic? Maybe they, too, will laugh at the workaholic who has gone to the opposite extreme. Are they sticklers for detail? Tell them about Winston Churchill who, in his obsession with correct grammar, once said, "This is something up with which I shall not put!"

Are your listeners peer-group oriented? Tell them about an embarrassing situation—your first date, a blooper you made at school or work, the time at church when you put a

120

five dollar bill in the collection plate and took out change. They will identify with you, possibly laugh at themselves and realize that sometimes they put too much stock in what people think about them. You've not only entertained them; you've helped in their personal development.

FELT NEEDS

Closely related to psychological make-up is the area of felt needs. A real need is a genuine necessity; a felt need is something one feels or thinks is a genuine necessity, but which may not be. Food, air and water are real needs. A steady job is usually a real need. Cravings for chocolate pie or a strawberry milkshake may represent felt needs that are not real needs, especially for the dieter. A desire for a million dollars in the bank may be a felt need that is not a real need. Some felt needs are also real needs, such as a warm fire to someone who is frostbitten or a word of encouragement to the discouraged.

The successful communicator seeks to establish contact with his or her audience at the point of felt need. So does the successful humorist. Are your listeners dieters? Tell them of the new fad diets mentioned in the last chapter. Are they struggling financially? Tell them about the beggar who always chose the nickel or the man who got rich from the "Last Day to Send in Your Dollar" ads. Are they interested in better relationships with their mates or children? Tell funny stories about marriage and the family. As employees, do they feel misunderstood by their employers? Are they frustrated by their boss's attitude of superiority? Tell them. . .

> Jack was eager to hear his boss, Mr. Creedle,
> evaluate a project he had just finished. As

121

Mr. Creedle proceeded to point out what he considered to be several minor flaws in the project, Jack bristled. Mr. Creedle seemed to think he was always right.

"Mr. Creedle," Jack asked in frustration, "have you ever been wrong at anything?"

"Why yes, Jack," Creedle replied. "One time several years ago I was wrong."

"When was that?" Jack asked.

"It was the time I thought I was mistaken about something, but I wasn't."[6]

Remember that laughter is a release of tension. By using humor in the area of a person's felt need, you may not need to build tension, but rather can deal with the existing tension. Learn to tap into your listeners' felt needs and you'll have a direct connection to their funny bones.

RELIGIOUS CONVICTIONS

Your audience's religious beliefs can be an invaluable tool. The key is to employ your humor gracefully and tactfully without offending. Jokes that make fun of or denigrate someone else's religious convictions are surely in poor taste. Yet, sometimes an insider speaking to fellow believers can successfully spoof an aspect of their own religion because it may be considered family humor. Everyone takes it well.

For example, Judaism has too often been the butt of tasteless jokes by non-Jews. The tragic results of avid anti-Semitism through the ages intensifies this concern even more. Very often, however, Jewish comedians speaking to Jewish audiences can spoof elements of Jewish life or tradition and get a tremendous response. The audience considers it a family affair and everyone laughs together at themselves.

Similarly, jokes about Protestant situations are probably in best taste when told by Protestant speakers to Protestant audiences. Likewise with Catholics. Yet, if a friendly rivalry exists between two denominations, and hostility or possible offense is not an issue, then some jokes may be appropriate in audiences of mixed denomination.

> A member of a Baptist family died while the pastor was out of town. The family asked the local Methodist minister to conduct the funeral service. He said he would have to check with his Bishop. He wired the Bishop: "Could I bury a Baptist?"
> The Bishop wired back: "Sure, bury all the Baptists you can!"

Since religious convictions are often dear to the hearts of people, be sensitive when composing or delivering humor. Never maliciously or satirically make light of something that someone else holds sacred.

CURRENT ISSUES

News items can be great sources of humor, provided they are treated tastefully. Jokes about Jonestown, the Vietnamese boat people or a presidential assassination are best left untold. On the other hand, less volatile issues can provide amusing subject matter. What is news in your area? A political race? The opening of a new airport? Make light comments about politicians or pilots. Did the local college football team just win a game after losing ten straight?

Speculate about a Rose Bowl bid. Did your county finally get electricity and indoor plumbing? Joke about the new bills you have to pay.

In 1940, Danny Thomas was master of ceremonies at the Morocco Club in Detroit, and Bob Hope was scheduled as a guest celebrity. Thomas recalls, "Bob came in and we got him on right away. He taught me a great lesson because he's always very well-dressed, you know, but mud and rain had gotten on his slacks from the storm outside. So the first thing he did, he looked down at his wet pants cuff and said, 'Those Detroit cabdrivers come mighty close.' The audience really broke up. The joke itself wasn't all that hilarious, but the point was, it was topical. It took advantage of that situation."[7]

While speaking to a student group at Central Missouri State University, Rusty decided to establish rapport by mentioning the school mascots, "The Fighting Mules." He began his talk with, "It's great to be here tonight at CMSU, the home of the Fighting Mules!" He said it seriously, but the audience laughed heartily. Someone explained to Rusty that school spirit definitely was lagging at CMSU and no one took the "Fighting Mules" very seriously. Rusty unintentionally had milked humor from a local issue.

Perhaps the weather is an issue to which you can refer.

◆ Spring in Indiana is when the furnace clicks off
   and the sump pump clicks on.[8]

◆ April showers may bring May flowers to other
   parts of the world, but not to Minnesota.
   There the season song goes: "April blizzards
   freeze your gizzards."[9]

Speaking of April, timeliness is valuable in referring to issues. Here are two pieces that should make hits around the fifteenth:

Have you heard about the new "quickie" Federal Income Tax form? It has only three questions:

A. How much money did you make last year?

B. How much do you have left?

C. Send "B."

Columnist Art Buchwald composed the "Taxpayer's Prayer":

Heavenly Father, we beseech you in our hour of need to look down kindly on your humble taxpaying servants, who have given all we possess to the almighty Internal Revenue Service. Grant us that we have completed our Form 1040 correctly so no power will find fault with it. We pray to God that we have added lines 7 through 20 accurately, and that we have subtracted line 30 from line 21 so our adjusted gross income is computed to their divine satisfaction. We ask you, O Lord, to protect our exemptions and bless our deductions as outline in Schedule A (Form 1040, see pages 17 through 20 of instruction booklet). Have mercy on those of us who failed to wisely estimate our payments during the year and must now borrow from Peter to pay Paul. Blessed are they who spent more than they earned and contributed so much to the economy. Give us the strength, Lord, so that we may dwell in a lower tax bracket forever and ever (as outlined in Publication 17, the revised 1981 edition). Yea, though we walk through the shadow of bankruptcy (see Tax Tables, tax rate schedule x, y, z, or, if applicable, Schedule D or Schedule G or maximum tax form 4726), there is no one to comfort us.[10]

If your fancy is politics and your audience is sympathetic, these may be appropriate:

◆ At a party in Washington, D.C., several guests were involved in informal conversation. One asked, "Say, have you heard the latest White House joke?"

"No," another answered. "But before you tell it, I think you should know that I work for the White House."

"That's OK," the first guest replied. "I'll tell it *very* slowly."[11]

◆ Someone asked Rev. Edward Everett Hale, while he was chaplain of the U.S. Senate, if he prayed for the Senators.

"No," Hale replied. "I look at the Senators and pray for the nation."[12]

◆ A visitor to Washington, D.C., had to make a brief stop near the Capitol. As he parked his car and got out, he saw a man standing nearby. "I have to leave my car here for a few minutes," the visitor said. "If you're going to be here, would you mind watching it for me?"

"Did you realize that I'm a United States senator?" the bystander asked.

"No, I wasn't aware of it," the driver responded. "But that's OK. I'll trust you."[13]

HEROES OR LOCAL PERSONALITIES

Steve Allen comments on the value of linking humor to personalities known by members of the audience:

I have learned that people will laugh loudest at a joke that affects some member of their own group, even though the joke might not be particularly noteworthy. When I make a benefit appearance or address some particular organization, I usually make it a point to acquaint myself with the names of a few of the important people connected with the group before which I am to appear. Then any little quip that detracts mildly from their dignity usually gets an enthusiastic reception.[14]

If you are a visiting speaker, you can use this technique to establish rapport and loosen your audience. If you are conversing with or speaking to people you know, you can laugh together at a bit of friendly fun poked at one or more members.

Or, if you are a prominent member of the group to which you are speaking (a manager, teacher, employer, etc.), that can enhance your ability to get laughs. Sometimes an audience is slightly tense with excitement when it is addressed by a superior. Frequently a small quip provides a release that produces laughter. Even if you are not a leader of the group, your rapport and familiarity with the members can work to your advantage. People like to have fun with their friends. Generally, the greater the rapport and familiarity between a speaker and his or her listeners, the easier it is for humor to be successful.

We've considered the importance of knowing your audience. We've looked at factors such as intellectual level, psychological make-up, felt needs, religious convictions, current issues, and heroes and personalities. These relate to the attitudes the audience members bring with them. But sometimes people overlook additional important factors, which relate to the physical arrangements of the location in which humor is used. Room size, crowding, lighting and temperature can greatly influence responsiveness to humor.

PHYSICAL ARRANGEMENTS AND RELATED FACTORS

Perhaps the most important physical arrangements factor is crowding and room size, because laughter helps stimulate more laughter. Some people feel shy about laughing where others can hear them. If, however, others around them are laughing, it is much easier for them to cast off their inhibitions and join in the laughter.

Also, some people are more apt to think a story is funny if they know that other people think it is. They usually do not consciously wait for others to laugh to determine if they feel the joke is good. Rather, the process is instantaneous, without a conscious decision.

This is why many television comedy shows are taped

before live audiences or use laugh tracks, so-called canned laughter. Such laughter encourages the viewer at home to laugh, too. Steve Allen comments on the psychology of crowd laughter:

> It's a simple matter of mass psychology. The appreciation of humor is, at heart, an emotional matter. You won't laugh at the most amusing joke in the world if you're not "in the mood." And when are you more in the mood for laughter; when you're sitting in a room by yourself or when you're with a large group of friends?
>
> Danny Kaye was very funny in the movies. His pictures usually made me laugh so loud I embarrassed my companions. But one time I saw one of his films at a drive-in theater. I didn't laugh aloud once. I didn't hear anyone else laughing.
>
> Fred [Fred Allen, a famous radio comedian; no relation to Steve] knew that a joke with which he could make a friend chuckle on the street would make an audience of fifty laugh deeply, and could make an audience of five hundred roar for perhaps half a minute.
>
> But sometimes people say, "Why didn't they just *try* a comedy show without an audience?"
>
> They have. Henry Morgan did once: just once. The script was marvelous and Henry was in top form. But at home I didn't crack a smile. Next week Henry performed before his usual crowd and I laughed aloud.[15]

We, and many others, have found that generally the larger the crowd and the more tightly people are packed into a room, the greater the response to humor. Tell a good joke to a group of ten people. If they are friends, you may get a good laugh. If they are not familiar with one another, you may get chuckles or polite smiles. Tell the same joke to a similar group of fifty people—even fifty who are not friends—and chances are that the laugh will be greater.

Why? Suppose that only 20 percent of a given group laugh at a given joke. If the audience has ten people, then only two laugh, and they may be stifled by the silence of the others. In a crowd of fifty people, however, ten people initially laugh at the joke. Ten may seem a more respectable response. Besides, their laughter makes more noise than that of two and may encourage the borderline laughers to chuckle or laugh. The joke that seemed to bomb with ten is moderately successful with fifty.

Imagine the same joke with an audience of five hundred. A hundred people laugh, thus priming the pump. Even if they only snicker, the sound of a hundred snickers may be loud enough to make the borderline laughers feel comfortable laughing. This probably accounts for the frequent phenomenon of laughter building in a crowd. It starts small and then rolls and grows until nearly everyone is laughing. People are encouraged to laugh when others around them are laughing.

Isaac Asimov, the noted science fiction writer and student of humor, makes another point about crowd size. Suppose you have a joke or funny story that you have used successfully before (i.e., you know it can work), but you are unsure how many in your current audience have heard it. Asimov says that, the larger the crowd, the greater risk you can afford to take. If only 25 percent of an audience has not heard your story, in a crowd of eight that means only two potential laughers. In a crowd of eight hundred, however, two hundred may laugh and even the six hundred non-laughers may be impressed.[16]

130

Now consider the factor of room size. Fifty people in a room designed to hold fifty or sixty may respond very positively. The same group in a room that holds five hundred may not. People may be so spread out that they cannot readily hear others laughing. Even if the fifty are gathered together close to the speaker (which helps), the room may be so large that their laughter seems to dissipate into thin air. Similarly, put an audience of five hundred in an auditorium designed for five hundred and response may be good. Put them in a field house that holds five thousand or outside in a stadium, and your jokes may die.

Why does crowding enhance response to humor? First, as mentioned earlier, crowding provides numerous potential laughers whose laughter can encourage the borderline laughers to respond (by lowering their inhibitions or creating the impression of humor).

Second, crowding creates a certain tension. People seated close together may be conscious of not wanting to bump the person next to them, not burping loud enough for their neighbor to hear, or any other assorted fears, which create a tension. Laughter affords an opportunity to release that tension, shift in one's seat, etc. The greater the crowding, the greater the tension and the more eager the listeners may be—even subconsciously—to release that tension. Hence the greater the laughter.

Third, crowding enhances a speaker's or comedian's image. Listeners often base their opinions of a speaker or entertainer on what other people think about that person. If the room is two-thirds empty, the listener might reason, *This person isn't successful. I probably won't like it very much.* This may not be conscious, but an attitude that develops as he sizes up the situation. Put him in the same size crowd in a more suitable room, and the audience may think, *The speaker packed out the place* and hence be more receptive.

A fourth reason that crowding enhances response relates to acoustics. Generally, the more echo in a room, the greater the response to humor. Resonant acoustics create the impression that more people are laughing, thus encouraging more laughter.

Some of these comments relate only to speakers or entertainers telling jokes to their audiences. You my ask, "How does this relate to using humor at a party in my living room? Should I tell jokes only if the party is packed to overflowing? Should I remove all the drapes, carpets and stuffed chairs to create a better echo?" Not at all! We merely encourage you to be aware of these factors so you can use them to your advantage when possible. And, if an audience doesn't respond as positively to your humor as you had hoped, do not necessarily conclude that your material or delivery were flawed. Poor physical arrangements may be to blame.

LET THOSE LIGHTS SHINE

Other physical arrangements that affect response to humor are lighting, seating and temperature. A great deal of verbal humor is conveyed through gestures and facial expressions. Poor lighting can prevent your listeners from seeing your face clearly, and may diminish a great potential impact. Or if the seating obstructs the audience's view, your expressions and gestures may lose their impact. In a lecture hall or theater, this is especially important. Generally, if more than ten rows of chairs are on a level floor, it helps to speak from a riser, platform or stage, so more of the audience can see more of you.

The best chairs are comfortable enough for the listeners to relax, but not so comfortable that they fall asleep. Chairs that are too uncomfortable may keep them awake and create tension that can be released through laughter. . .but they also may cause the listeners to focus their attention on their own posterior agony, rather than on your humor.

Room temperature is important, too. If it's too hot, they may become drowsy. If it's too cold, they may shiver and think more about their discomfort than your jokes. You want the audience members to be comfortable and relaxed, but alert.

PARDON ME. . .

Distractions and interruptions can kill good humor. We have attempted to try new material on our relatives at large gatherings, such as Thanksgiving dinner. Many a fine punch line has been lost because someone shouted from the kitchen, "Who wants coffee?" or "How many want ice cream with their pie?"

Why are interruptions and distractions so lethal? Because they allow listeners to focus their attention elsewhere and dissipate their tension (through shifting in their seats, answering the questions about coffee and ice cream, etc.).

Steve Allen shares some insights into the distractions that compete for the attention of a television comedian. He contrasts the television studio with the radio studio, in which the only thing between the comic and the studio audience is a microphone. In a television studio, however, the comic competes with stage hands, cameras and dollies, cameramen, lights, props, stage managers (who speak audibly into their headsets in response to orders from the control booth), plus assorted musicians, actors and dancers. It's much tougher. Allen says that sometimes trying to get a television studio audience to laugh can be ". . .a little like working at the Palace (theater) while between you and the footlights the Harlem Globe-Trotters mapped out a few fast-moving plays."[17]

And don't forget the time factor. After an audience sits for some time, you may find their responsiveness to humor dwindling, for. . .

> The mind can absorb only as much as the seat can endure.

An experience Rusty had illustrates the effect of physical arrangements on an audience's response to humor. One evening at a university in North Carolina, he spoke to three different audiences at three successive fraternity meetings. He opened each talk with the "Meathead" story.

The first fraternity was a chapter of Rusty's own fraternity, Lambda Chi Alpha, which usually increases responsiveness. They met in a classroom that had two doors, one in back and one in front, to the right of the speaker. The room was about two-thirds full with nearly forty-five men. As Rusty began the story, latecomers started to arrive. Nearly every one used the front entrance—the one nearest the speaker and in full view of the audience. In fact, the latecomers had to walk in front of Rusty to get a seat. Response to the joke was warm, but not nearly as good as might be expected. Rate it a *B*.

The next meeting was in progress when Rusty arrived. It was in a boardroom with a large table and was packed with thirty to forty men. Many were standing. The only entrance was in the back and, since the meeting had been underway for some time, there were no latecomers. The walls were wooden and reflected sound superbly. The conditions were ideal, and response to "Meathead" was loud and raucous. Give it an *A*.

The third meeting was in a fraternity house barroom. The floor was bare concrete and the men sat in a circle on folding metal chairs. They had just finished a business meeting that had run overtime and obviously were tired. Some had to leave because the meeting had run late; fifteen to twenty stayed. The room was about half full. The lighting was poor, with one shaded bulb hanging from a wire in the center of the ceiling, so Rusty had difficulty seeing the men's faces and they, seeing his. The bar opened into another room, which offered distractions as people came and left. The "Meathead" story received only a modest laugh. Rate it a *C*.

In summary, knowing your listeners is essential to successful humor. The more you know before you tell your story, the better your chance of hitting their funny bones. Of course, you can't know or control every factor, but be aware of them as you prepare and as you evaluate your response. Ask yourself questions such as:

"Where are my listeners intellectually?"

"What is their psychological make-up?"

"What are their felt needs?"

"What are their religious convictions?"

"What current issues are on their minds?"

"Who are their heroes?"

"Which personalities in the audience can I mention to generate laughter?"

"What about the physical arrangements and related factors?"

"Will they be crowded or spread out?"

"Are the lighting, seating and temperature suitable?"

"Can I position myself away from the entrance to keep distractions to a minimum?"

"Will I be sensitive to their fatigue and attention span?"

If your humor doesn't go over with every crowd, do not become discouraged. It may be that particular audience or situation. Remember, "You can please some of the people all of the time. . ." Keep trying!

Thus far we've looked at the first two of the four ingredients for humor: good material and a knowledge of the audience. Now we turn to the third factor: an effective delivery.

CHAPTER 9

~~~~~~~~~~~~~~~~

DELIVERING
YOUR STORY
WITH A PUNCH

~~~~~~~~~~~~~~~~

A NEW PRISON INMATE found that every night after dinner, his fellow prisoners stood, one at a time, and called out numbers. After each number, the inmates laughed uproariously.

"What's going on?' the new inmate asked.

"We're telling jokes," a prisoner replied. "But we've heard our jokes so many times that we have them memorized. Rather than go to the trouble of telling a story all the fellows know, we just holler out a number from our jokebooks; saves lots of time."

Eager to be accepted by his new associates, the newcomer rose and called out a number. Dead silence. He tried another number; more silence. Again and again, his efforts failed to draw a snicker. Finally he broke the chill by asking, "OK, what's the deal? Why isn't anybody laughing?"

A prisoner nearby replied, "Some guys just don't know how to tell a joke."[1]

The third essential quality that the successful humorist must cultivate is an effective delivery. Your material might be tops. You may know your audience inside and out. But unless you deliver your lines with style and timing, your stories can fall flat.

A humorist is a persuader, inducing listeners to laugh. He or she must create an atmosphere that is conducive to laughter—much in the same way a salesman attempts to create an atmosphere that is conducive to buying. Of course, some salesmen are better persuaders than others.

> A summer resident in a mountain resort visited the local grocery store to purchase a pound of coffee. After giving the man his coffee, the owner of the store asked if he'd like to buy some salt. "Why, no, thanks," the customer replied. "I don't think I need any salt today."
>
> "I can give you a great deal on salt," the proprietor said, pointing to shelves sagging from the weight of boxes and boxes of salt.
>
> "Good grief!" the customer responded. "You sure must sell a lot of salt!"
>
> "No," the owner replied, "I hardly sell any. But the guy who sells me salt. . .can *he* ever sell salt!"[2]

A successful salesman works very carefully on his delivery. He knows that how he presents himself—his voice, diction, timing, gestures and body language—plays a major part in producing the right atmosphere.

Likewise, timing, diction, voice level, facial expressions and gestures can make or break a good story. How do you time a punch line for the maximum effect? Is timing everything? What about body language? What if you feel like a goon when you're delivering your story? How do you

138

keep from stumbling over the lines? These are some of the questions we'll consider in this chapter.

One of the best ways to sharpen your delivery is to watch successful humorists. Many successful comedians have honed their skills by observing other pros. Danny Thomas relates that in his early years he picked up a valuable tip from watching Bob Hope's delivery. As previously mentioned, Thomas appreciated the way Hope related his humor to a local situation in a Detroit nightclub. But, even more important, Thomas says, "I never realized until that night what *authority* meant, and how important it was to size up and understand your audience. Up 'til that time I had never really done that. I just rattled off my jokes and stories. But Bob Hope taught me that night that the most brilliantly written material in the world can fall flat unless the delivery is authoritative."[3]

How can you develop an authoritative delivery? Practice, practice, practice.

PRACTICE, PRACTICE, PRACTICE

> A couple phoned a neighbor to extend birthday greetings. They dialed the number and then sang "Happy Birthday" to him. But when they finished their off-key rendition, they discovered that they had dialed the wrong number.
> "Don't let it bother you," said a strange but amused voice. "You folks need all the practice you can get."

And *you* need all the practice you can get! Remember, when you see successful comedians in action, they most likely have honed and refined their material through myriads of practice sessions and live performances. When they appear on television or in a large, prestigious theater, they usually deliver their best material. They probably tested it before smaller audiences to learn what works and to eliminate the bugs. They know their routines so well that their delivery appears spontaneous, effortless and author-itative. Don't get discouraged if you can't match it. With practice, you can develop your own effective delivery. Try out your material on yourself, a friend or a sympathetic audience before using it in a more difficult situation.

Joan Rivers is one of the most successful comediennes in the United States. Her big break came on her first appear-ance on "The Tonight Show," starring Johnny Carson, in 1965. When she appeared on "The Tonight Show," she pre-pared for weeks, even if her slot lasted only a few minutes. Before one appearance, she tested her jokes for two weeks at a Santa Monica club. Then, the day of the appearance, she read a three-page typewritten script of her carefully rehearsed routine to one of Carson's talent coordinators. They interacted and made appropriate changes. She even suggested lines that Carson might use to interrupt her— lines that would lead to additional jokes by Rivers. That night on the air, reported *Time* magazine, she came across with "fizz and sparkle, giving not a hint that she. . .[had] traveled the same ground many times before."[4]

THE RIGHT WORD

Linda likes to explain her new ideas with zest and in ways that help people remember them. If she plans to be with someone whom she desires to persuade to a certain point of view, she may mentally practice for hours to carefully hone her expression. Since she loves humor and values it as an important communication tool, she zealously practices pieces of humor to aid her argument. Most of her humor is spontaneous, however, as she has developed the art of seeing the funny side of things.

It can help to write out stories or jokes word-for-word and read them aloud as you practice. This allows you to hear exactly what your listeners will hear and to fine-tune your word choices and phrasing. Does a word sound cumbersome? Replace it with an easier synonym that won't confuse listeners or distract them. The right word can make all the difference.

> At a posh Manhattan dinner party, a Latin American visitor was telling the guests about his home country and himself. As he concluded, he said, "And I have a charming and understanding wife but, alas, no children." As his listeners appeared to be waiting for him to continue, he said, haltingly, "You see, my wife is unbearable." Puzzled glances prompted him to try to clarify the matter: "What I mean is, my wife is inconceivable." As his companions seemed amused, he floundered deeper into the intricacies of the English language, explaining triumphantly, "That is, my wife, she is impregnable!"[5]

Yes, the right word matters, and so does the proper phrase.

> A number of years ago, the dean of women at a large co-ed university was speaking to an assembly of the student body. She began her

141

remarks by saying, "Young men and women, the president of this university and I have decided to stop petting on this campus."

To avoid a red face or a lead balloon, strive for the best phrasing. Is a particular phrase too long? Will it lose your listeners? Condense it. Is it difficult to enunciate clearly? Does it sound unnatural? Rewrite it using words that seem more natural to you and your potential listeners. Remember that success in humor can depend on split-second timing. Cumbersome phrasing can make you tongue-tied, throw off your timing and kill the punch line.

Once you have developed your story—written it out, polished the words and phrases—then memorize it and practice it aloud until it doesn't sound memorized. Is it imperative that you memorize humorous material? No. Some people can tell humorous stories off the cuff and get laughs. But memorizing can help prevent rambling or sloppy pauses that come from having to rearrange a story in your mind as you tell it. It can help you make every word and phrase count and prevent you from falling prey to the pitfalls of obscure wording or cumbersome phrases. It can allow you to read the audience more closely and pay greater attention to your delivery, timing, gestures, etc. It also can help ensure that your punch line comes off smoothly.

As a simple illustration of the value of correct phrasing, word choice, practice and memorization, consider two endings in a story about Whistler's mother: (1) Whistler returns home and says, "Hey! Mother's off her rocker!" because he sees her scrubbing the floor down on her hands and knees. (2) Whistler enters the room and sees his mother down on hands and knees, scrubbing the floor. "Hey," he cries, "Mother's off her rocker!" Obviously, the second version packs the punch. The first version could be the result of poor preparation by the humorist. Practice and memorization could solve the problem.

TIMING

Timing can make or break your humor. One amateur observer said that for professional humorists, "Timing is everything." While we do not agree that it is everything— certainly good material and a knowledge of one's audience are important, too—timing is certainly crucial. The right pause before a punch line can allow tension to peak so that the release of tension—the laughter—is maximum.

Milton Berle once showed a friend the value of timing, explaining that it is almost more crucial than material. During a routine, Milton worked into a joke, built up suspense and paused before the punch line. Then, instead of delivering the correct line, he substituted the meaningless phrase, "last Thursday." The crowd roared. Berle had done such a stellar job of delivering the line "last Thursday" that the audience members laughed before they realized the laugh was on them.[6]

Jack Benny was a master of timing. A pause here, a wry glance there, even an extended delay could serve to heighten tension or draw a second round of laughter after the first had subsided. And Bob Hope says, ". . .timing is my greatest asset."[7]

The key to good timing is knowing what is happening in the mind of your listeners. Do they need more time to have their curiosity aroused or to significantly digest a piece of information, so they are ready for the twist? Would an added moment build the suspense? By being sufficiently in tune with your own thought process and response, you often can guess the audience response.

You can practice good timing by visualizing the thinking process of your listeners. Often they give clues. They may suddenly become quiet and expectant. Other times, eyes suggest, "What next?" or "So. . .?" These clues suggest that they have completed a thought process and are awaiting that next special phrase. Remember, if you move ahead of this process, they may not fully appreciate the humor, because they have not assimilated your build-up material. If you move too slowly, the audience may second guess you or, worse yet, be distracted by other thoughts.

Consider this illustration:

> A hopeful young lady visited a computer dating service and listed her requirements for a prospective date. She was a very precise person and knew exactly what she wanted in a date. She wanted someone who liked people, was small, preferred formal attire and enjoyed water sports. The computer followed her wishes to the letter. It sent her a penguin.

Perhaps you can see how timing could affect response to the above story. It probably is best to pause two to four seconds before the final sentence. This allows listeners to assimilate what you have said and gives time for their curiosity to mount. If you tell the story without the pause, you may go too fast for the assimilation to occur and curiosity to develop. But, you say, you tried it both ways and neither got a laugh? Relax! Maybe it will work with another audience, or perhaps you can practice timing with another story.

Again, the best way to develop a sense of timing is through observation, practice and testing. Watch other humorists to see how they time their lines. As you listen, ask yourself: "Why did they pause at that particular point?" "Could they have drawn a bigger laugh if they waited longer or started up sooner?"

Then try your own material. Ask a friend who is a good communicator to evaluate your timing. Test it on different audiences and try slightly different timing approaches to find the most successful.

HOW'S THAT AGAIN?

Several other factors, such as voice level and diction, can help your delivery. Is your voice clear and easy to understand? If not, practice reciting your lines until they come out clearly. Diogenese, the Greek orator, developed his speaking skills by practicing with pebbles in his mouth until he could enunciate clearly.

> A farmer was quoted in the Town Gazette as having "2,008 pigs." He showed up the next morning to declare to the editor, "That's a misprint! I didn't say I have 2,008 pigs. I told your reporter that I have 2 sows and 8 pigs."
> —Bob Horner

Do you speak in a monotone? Practice varying your pitch and intensity. If you feel that it sounds forced, ask a friend to listen. Often what seems unnatural or exaggerated to you can come across superbly to an audience. If appropriate, talk rapidly to keep your listeners' attention. And remember that varying your voice level, intensity and speed can be just what you need to make your point.

> A janitor was straightening up after a political rally and came across the politician's speech

145

manuscript, which inadvertently had been left on the lectern. Along the margins were various instructions such as "Pause here. Look left and right for effect," "Wipe brow here," "Gaze upward," "Shake fist."

Near the end was a long paragraph of text. Opposite it, the politician had written in large capital letters: "ARGUMENT WEAK HERE. RAISE VOICE. YELL LIKE THE BLAZES!"[8]

BODY LANGUAGE

Body language—facial expressions, hand gestures, motions, etc.—can be a great help in communicating humor. Body language provides a visual aid, and any appropriate visual aid can help in communication.

> One university student decided to give a speech for his speech class on "How to Skip Class." Just after he began his presentation, the professor asked if he had any visual aids to clarify his points. "I almost forgot!" the young man replied, and he stepped out into the hall. He never came back.[9]

Gestures can help your listeners grasp the scene you are trying to set. Does your story involve someone painting a house? Mimic the arm motions of wielding a paintbrush or roller. Is your protagonist putting on spray deodorant? Spray a few imaginary squirts under each arm.

Use your hands to emphasize particular points in your story. Generally, for a small audience your hand and arm motions should be closer to your body. For larger crowds,

146

extend your arms and make your motions more pronounced. It will help keep the crowd's attention. And there's another good reason to use gestures. . .

> Veteran speakers usually gesture freely and
> walk around and around on the platform.
> They know that a moving target is harder to
> hit.[10]

Facial expressions also are a good tool in delivering humor. In most cases it is best to keep a straight face—rather than laughing—until after the punch line. It helps to build the suspense. But don't feel that your face must be perfectly straight. Maybe a grimace, a wink, a wide-eyed shock or a frown would help set the mood.

Jerry Lewis is a master of the facial expression. His crazy facial contortions sometimes draw greater laughs than his lines. Comedian Robin Williams is just as crazy or more so. Milton Berle's buffoonery captured millions of viewers in the early days of television. Jack Benny once passed the ultimate test of facial comedy. A stagehand in Las Vegas asked him how long he could be onstage without uttering a word and still get laughs. Jack gave it a try. That night, when he walked onstage, the spotlight hit him. He froze and gazed upward as if to say, "Where did that come from?" The audience members started to laugh. Jack then looked at them as if to say, "What's so funny?" and their laughter grew. He looked into the wings with a puzzled look as if to say, "Why are they laughing? I don't know. Do you?" More laughs. He stepped up to the microphone and deadpanned the audience. Hysterical laughter. He looked at his watch, began to tap his foot and put his hands on his hips. The audience roared with each move. For seven full minutes he uttered not a word. He did it all through facial expressions and gestures.[11]

Maybe facial expressions come easily for you. Use them to your advantage. Maybe they don't. Practice them in front of a mirror. Then try them out in your story-telling—perhaps a few at a time so you gradually build confidence. Remember that what may feel awkward to you often comes across to others as perfectly appropriate.

TELEGRAPHING PUNCHES

As you employ gestures and facial expressions, be careful not to telegraph the punch. Remember, the suddenness with which you introduce the unexpected twist is essential to its success. The audience may know that a punch line is coming, and sensing that it is coming often heightens the anticipation. But if people figure out the punch line in advance, much of the laughter may be lost.

A professional boxer learns not to telegraph his punches—not to let his opponent know which punch is coming next. A basketball player learns to fake one way and pass another or turn his head one way and pass another. The objective is to keep his opponent guessing. Likewise, humor requires bluffing, much like a successful card player might use.

> The tourist was amazed when he walked into the Las Vegas casino and saw a dog seated at a table playing poker with three men. "Say, can that dog read his cards?" the stranger inquired.
> "Yeah, but he's not much of a poker player," one of the men answered. "Whenever he gets a good hand he wags his tail."[12]

Learn to use body language, gestures and animated

facial expressions to enhance your humor—just don't tip your hand and ruin the punch line.

Here is a story that lends itself to a good bit of acting out:

> Bill once had a summer job as a truck driver. Twice a week, he hauled loads on the interstate between Cincinnati and Atlanta. He always stopped for lunch at Joe's Diner, a friendly little truck stop about halfway between the two cities.
>
> One day Bill parked his truck, walked into Joe's Diner, sat down on a stool at the counter and ordered lunch. Off in the distance, there was a roar and a cloud of dust. As the roar got closer, out of the cloud of dust came twelve gang members on motorcycles. The bikers parked their cycles and stomped into the diner. They formed a semicircle around Bill and began to snap their fingers in a rhythmic cadence. Bill sat at the counter, unperturbed, eating his lunch. Then the leader of the gang silenced his men, pointed at two of them, pointed at Bill and snapped his fingers. The two Hell's Angels went over to Bill. One of them poured iced tea over Bill's head. The other picked up the mashed potatoes and smashed them into Bill's face. Then the two of them knocked him off the stool and beat him to a pulp. Bill never said a word. He got up, brushed himself off, paid Joe for his lunch and left.
>
> The leader of the motorcycle gang swaggered over to Joe and said, "That guy's not

much of a man, is he? He didn't even stand up for himself."

"No," Joe replied as he looked out the window, "and he's not much of a truck driver either. He just ran over twelve motorcycles."

Now, re-read the above story and imagine telling it to a group of friends. What facial expressions would you include to make it more effective? Maybe you'd portray the gang members as angry, Bill as cool and calm, Joe the proprietor as wide-eyed.

What gestures and body language would you employ? Maybe you would act like a motorcyclist riding a chopper with butterfly handlebars. You could snap your fingers and then silence the gang. You could point to two of the men, then to Bill and snap your fingers. You could pour the iced tea, smash the mashed potatoes and beat Bill to a pulp. Then as Bill, you could pick yourself up, brush yourself off and pay your bill. As Joe, you might peer out the window, squint slightly, crane your neck and cup your hand over your eyes.

What about variations in your voice? You could imitate the roar of the motorcycles as they approached and the cocky boast of the leader of the pack. Your delivery would help set the mood for the punch line. The crowd would laugh with approval!

ADAPTING TO DIFFERENT
AUDIENCES AND SITUATIONS

Successful communicators adapt their delivery to each audience and situation. So, too, must the humorist. Flexibility is the key. Develop and learn your material, but be ready to think on your feet.

Once Rusty was speaking to a group of fraternity men at a Texas university. He began with the humorous automobile accident insurance claims from Chapter 1. These stories nearly always work well, and that day he used them out of habit. As he began, he suddenly remembered that, just before he was introduced, someone had told the group that a member of the fraternity was in a bad car wreck the night before and hospitalized with semi-serious injuries. Rusty had to think fast. He might offend his audience. But it was too late to stop, and the success of his talks often depend greatly on the first impression.

Fortunately he had the presence of mind to dig himself out of the hole. "You know," he said, "I just realized that, in light of the auto accident last night, these stories might not be the most appropriate. I certainly don't mean to cause offense. On the other hand, maybe you can tell them to your friend when you visit him in the hospital. He'll probably get a kick out of them, and you'll cheer him up!" The men smiled and the stories got their usual warm response.

You may not always be that quick-thinking (Rusty isn't either), but you can develop that skill with experience. Remember, flexibility is the name of the game in presenting humor.

BE BRIEF

Brevity is an art that the humorist must cultivate and apply as the situation warrants. Only a skillful story-teller can hold a listener's attention for a long time. It is better to begin with shorter stories. Or, if you use a longer story, insert several intermediate humorous lines to keep them with you.

If you are telling several jokes, be aware that many consider it a crime to bore an audience. (Undoubtedly an

151

audience member came up with that line.) Practice will help you learn when to stop and when to continue. It is best to stop while you're ahead and leave them eager to hear you the next time—best for your audience and for you.

◆ In mentioning brevity, it is worth noting that the shortest inaugural address was George Washington's—just 135 words. The longest was William Henry Harrison's in 1841. He delivered a two-hour, 9,000-word speech into the teeth of a freezing northeast wind. He came down with a cold the following day, and a month later he died of pneumonia.[13]

◆ One orator said, "I have discontinued long speeches on account of my throat. . .several people have threatened to cut it."[14]

◆ One famous speaker was advised to lecture for five minutes and if he couldn't strike oil, to stop boring.[15]

◆ Will Rogers was presiding as toastmaster at a meeting being addressed by a tediously long speaker. At the conclusion, Rogers told the crowd, "You have been listening to that famous Chinese orator, On Too Long."[16]

A few additional tips regarding brevity: Avoid spending excessive time on one topic. Varying the topics will help keep your listeners with you. Also, if you find great success, some in the audience may begin to resent you. Try making yourself the butt of one or two jokes to lure them back to your side. In fact, making yourself the butt of the joke can get you out of many difficult situations, as the following story illustrates:

> Billy Graham was once scheduled to speak at a large church convention in Texas. People from all over poured into the auditorium. As the program participants mounted the platform, the audience looked in vain for Graham. His plane had been grounded several hundred miles away. As the audience was not informed of this until his substitute was introduced, the speaker began under a decided handicap. He tried a story to alleviate the disappointment.
>
> "My replacement of Billy Graham as speaker today reminds me of a church that announced a strawberry festival one year. They invited everyone to participate and eat all the strawberries and cream they wanted. Huge crowds came from near and far. During the festival, the chairman rose and announced, 'I'm sorry to report that our strawberry crop was a total loss this year. We're sorry, but we don't have any strawberries. However, we do have plenty of prunes.'" The speaker's story not only brought down the house, but also helped relieve the crowd's disappointment.[17]

That speaker adapted well to his audience.

MIDSTREAM CHANGES

Sometimes you need to adapt in the middle of your story. Suppose, as occasionally happens, your listeners laugh at an intermediate point. If you wait for that laughter to die

153

down, they may unwind and not laugh as hard at the punch line. So use that laughter to your advantage. Be grateful that they are following you closely enough to be laughing, but keep moving so that the tension doesn't have time to completely dissipate. You often can use the first laugh to intensify the second. Above all, do not stop after the first laugh and say, "Wait! That's not the punch line. We're not there yet!" That usually will put your story six feet under.

Frequently you will have interruptions during your stories. Some interruptions (such as shouts from the kitchen while you're waxing eloquent at the dinner table) will kill any chances for continuing. It is best to stop and wait for a better setting. Other times, someone will cough or move a chair across the floor as you utter a key word. You realize that, unless your listeners catch that word or phrase, they'll never understand the punch line. Yet you fear that the interruption obscured it. Simply repeat the phrase without calling attention to why you are doing it. If you glance at the person who coughed or sneer at the one who moved his chair, you may lose the audience. If you pause and, with stifled discontent, repeat the key phrase, you may offend them. But if you pause naturally, as if to take a breath, begin again by repeating the key phrase and continue as if nothing happened, you may compensate for and cover the interruption.

Suppose someone enters the room during your story. If he enters through the back door and you suspect that few in the audience are distracted, continue without pausing. On the other hand, if the latecomer enters by a front door in full view of all, or if he makes a lot of noise as he enters, you may need to think quickly to hold the crowd's attention. Draw brief attention to the intruder in a lighthearted, non-offensive way.

One speaker we know glances at the latecomer and

says, "Welcome! You might want to get the notes, as we'll have a test on this at the end of the meeting" or (for a classroom) ". . .this will be on the final exam." Usually the audience and latecomer laugh and the speaker can resume his story. Sometimes a dog or cat will wander by the speaker. A creative and quick-thinking speaker can play with the animal for a moment, then hand it to someone to remove and continue the story. One time when Linda was addressing an outdoor audience in Korea, a chicken walked up. The audience started to laugh and Linda, who doesn't take herself too seriously, laughed right along with them. The key is to acknowledge the interruption, remain unflustered, and gently and tactfully draw the listeners' attention back into focus.

One final tip on delivery: Leave 'em laughing. Once you deliver your lines and gather your laughs, be satisfied. Avoid the temptation to squeeze out more chuckles by repeating the punch line. Reruns are usually duds.

But suppose they don't laugh. What do you do then? How do you avoid the pain, the embarrassment, the sense of rejection and even the fear of future rejections that come when your story falls flat? And how do you get your audience back?

What do you do when your story bombs? Stay tuned. . .!

CHAPTER 10

~~~~~~~~

WHAT TO DO
WHEN IT BOMBS

~~~~~~~~

PASSENGERS ON A JETLINER were relaxing in their seats for the long flight. The voice over the loudspeaker had just announced that the aircraft had reached its cruising altitude and that passengers were free to unfasten their seatbelts and move about the cabin. Then the voice continued.

"Ladies and gentlemen, we are proud to announce that you are flying on the maiden voyage of one of our brand new fully automated jetliners. These new jetliners are the pride of our fleet and have no need for pilot, co-pilot or navigator. All human error has been eliminated. You needn't be alarmed, as everything—from cabin pressure to speed and altitude—is completely controlled by our computer. We're excited about the world's first fully automated airplane, and we hope you are, too. So just sit back and relax, and remember, nothing can go wrong. . .nothing can go wrong. . .nothing can go wrong. . . nothing can go wrong."

If you carefully follow all the guidelines in this book whenever you tell a joke or humorous story, nothing can go wrong. Right? Wrong! Sometimes, no matter how well you prepare and practice, even the best material falls flat. What do you do?

Imagine telling the above story to a group at a dinner party. Dinner is over, everyone has gathered in the living room, and you are eager to try your latest chestnut. You tell the story, deliver the punch line, ". . .nothing can go wrong. . ." Then, dead silence. A few polite smiles, but not a trace of laughter. Your story has bombed.

What would you do? Crawl behind a sofa and hide? Perhaps you would feign a heart attack, hoping to garner the sympathy to assuage your embarrassment. You might be overcome by an intense desire to burn this book.

Don't! Regardless of how uncomfortable you feel in such situations, realize that you are not alone. Even the pros bomb now and then. But they know a few good techniques for on-the-spot recovery—which you can develop. And you can look on the entire situation as a learning experience. Later, think back over it to discover what went wrong and why. Believe it or not, there are also ways to cope inside— to handle the feelings of hurt or rejection that can creep in or even overwhelm us when we feel we are not well-received. So read carefully and tuck away some good ideas for "What to do when it bombs."

ON-THE-SPOT RECOVERY
Quick recoveries require quick thinking. Here's a fellow who found himself in an embarrassing situation and used quick thinking to his advantage. At least he hoped it would work to his advantage.

An old fisherman sat on the riverbank with his pole in hand and line in the water. He obviously was waiting for a nibble, even though fishing season had not officially opened. A game warden observed him from a distance, then strolled up and quietly stood behind him for several minutes.

"You the game warden?" the fisherman asked, glancing over his shoulder.

"Yep," the warden replied.

Cool as could be, the old fisherman started to move his pole gently from side to side. After a couple of minutes, he lifted the line out of the water to reveal his bait, a small minnow wiggling on the hook.

"Just teachin' him how to swim," the old fisherman explained.[1]

"But," you might ask, "suppose I can't think that quickly when my story bombs?" The key is to think in advance—think through possible approaches to the problem and have them ready to use. Here are three techniques for successful on-the-spot recovery: (1) keep moving; (2) acknowledge the bomb; (3) spin off to more humor.

Keep moving. Sometimes when your punch lines falls flat, the best thing to do is remain calm, maintain your composure and keep on talking as if nothing had happened. Sound far-fetched? It is not. If you have not tipped off your listeners that a humorous punch line is coming, often they won't know what they missed. This approach works especially well in speeches in which you can naturally move on to related material. Of course, if you are swapping jokes or relating a personal experience at a gathering of friends, or if, in your speech, you already announced or hinted about the funny story, "keep moving" may not be the best advice. But if you can keep moving, you often can cover your tracks with the content of your talk.

If the speech is well-written, you may have included a perfectly logical transition from the joke into your next thought. Even if the transition lacks polish, if you keep moving, some (or even many) individuals who might mentally stumble over your thinking will assume they had a brief lapse in their own attention. They may even resolve to set their minds in gear to follow you more closely. We're not encouraging you to use fast talk to cover for poor logic. Rather, we're saying that the listener who fails to get the point of a funny story may not know it was supposed to be funny if no one tells him. It's not a bomb unless your listeners realize it's a bomb. So if you suspect that most in your audience are unaware that they were supposed to laugh, just keep moving!

Acknowledge the bomb. If, however, you suspect that the bulk of your silent audience realizes you intended for them to laugh, it is usually appropriate to acknowledge the bomb. In such situations, the listeners often feel tension. Some may identify with the faux pas, having committed similar blunders themselves, and recall their feelings of embarrassment and isolation. Others may feel sorry or embarrassed for you. Still others may feel awkward because the orderly flow of things was interrupted; people didn't react as you had anticipated. They may wonder how you will get things back on track—or if you can.

All of these audience responses create tension. By skillfully and sincerely acknowledging your blunder, you can break the tension and draw a laugh. If you succeed, you win the respect of your audience and gain points. For instance, after the punch line, when no one laughs, you can pause a second or two, look around, let the tension of

160

silence mount, then say, "Well, I guess *that* one went over like a lead balloon!" Delivered with the appropriate facial expression—perhaps a wry smile to convey that you're poking fun at yourself rather than at them—the line can draw chuckles or even loud laughter. The audience is relaxed and you can proceed.

Another line that can work effectively, if delivered with a slight shrug or flip of the hand, is "(Pause). . . Well, I didn't think it was funny, either!" Or, if your rapport with the audience is very good and they are jovial, you might say (after the obvious awkward pause), "OK, now, I'm going to give you another chance!" Then proceed to tell another anecdote. If the rapport and mood are right, people might laugh as soon as you say you're going to give them another chance. They will see your offer as a friendly put-down. If, however, they feel the least bit offended, your comeback may bomb as well. They might interpret your offer as a serious put-down of their intelligence (i.e., their ability to get jokes).

One final way to acknowledging the bomb is to claim, "I'm just testing some new material here." You may or may not get away with it.

For the quick thinker, here is a third technique for on-the-spot recovery:

Spin off to more humor. Pick up on something—an idea from your story, a current situation, a person in the audience, etc.—that enables you to move quickly to another humorous line or anecdote. Without specifically acknowledging the bomb, and ideally, without missing a beat, attempt to insert new humor or a new twist to keep your audience with you. Often the fact that your original line bombed, and that you know it bombed, will be obvious to your listeners, perhaps by what you say, by your sly facial expression or by the twinkle

161

in your eye. But your new humor should come so deftly that your audience can't help but laugh.

Quick thinking can pay off in any potentially embarrassing or difficult situation.

◆ "Skipper," the sailor said to his captain as he saluted, "a special message just came in for you from the admiral. I have it right here."

"Read it to me," the captain ordered.

The sailor read: "You are without a doubt the most idiotic, lame-brained officer ever to command a ship in the United States Navy."

The skipper responded, "Have that communication decoded at once."[2]

◆ A young minister, just out of seminary, decided to take a job on the police force for a few months, in hopes that the experience would be useful to his work. After passing the physical, he took the oral exam, which was designed to test his mental alertness and his ability to think and act quickly and wisely in an emergency.

One of the questions he was asked was, "What would you do to disperse an agitated crowd?"

His quick reply: "I'd take up a collection."[3]

When Rusty speaks on university campuses about love, sex and marriage, he frequently begins by saying, "One of the main purposes of sex is pleasure. . .(pause). . .P-L-E-A-S-U-R-E (spelling it out)." Then he follows with, "I sound like a Rolaids commercial!" (as in "how do you spell relief from acid indigestion? R-O-L-A-I-D-S!"). Often the line draws a laugh, but occasionally it fails, possibly because some are unfamiliar with the commercial or because the line just doesn't strike them as humorous. If it bombs, Rusty has learned to follow with, "Now, they do have Rolaids here in (city), don't they?" The wry jab usually generates some laughter and the audience is back in step.

As you probably can surmise, spinning off to more humor is not always easy. Bright ideas do not always come to you when you need them. But try to stay alert, use them when they do come and remember the successful ones for future use.

WHAT NOT TO DO WHEN IT BOMBS

When your story bombs, do not try to explain the punch line or the humor. If your listeners got the joke, but didn't think it was funny, your explanation may offend them. If they did not get the joke, they may be embarrassed or indignant, interpreting your subtlety as stupidity. In any case, your explanation will probably detract from the suddenness necessary to incite laughter. Better to move on to new material.

One exception to this prescription is situations in which you can use the explanation to acknowledge the bomb or to spin off to new humor. This risky approach usually works only when the speaker has excellent rapport with the audience and the crowd is in a lighthearted mood. Johnny Carson sometimes uses this technique in situations where it is obvious to all that the audience caught his punch line, but simply felt it wasn't funny enough to laugh at. He then pretends that they didn't get the joke and proceeds to explain it. If Carson were to apply this technique to the story about the captain receiving the critical message from the admiral, he might say something like this:

". . .The skipper responded, 'Have that communication

decoded at once.' "...dead silence...pause...Carson looks puzzled, glances at two or three sections of the audience, perhaps glances behind him, as if to see if something had distracted the audience's attention. Then he follows with, "You see, the skipper didn't want to believe that the admiral would really say all those terrible things about him... (pause)...He thought the message must have been part of a secret code... (pause)...You see, in the Navy, they often send messages in *code*...(pause)...and in order to understand them, they have to be *de*coded...(pause)...and that was a *joke*...(pause)... Maybe *you* need to have it decoded!" With the right chemistry, the jokester can use the explanation to generate laughter.

Consider another approach to avoid when your story bombs. Occasionally, the same story has two or three alternate punch lines. If one fails, you may be tempted to chime in with, "There's this other ending that goes like this..." In most cases, don't. Chances are the tension has already dissipated and your alternate line will bomb as well. Try another story.

A final principle to remember if your story bombs, especially if it is good: people may be all laughed out. It may be time to ask, "What did you think of the football game the other day?" (or soap opera, President's speech, or whatever you choose).

ANALYSIS:
WHAT WENT WRONG AND WHY

In doing the post mortem on any anecdote or joke, it is important to learn what went wrong and why. When you are alone, or perhaps with a friend whose advice you respect, analyze the incident. Was the problem with your material? Did you misread your audience? Was your delivery flawed? Here are some questions to ask as you think through each area:

Material. Did I depict a commonly understood situation? Did I allow for the tension to develop or play off of existing tension? Did I introduce the twist suddenly and unexpectedly? Was my story too long; did I bore them? or was it too short; did I fail to paint the necessary picture or omit a crucial detail? Does my phrasing need work? Could my sentences be tightened? Are any words too complex? Does the humor turn on a written twist that the listening audience might miss?

Audience. Was I familiar enough with the audience? Did we have enough rapport to use that type of humor? Did they understand the story's setting? Was my material too intellectual or too simple for this audience? Did I misjudge their social class? Were they in the right mood for that kind of story?

Many professional and college football teams hold a voluntary pre-game chapel program on game days. Once Rusty spoke at the University of Miami team chapel on "How to be Successful and Satisfied." He began with two jokes that were proven winners, but not one player even cracked a smile. In fact, they appeared unresponsive to all humor in the talk. Yet at the end, everyone seemed very warm, grateful and enthusiastic as they walked up to Rusty, shook his hand and thanked him for coming.

Rusty was puzzled about their lack of response to the humor. He frequently had spoken to athletes and his humor had been well-received. He asked Steve, a friend who had coordinated the program, if he had done something wrong. "Oh, that," Steve explained. "The players are always up-tight on game days. You didn't do anything

165

wrong—they just don't laugh before a game."

Other questions to ask about your audience in analyzing why your story bombed: Might I have offended some by allusions or statements regarding politics, religion, morality, etc.? Could I have improved my story by referring to a local personality? And what about the physical arrangements? Was the lighting appropriate? The temperature? Were they packed into the room or scattered like marbles in an airplane hangar? Was I close enough to the audience to generate interest and enthusiasm? Were there interruptions or distractions? Were my listeners fatigued? Was their attention waning?

Delivery. Did I appear relaxed or nervous? Was my delivery authoritative? Did I stumble over my lines? Do I need to work on my timing, diction, or voice level? Would more practice help? What about my gestures? Would more energetic hand and body motions liven up the crowd? Or were my gestures inappropriately exaggerated for such a setting? Would a change in facial expression help? Did I telegraph my punch, perhaps by smiling at a key phrase that unintentionally clued the listener? Did I laugh at the wrong time?

Asking these kinds of questions can help you discover why a story bombed and how you can improve. Above all, don't give up! Remember that the right material, a knowledge of your audience and an effective delivery usually can help you become successful in humor. The same material in a different audience and situation can work wonders.

We've considered techniques for on-the-spot recovery and ways to learn and improve. But an important question remains: When your story falls flat, how do you cope on the inside? How do you keep from feeling insecure or rejected? And how do you avoid the fear that it may happen again? Fear of failure can be paralyzing.

166

COPING ON THE INSIDE

The *Times of London* reported on a survey of 3,000 U.S. inhabitants concerning fear. "What are you most afraid of?" asked the team of market researchers. The results may surprise you. The fifth worst fear was the fear of flying. Tied for fourth place were the fears of sickness and death. Tied for third place were deep water, financial problems, and insects and bugs. In second place was fear of heights. And in first place, the human fear named more often that any other, was the fear of speaking before a group.[4]

Public speakers and humorists are on display. All eyes and ears are on them. Their every word, gesture, facial expression is open to public scrutiny. Is it any wonder that even experienced speakers and performers often get butterflies?

> One young man paced back and forth incessantly in a room adjoining an auditorium where a series of lectures was being given. A kind lady stopped him and said, "You seem quite nervous about going up to speak next."
>
> "Who, me? Nervous?" replied the man. "Not me. I'm not nervous. I make speeches all the time."
>
> The woman asked, "Then what are you doing here in the ladies' room?"[5]

Television newscaster Edward R. Murrow called stage fright "the sweat of perfection."[6] Most of us are concerned about how we come across to others, and a certain amount of apprehension before we speak or tell a story is natural. But how do we avoid excessive concern, which can keep us in knots and even immobilize us? And when our worst fears about story-telling or joke-telling are realized—when our story bombs—how do we handle the disappointment? How do we deal with feelings, large or small, of rejection, hurt or isolation? Everyone wants to be liked. How do we cope with the feeling that "they didn't like me"?

First, it's important to realize that laying an egg with your humor is not the end of the world. Things could be worse.

> When I was down in the dumps, my friend
> said, "Cheer up, things could be worse." So I
> cheered up and, sure enough, things got worse!

Remember, too, that just because your listeners didn't like what you did (i.e., your joke), that doesn't mean they don't like you as a person (though they might not).

Ultimately, though, the answer to fear of rejection lies not in advice such as, "It's not the end of the world," or, "They may still like you as a person." Rather, we believe that the secret is a healthy self-concept, a healthy view of who you are as a person. Security in your identity can give you the inner strength to stand in the public eye with confidence, to tell your story or deliver your lines with authority. And, if your story bombs, it can help you recover on the inside while you attempt to recover on the outside. With a healthy self-concept, you can withstand many kinds of rejection because at the core of your being, you can accept yourself. Your deep genuine love for yourself enables you to handle lack of love from others.

Remember again the four ingredients for successful humor: good material, a knowledge of your audience, good delivery and *a healthy self-concept*. A healthy self-concept is essential because it helps combat the fear of failure. The next chapter looks at how to develop a healthy self-concept.

CHAPTER 11

YOUR SELF-CONCEPT: HOW TO LIVE WITH YOURSELF AND LIKE IT

ONE MAN HAD an inferiority complex that was so bad that whenever he entered an elevator and gave the attendant his floor number, he always included, "If it isn't out of your way."[1]

Steve Allen writes, "All of us require the approval of others. Without it, in infancy, we literally wither and die. Comedians are perhaps distinguished from the rest of the human race by requiring the attention of others even more."[2]

Mel Brooks, the comedian, film producer and actor, attributes the aggressive strain in much of his humor, in part, to the fact that as a youngster he was not included in the social groups and activities of the older, bigger, more confident boys. His solution was to get people to like him by entertaining them. He became a jester.[3]

JUST ONE KISS

Many who try to be funny are actually, consciously or not, seeking the approval and the resulting self-esteem that come with getting others to laugh. Many professional comics admit that. Dudley Moore, the successful movie actor, explains his lifelong quest for approval. When he was six or seven, he spent a lot of time in British hospitals. One night, a nurse named Pat gave him a good-night kiss. Forty years later, Moore says, "I almost spin when I think about it. She was truly an angel of mercy, and that kiss was probably the first taste of real, unqualified, uncomplicated affection I had ever had. In many ways my entire life is based on recapturing that single moment of affection."[4]

As a youngster, Moore felt humiliated about his small height, clubfoot and short left leg. Kids laughed at him and called him Hopalong. "I felt unworthy of anything, a little runt with a twisted foot."[5] His parents felt guilty about his defect, so Dudley felt that he had done something wrong. His home lacked love, and his parents seemed characterized by fear and anxiety. *Time* magazine reports his avenue for self-esteem:

> In his early teens, Moore learned how to win
> affection, and the lesson has dominated his life:
> people like to laugh, and they reward those who
> can make them do so. Having discovered that
> vintage truth, he became the class clown. Says he:
> "I think that is every comedian's story."[6]

Today, Moore says that one of his main goals is to make people laugh. "I want to attract people. I want their warmth. I want their love."[7]

We all desire the approval of others. Sometimes the desire outweighs the fear of failure, so a person with low self-esteem takes the risks involved in humor. Generally, however, you need at least a measure of confidence to take the chance that your listeners won't understand, like or laugh at your jokes.

HOW YOU SEE YOURSELF. . .
IT MATTERS

A strong self-concept provides the inner security needed to withstand calamity, even rejection, and to overcome the fear of failure. And a greater self-confidence helps you improve at humor.

In fact, a healthy self-concept helps you relax and improve at whatever you do. For example, suppose that during a regular employees' meeting at your place of work, your boss says, "Before we consider our usual business, I want to recognize *(your name)*, one of our most outstanding employees. I want everyone to know what a fine worker you are. You are always on time, you never complain about extra work, and you even seek opportunities to improve our company. I never have seen anyone with such integrity, proficiency and enthusiasm. Thank you for being part of our company."[8]

Wouldn't you feel great about yourself and be motivated to be a better employee? When your self-concept improves, your performance as a person, and as a humorist, usually improves.

A Gallup Poll examining self-esteem in the United States revealed that those with healthy self-concepts are distinguished by several outstanding characteristics, such as:

"They are morally and ethically sensitive, and generous in giving."

"They are highly productive in their jobs, and far freer from the abuse of chemicals and alcohol."

"They are more actively involved in society's problems."

"They view success not in a materialistic way, but in terms of relationships."

"They have stronger families and marriages, and are more successful in interpersonal relationships."

"They handle stress more successfully and live healthier lives."[9]

The poll also found that only one-third of Americans report a strong self-esteem. We suspect that a good deal of human behavior, from strivings for success to involvement in interpersonal relationships, is motivated by the desire to enhance one's own self-concept.

Success and a healthy self-concept are somewhat symbiotic; they feed each other. Not only does a healthy self-concept contribute to success, but success enhances one's self-concept. And nearly everyone wants to be successful.

> President Calvin Coolidge once entertained some friends from Vermont in the White House. His friends were concerned that they display proper table manners to win the President's respect, so they observed Coolidge very carefully and followed his example in detail. The meal passed smoothly. Then coffee was served. Coolidge poured his into his saucer. The guests did likewise. Then Coolidge added sugar and cream. The visitors did the same. Coolidge then leaned over and gave his coffee to the cat.[10]

It would seem advantageous not to be ruled by our desire for approval, but to be secure enough not to depend solely on the response of others for self-esteem.

Gallup's finding that two-thirds of Americans indicate a less-than-strong self-esteem raises the question, "Why?" Probably many factors contribute to this lack of self-esteem, but consider four main ones: guilt, fear, problems in interpersonal relationships and lack of meaning in life.

GUILT

When people fail to achieve standards (moral, ethical, social, vocational, etc.) that they impose upon themselves or that others set for them, they often feel guilty. As a result, they may become anxious about their attitudes and behavior, question their self-worth and worry about punishment. If the guilt remains, anxiety can compound and cause serious disturbances. A person who feels guilty may strike out against authority and rebel, which often produces more guilt and anxiety. Guilt and fear of punishment can precipitate several neurotic and psychotic disorders. In severe cases, it can lead to depression, which often is characterized by feelings of worthlessness, and to self-hate. Self-hate can cause people to want to punish themselves or even to commit suicide.

Some psychologists maintain that guilt feelings arise from intricate guilt complexes. Usually the cause of guilt is thought to be something other than the patient, such as unrealistic or outdated moral codes, previous experiences, etc. Therapy often consists of leading the patient to discover his subconscious problem, or of convincing him that the problem is not in himself but in the code of behavior he is trying to follow.

Certainly many people are subject to unrealistic demands, and past experiences affect personal development. But it is reasonable to consider another possibility also: very often people *feel* guilty because they *are* guilty. If this is true, then therapy should consist, at least in part, of getting the person to admit his guilt. This isn't always easy. O. H. Mowrer, a psychologist at the University of Illinois, stresses the importance of being honest with oneself, but points out the dilemma that frequently results:

. . .Here, too, we encounter difficulty, because human beings do not change radically until first they acknowledge their sins, but it is hard for one to make such an acknowledgment unless he has "already changed." In other words, the full realization of deep worthlessness is a severe ego "insult," and one must have a new source of strength to endure it.[11]

Guilt, then, inhibits a healthy self-esteem. Also, if one is plagued with guilt, it is difficult to see the light side of life, let alone relate it to others. To deal with guilt, one must admit it, but that is difficult. What is the solution? Before we address that, let's look at the three other main barriers to a positive self-concept.

FEAR

Consider two types of fear: fear of death and fear of circumstances. Fear of death is one of humanity's greatest fears. If a person does not know what lies beyond the grave, he may become anxious. "Is it the end?" he wonders, "or is there some existence after death? If so, what will happen to me?" Uncertainly about death can generate uncertainty about the meaning of earthly existence. After all, if the ultimate outcome of our existence is nebulous, how can we be secure in our identity today? How can we answer the three basic identity questions: "Who am I?" "Why am I here?" "Where am I going?" Conversely, to have the death question settled may leave us free to take needed risks in life.

During Rusty's sophomore year in college, a student who lived in the room next to his was playing golf one afternoon. A thunderstorm came up, Mike was struck by lightning, and he died instantly. For some time after Mike's death, Rusty's fraternity was in shock. Young men were struggling with, "What is life all about? What does it mean if life can be snuffed out in an instant? Is there a life after death? If so, how can I experience it?" Fear of death can bring people face to face with questions about their own identity.

Fear of circumstances is the fear of what's going to happen to us as a result of what's going on around us. This fear comes at exam time in school; or when a young person receives a letter addressed "Dear John," and his name isn't John; or when we still have some month left at the end of our money. It can eat away at the spouse whose mate walked out, at the parent whose child was arrested for drunk driving, at the employer who learns that his employees have been embezzling, at the coach or player who worries about losing the big game. These fears can compound to affect self-esteem. A person might wonder, "Why are these things happening to me? What will become of me?"

Sometimes the poor self-concept engenders the fears; sometimes the fears hamper the self-concept. Nevertheless, fear is not conducive to inner happiness. A person in bondage to fear is often blind to the lighter side of life. Laughter can release worries; conversely, serious worries can consume laughter.

What is the solution to fear of circumstances? To realize that many things we worry about never happen? Perhaps. But some of them do. To try to laugh them off? We still may have to face and deal with them. Let's not kid ourselves; humor may relieve tension, but it is not—nor was it meant to be—a final antidote to our real problems. How then do we handle fear of circumstances? We soon will see, but first. . .

PROBLEMS IN
INTERPERSONAL RELATIONSHIPS

In his book *Reality Therapy*, California psychiatrist William Glasser says that humans' two basic needs are for love and for worth; we all want to love and be loved, and we want to feel a sense of worth to ourselves and others. Glasser feels that many psychological problems are due to a failure to act responsibly, and that each of us needs to become involved with at least one other person who cares for us and for whom we care. This person should accept us unconditionally, but be willing to confront us when we act irresponsibly. Without "this essential person," he writes, "we will not be able to fulfill our basic needs."[12]

Glasser cites several cases to support his point. One involves a young woman and an experienced pilot whose airplane crashed in the snowy wilderness of northern Canada. Though they had little food and insubstantial shelter, they survived for forty-nine days before they were rescued. Glasser says that their interpersonal involvement with each other and meaningful relationships with friends at home kept them going.

Certainly sincere interpersonal relationships are important. They can enhance our sense of worth. But people—even our closest friends—can let us down and err in judgement. We may look to other people to affirm our self-worth, but what do we do when they fail us? Before we suggest an answer, let's consider the fourth factor.

LACK OF MEANING

UCLA psychologist James C. Coleman writes that as the twentieth century person struggles "with the baffling question of his own existence. . .science falls short of providing full answers. . .It can tell how but not why."[13] In his standard textbook, *Abnormal Psychology and Modern Life,* he continues:

> With the advent of the space age, man is confronted with a new perspective of time and space, and the problem of finding the meaning of his existence in a universe in which the earth and even the whole solar system may be no larger in relation to the whole that an atom is to the earth. At the same time, materialistic values—based on the belief that scientific progress would automatically lead to man's happiness and fulfillment—have proved sadly disillusioning. As a result, many people are groping about, bewildered and bitter, unable to find any enduring faith or to develop a satisfying philosophy of life. Despite their fine automobiles, well-stocked refrigerators, and other material possessions and comforts, the meaning of life seems to be evading them. In essence, they are suffering from *existential anxiety*—deep concern about finding values which will enable them to live satisfying, fulfilling, and meaningful lives.[14]

In the 1940s, more than thirty-one thousand Allied soldiers were detained as prisoners in Japan and Korea. A study of these soldiers showed that many of them suffered from lack of hope. Although they were offered sufficient food, more than eight thousand died. Dr. Harold Wolff maintains that many died from despair. He writes, "Hope, like faith and a purpose in life, is medicinal. This is not merely a statement of belief, but a conclusion proved by meticulously controlled scientific experiment."[15]

A clear purpose for life can assure people that they are

177

significant human beings, that they count for something. This, in turn, can release them to look on the bright side.

We've considered four factors that can inhibit a healthy self-concept: guilt, fear, problems in interpersonal relationships, and lack of meaning in life. The guilty person says, "I have erred. I feel bad about myself." The fearful person asks, "What will happen to me?" The one struggling with an interpersonal relationship wonders, "Does this person like me?" The one searching for meaning in life asks, "Am I a significant person?" How can these questions be answered? How can these factors be overcome? How can one develop a healthy self-concept?

HOW TO DEVELOP A
HEALTHY SELF-CONCEPT

One way to seek a healthy self-concept is to look for it through other people. Their emotional feedback helps us form an image of ourselves. The ways our family members, friends and co-workers treat us either encourage or discourage a positive self-concept.

> One man told his friend, "I looked up my
> family tree and learned I was the sap."[16]

Do any of your family members treat you like a sap? Chances are that influences the way you see yourself. Do your friends treat you with respect, or are you often the butt of jokes? Do they see you as socially desirable, or do you get the feeling they'd rather you wouldn't show up?

> One fellow mailed his photograph to the
> Lonely Hearts Club. A few weeks later, the
> reply came: "We're not that lonely."[17]

178

Do your co-workers or business associates look up to you, or do they seem to see you as a means to their end? And what about people in the groups in which you use humor? How do they respond?

Comedian Jimmy Durante was well-known and fondly appreciated for his enormous nose, yet his schnozzola was a source of great agony during his childhood. People always stared or called attention to it. Durante recalled, "All through life, even when I'm making a fortune on account of the big beak, and while I'm out there on stage laughin' and kiddin' about the nose, at no time was I ever happy about it."[18]

Durante's biographer relates a touching story:

Not long ago Durante received a letter from a boy: "I've got a big nose, Mr. Durante. Everybody laughed at my nose. But then I saw you, Mr. Durante, in a movie. And when you kept laughing about your nose, it made me feel good all over. And the other fellows call me 'Schnozz,' and I'm awful proud."

Durante sat silently at the breakfast table for a while, then he called out happily to his housekeeper, Maggie Arnold, "A big load has just fallen off'n me, Maggie, like an awful curse!"[19]

The boy affirmed Durante and his nose as being worthwhile because his situation was used to help another. The comedian accepted and believed the affirmation, so his self-esteem was enhanced.

Anyone you contact—store clerks, police, ticket-takers, telephone operators, receptionists—can influence your self-concept.

179

> Rodney Dangerfield says, "I don't get no
> respect. Why, I even phoned the Suicide
> Prevention Hotline and they put me on hold!"

The problem with relying totally on others for our self-esteem is that of uncertainty. If more people affirm us than criticize us, we may have a healthy self-concept. If the opposite occurs, we may not. And people can be fickle; they might like us one minute and ignore us the next. They might laugh at our humor one week and seem disinterested the next. We all want the approval of others, but is there a more dependable source of self-esteem?

Some say that if we believe we have self-esteem, we will have it.

> One young man was riding his bicycle across
> a university campus. A passerby saw that a
> message on the front of his T-shirt announced
> his occupational goal: "I AM GOING TO BE
> A DOCTOR." As the cyclist rode on, the
> passerby noticed a sign on the rear of his
> bicycle: "I AM GOING TO BE A MER-
> CEDES."[20]

But suppose you try to believe in yourself and find you can't? Or that you can in some areas and can't in others? Is will power alone a dependable source of self-esteem?

Some people base their self-esteem on their success.

> A Notre Dame football star appeared in court
> as a witness in a civil suit. The judge asked,
> "Are you a member of this year's Notre Dame

football team?"

"Yes, Your Honor," the athlete replied.

"What position do you play?"

"I play center, Your Honor."

"How good a center are you?" the judge inquired.

"Sir," came the confident reply, "I'm the best center Notre Dame ever had."

The Notre Dame coach was in the court and was quite surprised by the reply. Though an excellent ballplayer, he always had seemed modest and unpretentious. Later, he asked the player why he had said what he had.

"I didn't want to, coach, but there was no choice. I was under oath."[21]

But again, success is fickle. Teams can lose, economic circumstances can change, applause can dwindle. Sometimes the success itself leaves people dry. Consider these examples from the lives of several famous comics.

WHEN YOU'RE HOT
AND WHEN YOU'RE NOT. . .

Joan Rivers is often afraid of losing her money. She speaks of her great fear of winding up in a nursing home. Joan says, "I wake up at night and say, 'What if I'm not funny in the morning? It's gone. It's over. Goodbye to the house, goodbye to Melissa's horses and the dogs, make sushi out of the goldfish.' I always think it is just going to go away. Success is very fickle, and you must never think it is going to last forever, because it will not. Every time I go onstage, I say a little prayer, 'Thank You, God.' "[22]

Richard Pryor comments on some of the fears common

to those who appear in public, "Audiences are really something else. When you're apprehensive and show a little fear and doubt because you're not getting any laughs, man, an audience will eat you alive. They sense fear, and it's like being in confrontation with a wild animal that senses you're afraid. In both cases, you're doomed."[23]

Steve Allen notes, "It is always fascinating to observe in the character of so many leading funnymen the great sensitivity that led them to erect a humorous defense. Far from being the overconfident buffoons the layman might think, most of the leading comedians are somewhat shy, pessimistic worriers whose greatest fault is a lack of confidence rather than an excess of it."[24]

Many successful comics hide their fears and insecurities behind the wall of their comedy. Many have difficulties in social relationships. Author Leo Rosten speaks of Groucho Marxs' emotional isolation, "I never heard him laugh out loud, *never*, even at jokes or comedians he enjoyed. His natural expression was edged with sadness, but in public he donned the mask of a sardonic owl. He hid his emotions. Even his wives and children were not his confidants. He was, in truth, a melancholy man, often depressed, as many comedians are."[25]

On a St. Louis radio program, Red Skelton was asked, "If you had the opportunity to write—in a sentence or two—Red Skelton's philosophy of life—what would it be?"

"Don't love anyone," Skelton replied. "Like everybody. Because love can hurt."[26]

Shortly before Peter Sellers' death, his fourth wife, actress Lynne Frederick, shared this observation about her husband: "His mind is in a constant state of turmoil about what his purpose is on this planet and whether it's all worthwhile."[27]

Mel Brooks says, "Humor is just another defense against the universe."[28]

Michael O'Donoghure, a former editor of *National Lampoon* who has written sketches for "Saturday Night Live," says that his own morbid humor is appropriate to "a violent, desperate time. Humor is a release of tension, and you react to what is happening around you. The world is ready to nuke itself out. That's why my humor is preoccupied with death—Dick Van Dyke and Donna Reed just don't cut it anymore. I believe that life is a joke and death is the punch line."[29]

We are not claiming that all comedians are tortured souls. Even those who struggle with inner torment still find themselves enjoying the laughter of a warm, responsive crowd. But after the crowd has gone and the lights are out, the comic must live with himself. "Even in laughter the heart may be in pain," notes a biblical proverb, "and the end of joy may be grief."[30] The writer of the Old Testament book of Ecclesiastes tried to find ultimate happiness through many means, including humor. He concluded, "I said of laughter, 'It is madness,' and of pleasure, 'What does it accomplish?' "[31] Humor can be the anesthetic that deadens the pain of an empty soul. Yet eventually, the anesthetic wears off.

Where can one find a dependable basis for a healthy self-concept? If other people, our own willpower and our own success are insufficient *in the long haul*, where do we go? There is an answer. . .

CHAPTER 12

~~~~~~~~

MIRROR, MIRROR

~~~~~~~~

AN ARMY BASE was planning war games and the leaders did not want to use live ammu-nition. They instructed the men to imi-tate

the sounds of weapons. For rifle shots, the soldiers were to say, "Bang, bang." For knife thrusts, "Stab, stab." For hand grenades, "Lob, lob."

The games were in progress and one soldier spotted the enemy. He shouted, "Bang, bang," but nothing happened. He dashed forward and said, "Stab, stab." Still no response. He moved back and yelled, "Lob, lob," but nothing happened. At last, he walked up to the enemy and complained. "Hey, you're not playing fair. I said 'Bang, bang,' 'Stab, stab' and 'Lob, lob,' but you haven't fallen dead yet!"

The enemy answered, "Rumble, rumble. I'm a tank."[1]

How can you see yourself as a tank? How can you develop a healthy self-concept, and thus affect your success and your outlook on life?

A Boston stockbroker advertised for a "Harvard graduate or the equivalent." A Yale man responded. "When you speak of an equivalent," he asked, "do you mean two Princeton men or a Yale man half-time?"[2]

A bit cocky? Perhaps, but his view of himself probably helped him in life. How do we establish a positive attitude toward ourselves? If others' opinions of us cannot form a consistently stable basis for our self-concept (as we saw in the previous chapter), where do we look?

> On a foggy night at sea, the ship's captain saw what appeared to be the lights of another ship heading toward him. He instructed his signalman to contact the other ship by signal light. He sent the message, "Change your course ten degrees to the north."
>
> The reply came, "Change *your* course ten degrees to the south."
>
> The captain responded, "I am a captain. Change *your* course ten degrees to the north."
>
> Response: "I am a seaman first class. You change *your* course ten degrees to the south."
>
> The captain was furious. He had his signalman reply, "I am a battleship. You change *your* course ten degrees to the north."
>
> Reply: "I am a lighthouse. You change *your* course ten degrees to the south!"[3]

Where can we find a lighthouse, a stable point of reference by which to evaluate who we are, why we are here and where we are going?

THE TOTAL PERSON

Human beings are composed of three dimensions: a physical dimension (the body); a psychological dimension (the mind: intellect, emotion, will); and a spiritual dimension (the spirit). More and more psychologists and psychiatrists are seeing the need to focus on all three areas—the total person—to develop a positive self-concept.

Kenneth Pelletier, an Oakland psychologist, has a Ph.D. in clinical psychology from the University of California at Berkley and specializes in psychosomatic medicine. He comments on the value of this concept, "The best understanding of disease comes when we consider the whole person. We need to see a person physically, psychologically, and spiritually to gain as full an understanding of his life as we can. There is a new approach emerging in the healing professions today that takes such a holistic focus. Those who take this view. . .look at the patient as a person, rather than limiting themselves to his symptoms."[4]

Once, when Rusty spoke on love, sex and marriage at Memphis State University, he alluded to the importance of the total person concept in interpersonal relationships. After the talk, a man in his mid-forties (who had returned to college to finish his degree) made a revealing point. "My wife and I have been married for twenty-five years," he said. "We've had a physical relationship, somewhat of a psychological relationship, but no spiritual relationship at all. I see now that we could have avoided many problems if we'd related on all three levels."

The physical fitness craze has prompted millions to try to improve their physical condition. Executives play basketball or raquetball in place of the three-martini lunch. Homemakers jog through their neighborhoods after the family is off to work and school. Health food stores abound. Soft drink companies compete with caffeine-free sugar-free beverages. Food companies promote low-salt, low-choles-terol products. Western society is very conscious of physical development.

Interest in psychological development abounds as well. Counseling centers are numerous and busy. Self-help books pepper the newsstands. Psychiatrists and psychologists are frequent guests on television talk shows. Some have their own radio call-in programs. The male midlife crisis nearly equals female menopause as a subject of psychological scrutiny. Psychological well-being is a hot topic.

Interest in the spiritual dimension is also keen, and that is the area we would like to consider here. While we strongly believe in the importance of physical and psychological health, we feel that spiritual development is a vital key to the development of a healthy self-concept.

Of course, people follow many approaches to the spiritual dimension of life and to enhancing their self-concepts through it. But we believe there is one true path to a full relationship with God—and that path is through His son, Jesus Christ. While Linda came to an understanding of this perspective as a child, Rusty did not appreciate it in his life until in college. Perhaps his story will best explain what we found:

AN ALTERNATIVE

As a high school student, I looked for success through athletics, academics and student government, and I found it. I attended one of the nation's leading prep schools. John F. Kennedy and Adlai Stevenson were alumni, as were playwright Edward Albee and actor Michael Douglas. David Rockefeller spoke at our graduation; his son was in my class. Many graduates went on to Harvard, Yale and Princeton.

In school I lettered in basketball and track. Our track team was undefeated. I ranked in the top of my class academically and participated in student government. I mention these details not to boast, but to draw a contrast. Success in those areas had not brought personal satisfaction. I was still somewhat of an introvert, at times afraid to introduce myself to a stranger or to ask a young woman for a date. Guilt, anxiety and a poor self-image often prevented me from taking risks. I put up a front of confidence and security. But when I was honest with myself—which wasn't always—I knew that I was uneasy in relationships.

During my first year at Duke University I still struggled with many of these areas. Then I met a group of students and was attracted by their love, joy and peace. I especially appreciated their acceptance of me just as I was. Though they were sharp, attractive and successful, I didn't have to impress them with a list of my accomplishments. Even in dating the women, I didn't feel pressured to put on the "macho" image. They seemed to like themselves, and they liked me, too.

I knew I wanted what they had. They told me they were Christians; they had found a personal relationship with God. I didn't understand that and couldn't believe it all right away. But I kept returning to their meetings because I was curious, and because it was a good place to get a date. Especially because it was a good place to get a date!

As I spent time with these people, I saw how their faith affected their lives and relationships. Eventually I learned that a relationship with God could be the key to establishing a healthy self-concept. I saw that God could remove the four barriers to a healthy self-esteem: guilt, fear, problems in interpersonal relationships and lack of meaning. Through a relationship with Him, I could find complete forgiveness, peace in difficult circumstances or when facing death, a faithful friend and ultimate meaning in life.

HE LOVES ME. . .

My friends explained how all this could come about in my life. They told me that God loved me and wanted me to have the most fulfilling life possible. They helped me see why I and many others were not experiencing it.

> A father frequently took his four-year-old son on walks through the city park. This park contained a large statue of Gen. Robert E. Lee riding his horse, Traveler. The father had a fond respect for General Lee and wanted his son to have the same affection for the general. On each walk they would stop in front of the statue of General Lee on his horse and the father would tell his son, "Say hello to General Lee." The little boy would wave his hand and say, "Hi, General Lee."
>
> For several months, this ritual continued with each visit to the park. Then one day, after greeting General Lee, the boy asked his father, "Daddy, who is that man up there riding General Lee?"

One of the main reasons many people do not accept God in their lives is that they don't understand who He is and the great benefits of receiving Him. Just as the young boy confused the horse and General Lee, many are confused about who God is and what is involved in coming to know Him. God is a loving parent, and simple faith or trust is all that is necessary to begin the great adventure of knowing Him personally. Consider some of the things God can do in one's life:[5]

God can give wisdom for decisions.

God can provide resources to help dreams come true.

God can give protection.

God can provide security.

God can provide inner strength to face difficult circumstances.

God can give love to overcome the wounds of life.

God can heal damaged emotions that cripple usefulness.

My friends explained that Jesus of Nazareth came, in part, to help us understand what God is like. They quoted Him as saying, "God so loved the world, that He gave His only begotten Son, that whoever believes in Him should not perish but have eternal life."[6] He went on to say, "I came that they (people) might have life, and might have it abundantly."[7] In other words, God loved me unconditionally, as those students had, only better.

The more I understood this, the more I saw how it could affect my self-concept. I realized that even if everyone else rejected me, I could be secure in the knowledge that God still loved me. I could be freed from the fear of what people thought.

> A student took a final examination shortly before Christmas. The exam consisted of one extremely difficult question. The student

agonized over the test and finally realized he didn't know the answer. In desperation, he wrote on his paper: "God only knows. Merry Christmas!"

When the professor returned his paper, the student read the following notation: "God gets an *A,* and you get an *F.* Happy New Year!"

Some people picture God as an impersonal force or perhaps a diffuse entity, as portrayed in common expressions such as "God only knows." The Bible pictures God as a personal being who loves us and wants us to establish a fulfilling, personal relationship with Him. Yet, some people have trouble believing in God. They feel that such belief must involve a blind leap into the dark.

A man was on the roof of his two-story house repairing his TV antenna. Suddenly he slipped and began to slide down over the edge. At the last second, he grabbed the rain gutter and held on for dear life.

"Help! Help!" he shouted. "Is there anyone down there who can help me?" he asked, desperately looking about. No answer. He then looked into the heavens and asked, "Is there anyone up there who can help me?"

The clouds parted and a deep, resonant voice came from the skies: "Believe, and let go."

"Is there anyone *else* up there who can help me?"

Like that fellow, I tend to be quite skeptical, so I was wary of believing something I couldn't see. My will would not follow what my mind could not accept. Then I learned that there were good reasons for believing; that there was quite a bit of evidence for the Christian faith. Evidences for the resurrection of Christ, His deity and His fulfilled prophecy provided a solid basis for belief. (To examine these, we recommend books such as Josh McDowell's *More Than a Carpenter* and *Evidence That Demands a Verdict.*[8])

UNPLUGGED

Even though it made sense to believe in a God who loved me, I still had a problem relating to Him. My friends explained that everyone initially exists in a condition of separation from their Creator. Some psychologists call this alienation: the biblical documents call it sin. Sin refers to a condition of being spiritually unplugged from God. If the plug of a floor lamp is pulled from the wall socket, contact with the circuit is broken and the light is extinguished. So it is with human beings. Some of the more obvious manifestations of separation from God are murder, thievery, war, etc. Some of the less obvious are worry, anxiety, lack of purpose in life, excessive self-centeredness, poor self-image, etc.

> President Calvin Coolidge was known for his brevity of speech. He tried to use as few words as possible. One Sunday after church, "Silent Cal" returned to the White House where his wife was confined with a cold. She asked whether he enjoyed the sermon.
>
> "Yes," Coolidge replied.
>
> "What was the sermon about?" the first lady asked, trying to engage her husband in conversation.

"Sin," the President explained.

"But what did the minister *say*?" Mrs.
Coolidge persisted.

"He was against it."[9]

God also is against sin. Why? Because He loves us and wants a relationship with us. That is why He created us, and that is the only way we can be fulfilled. Our sins (worry, fear, pride, lack of purpose, etc.) frustrate us and leave us empty, and they separate us from God. In fact, that separation is the root cause of human emptiness. One early Christian wrote, "All have sinned and fall short of the glory of God,"[10] and, "The wages of sin is death"[11] (spiritual separation from God).

Left to our own ends, we would have to spend time and eternity in this unfulfilled state. We are powerless to overcome our sin. But restoration is possible, because it doesn't depend on our efforts or sinlessness or ability to change.

PAID IN FULL

I considered this perspective, and fortunately it provided a solution. My friends explained that God had sent His Son, Jesus, the Messiah or Christ, to die on the cross to pay the penalty for my sins. That was certainly an example of great love—one person dying for others. And understanding His love for me could enhance my own self-worth. After all, if the King of the universe loved me enough to die for me, who was I to argue with Him? But Christ's death was more than a demonstration of God's love; it was a payment for sin.

Imagine that you are a traffic judge and also my parent. I'm caught for speeding and you try me, find me guilty and sentence me to a $100 fine or thirty days in jail. Suppose

I'm broke and can't pay the fine. As a loving parent, you might not want me to go to jail. As a just judge, you'd have to send me to jail. What would you do?

There would be an alternative—you could pay the fine for me. As my parent, you could step from behind the judge's bench, take out your billfold or purse and offer me $100. I could accept it, use it to pay the fine and go free.

I learned that, in the same way, God paid the penalty for our sins through Christ's death on the cross. All our sins—our guilt, self-centeredness, worry, insecurity, fear, jealousy, bitterness, murder, adultery, resentment—He took them all on Himself, dying a physical and spiritual death so that we could be forgiven. "God demonstrates His own love toward us, in that while we were yet sinners, Christ died for us."[12] "God took the sinless Christ and poured into Him our sins. Then, in exchange, He poured God's goodness into us!"[13]

Today, justice and accountability frequently are watered down, and the lines between right and wrong often are blurred. Tolerance is a popular buzz word, and some question the propriety of holding people accountable for their actions. This blurring may result from fear of punishment. But is there a better way to deal with that fear?

The biblical God is pictured as the standard of right and wrong, as the lighthouse that shows us the way to safety through troubled waters. He is a just judge who requires that sin be paid for. He is also the loving, tolerant father who gives His loved ones the freedom to rebel and who pays, with His Son's life, the fine for their transgressions.

As my friends explained the cross of Christ from this perspective, it took on a new significance. He died for me! This meant that I could be freed from the worries and insecurities I had struggled with. That was good news! But my friends said that it wasn't enough to know that God loved me, that I was separated from Him and that Jesus Christ had died and been raised from the dead for me. I needed to make a simple choice to make this real in my life.

THE CHOICE

In the judge illustration, I could refuse the $100 and go to jail if I wanted to. The choice would be mine. It's the same with Christ. Peace with God and ourselves is as simple as accepting His free gift of forgiveness and new life. If we *personally* acknowledge what He has done for us individually, we'll be able to enjoy the benefits of a relationship with God. If we refuse that gift, we'll miss out on those benefits. The choice is ours.

I used to think that God graded on the curve; that if I did enough good deeds, He would accept me. But I was never sure that I'd done enough. My friends explained that we come to God by His grace through our faith, based on what He has accomplished for us, not on what we have done for Him. Good works don't help us a bit. If they could, then we'd be able to boast about it.[14]

Jesus said, "Behold [i.e., listen], I stand at the door [i.e., the door to your heart or life] and knock; if anyone hears My voice and opens the door, I will come in to him."[15] The more I considered Christ's life and teachings, the more it all made sense. Finally, I said, "Jesus Christ, I need You. Thanks for dying for me. Thanks for rising again from the dead. I want to accept Your death on the cross as the provision for my sins. I open the door of my heart and ask You to come in. Thank You for coming into my life and forgiving my sins. Give me the fulfilling life You promised."

I heard no thunder, saw no lightning. Angels didn't rise in the background singing the "Hallelujah" chorus. And I certainly didn't become perfect overnight. But gradually I began to see changes. I found a new inner peace and freedom from guilt. I found a purpose for living and the power to begin becoming the person I'd always wanted to be. I saw my self-image improve and I felt freer to take risks. Of course, my life is not without problems and struggles, but the presence of the problem-solver—Jesus Christ—the load easier to bear.

Earlier, we referred to four barriers to a healthy self-concept. Consider how Jesus Christ can remove those barriers.

GUILT

The moment that a person comes into a relationship with God, his or her sins are completely forgiven. "As far as the east is from the west, so far has He removed our transgressions from us."[16] "Their sins and their lawless deeds I will remember no more."[17] He not only wipes the slate clean—He throws it away.

FEAR

Fear of death need not plague the person of faith. The moment he or she trusts God, an eternal relationship with God begins. "God has given us eternal life, and this life is in His Son. He who has the Son has the life; he who does not have the Son of God does not have the life. These things I have written to you who believe in the name of the Son of God, in order that you may know that you have eternal life."[18] Fear of circumstances can be overcome by His promises to meet our needs. "My God shall supply all your needs according to His riches in glory in Christ Jesus."[19] "Do not be anxious then, saying, 'What shall we eat?' or 'What shall we drink?' or 'With what shall we clothe ourselves?'. . .

But seek first His kingdom and His righteousness; and all these things shall be added to you."[20]

PROBLEMS IN INTERPERSONAL RELATIONSHIPS

Friends can let us down and err in judgment; the ultimate therapy is involvement with our Creator. He is faithful and righteous. He never lets us down and always has the best advice. He loves us. "I am convinced that neither death, nor life, nor angels, nor principalities, nor things present, nor things to come, nor powers, nor height, nor depth, nor any other created thing, shall be able to separate us from the love of God, which is in Christ Jesus our Lord."[21] When our relationships with God are secure and growing, we can relate more effectively to others.

LACK OF MEANING

Remember the eight thousand Allied soldiers who died from despair? Contrast them to Reverend Richard Wurmbrand, a Christian minister who spent fourteen years in Communist prison camps, was tortured for his faith and at times became so hungry that he sucked his fingers. Yet after his release from prison, he directed a nonprofit organization dedicated to taking the love of God to the people who nearly killed him.

Christ offers hope, meaning and purpose. One can hope in the fact that He will come again: ". . .they will see the Son of Man coming on the clouds of the sky."[22] He has admonished His followers to take His message to all nations: We are ambassadors for Christ.[23] That certainly is a meaningful task and a worthwhile life purpose.

Does what you are reading seem more upbeat and

positive than the somewhat depressing comments a few pages back? It should. For the Christian, life is an exciting adventure! some may feel, as Michael O'Donoghure expressed, that "life is a joke and death is the punch line." Yet we desperately wish everyone could see that, in reality, life can be an exciting short story with death as the happy ending. . .because it leads into an even longer, more exciting story that never ends.

WHAT ABOUT YOU?

Do you feel some of the needs we've mentioned? Has this made sense? Jesus Christ can make a positive difference in your life. Are you willing to let Him?

Have you received Christ? Do you know that He lives in your life? You *can* know. He said, "If you open the door, *I will come in*." Jesus Christ is no liar. You can take Him at His word and believe that if you ask Him to forgive you and enter your life, He will do just that. We're not talking about becoming a member of a church, joining an organization or promising God you'll live a perfect life. We're talking about accepting a free gift and inviting the risen Christ to live in your life.

Many who have desired to receive Christ have expressed their faith through prayer, which is simply talking with God. You can talk to Him in the quiet of your own heart. He is much more concerned about your attitude than your specific words. Below is a short prayer that many people use in receiving Christ:

Lord Jesus, I need You. Thanks for dying and rising again for me. I want to accept Your death on the cross as the payment for my sins. I open the door of my life and receive You as my Savior (the One who died for my sins). Thank You for forgiving me. Give me the fulfilling life that You promised.

Does that express the desire of your heart? If so, we encourage you to pray it (or something similar in your own words) right now, wherever you are, and Christ will forgive you and come into your life as He promised.

Did you ask Jesus to forgive you and enter your life? Did He do it? Of course He did (if you asked), because He said He would!

Don't worry if you don't feel different, or if you *do* feel different now. The Christian life is lived by faith in God's trustworthiness and in His promises (revealed in a living book, the Bible), not by feelings. Feelings come and go. Sometimes they are a result of believing God. At other times they reflect the complexities of human personality, rather than the work of God in one's life. Simply remember that Jesus will never leave you once He has entered your life. He said, "I will never desert you, nor will I ever forsake you"[24] and "I am with you always."[25] He gives you life for eternity.

If you have just received Christ, we would like to send you some materials (at no cost to you) that will help you begin to grow in your new faith. Please drop us a postcard or letter at the address below, telling us you have just made this decision, and we'll be happy to get this information to you.

Rusty Wright
Arrowhead Springs
San Bernardino, CA 92414

AN ENHANCED SELF-CONCEPT

We have stressed the importance of a healthy self-concept, as it relates to humor and to all areas of life. We would be remiss if we did not mention some practical ways that the Christian life can enhance one's self-image and give the power to develop a fulfilling life.

One of the most important things any Christian can do is study the Bible. To fill our minds with the Bible is to fill our minds with God's perspective on life, which enables us to begin to see ourselves as He sees us. And His opinion counts! As author and speaker Josh McDowell says, "A healthy self-concept involves seeing ourselves the way God sees us—no more; no less." Consider some of the things God says are true about you if you have trusted Him:

You are a child of God (John 1:12).

You have at your disposal all of God's wisdom to help you live successfully (James 1:5).

You can come to God and receive help whenever you need it (Hebrews 4:16).

You are a world ambassador (2 Corinthians 5:20).

You are completely forgiven (Colossians 1:14).

You have everything you need (Philippians 4:19).

You have a wonderful life ahead of you (John 10:10).

You are tenderly loved (Jeremiah 31:3).

You are precious in his sight (Isaiah 43:4).

You are a fragrance of Christ to God
(2 Corinthians 2:15).

When you wake in the morning, God is thinking
of you! (Psalm 139:18, TLB).

You have been inscribed on the palms of God's
hands (Isaiah 49:16).

Look at the birds of the air, that they do not sow
neither do they reap, nor gather into barns,
and yet your heavenly Father feeds them. Are
you not worth much more than they?
(Matthew 6:26).

Suppose you feel depressed or defeated. What practical
steps should you take? First, attempt to identify the cause. It
may be physical, such as fatigue, lack of sleep, or improper
nutrition. Or it may be spiritual. Learn what the Bible says
about you, your self-concept, your problems. Linda's book,
Staying on Top When Things Go Wrong (Tyndale House,
1983), goes deeper into these topics. (The above list was
adapted from that book.)

Learning what the Bible says will improve your attitudes about your self and your life. But such knowledge is
most effective if it is coupled with God's inner source of
strength, the Holy Spirit. The Holy Spirit is God's Spirit,
who lives inside every believer and provides power to live
the Christian life. The Spirit-filled life is one of the most
important topics for any Christian, so we recommend that
you read Bill Bright's book *The Holy Spirit* (Here's Life
Publishers). Here is one illustration adapted from his book:

A BREATH OF FRESH AIR

Many Christians wonder, "What do I do when I sin? How do I continue in unbroken fellowship with God?" Bright's answer is to practice "spiritual breathing." In physical breathing, we exhale bad air and inhale good air.

In spiritual breathing, exhaling involves *confession:* admitting our sins to God as we become aware of them. As we honestly confess our sins, we experience His forgiveness. "If we confess our sins, He is faithful and righteous to forgive us our sins and to cleanse us from all unrighteousness."[26]

Inhaling involves asking God to keep the Holy Spirit in the driver's seat of our lives according to His *command* and *promise.*

His command: Be filled with the Spirit. "And do not get drunk with wine, for that is dissipation, but be filled with the Spirit."[27]

His promise: He always answers when we ask according to His will. "And this is the confidence which we have before Him, that, if we ask anything according to His will, He hears us. And if we know that He hears us in whatever we ask, we know that we have the requests which we have asked from Him."[28]

We know that God wants us to be filled with (empowered by) the Spirit. He commands it. So we can ask Him to fill us and then believe according to His promise that He has done it. Spiritual breathing is a practical exercise that Christians need to apply many times every day.

Why have we spent so much time on the spiritual dimension in a book on how to use humor successfully? Remember that one key to successful humor is a healthy self-concept. We would be intellectually dishonest if we did not explain, for your consideration, the perspective that has helped us develop improving self-concepts. Also recall that many humorists look to humor to enhance their self-worth or mask their emptiness. We offer the thought that Jesus Christ can bring inner satisfaction and help people live and work *from* acceptance rather than *toward* acceptance.

We want to help you be a successful humorist. But what a tragedy it would be to spend an entire lifetime climbing the ladder of success only to reach the top and find that the ladder had been against the wrong wall.

CHAPTER 13

DIVINE ANTIDOTES

SOME ARE SURPRISED to find Christians enjoying humor. They seem to think that a Christian is supposed to be straight-laced, sober and sad. Yet who has more reason to laugh and rejoice than someone experiencing the blessings of an eternal relationship with the Lord? Besides, God obviously has a sense of humor. . .after all, He made all of us, didn't He?

And God created us with the capacity and need to laugh. Humor is an integral part of healthy psychological and spiritual development. With that in mind, here are some divine antidotes:

> Two young boys were forever getting into trouble. . .disrupting classes in school, teasing neighborhood children, taking what didn't belong to them. One day their mother asked the pastor over to see if he could talk some sense into them. Rather than threaten or reprimand them, the pastor decided on a more subtle approach. He would try to help the boys see that God is everywhere, that He is aware of everything and is displeased when they acted wrongly. But the pastor wanted the boys to come to this conclusion on their own, so he began by asking some questions.
>
> "Young men," he intoned after having the boys sit down, "I have a question for you.

Where is God?"

The two boys just sat there, unsure how to answer.

"Where is God?" the preacher repeated, a bit more firmly. "Surely you know the answer to a simple question like that!" The boys remained silent, too frightened to speak.

"I'll ask you one more time," the pastor said, this time even more firmly, "WHERE IS GOD?"

At that, the older boy jumped up and grabbed his brother. "C'mon, let's get out of here!" he whispered. "God's missin' and they think we did it!"

—Laura Raney

Children often have views of God, life and Bible stories that strike our adult funny bones. Comedian Dick Van Dyke compiled a book of some of the more humorous statements kids have made regarding spiritual situations. Here are a few choice anecdotes adapted from his very amusing book, *Faith, Hope and Hilarity:*

◆   A Sunday school teacher was telling her class the story of the Good Samaritan, in which a man was beaten, robbed and left for dead. She described the situation in vivid detail so her students would catch the drama. Then she asked the class, "If you saw a person lying on the roadside all wounded and bleeding, what would you do?"

A thoughtful little girl broke the hushed silence. "I think I'd throw up."

◆ One polite little girl was saying her prayers but interrupted them to say, "Pardon me, God, while I kick my ornery little brother."

◆ A young toddler who had received an Easter basket a week earlier was saying grace before dinner. "Bless us, O Lord, and these Thy gifts which we are about to receive from Thy bunny."

◆ One boy described to his younger buddies how great God is: "God is greater than Superman, Batman and the Lone Ranger put together."

◆ A small boy was hurrying to help his mother bring the clothes in off the line before the thunderstorm hit. Finally they had gathered the last armload and were about to close the door. The boy stood at the threshold, waved his hand at the heavens in a sweeping gesture and said, "O.K., God. . . let 'er rip!"

◆ Little boy: "Mama, who made the moon?"
Mother: "God made the moon."
Boy: "Well, then, who made the stars?"
Mother: "God made the stars, too."
Boy: "And who made the trees?"
Mother: "God made the trees, too, son."

The little boy obviously was becoming more and more frustrated with the same answer. Finally he asked, "Well, all I want to know is, doesn't Jesus ever do anything?"

◆ A Sunday school teacher was discussing the Ten Commandments with her five- and six-year-olds. After explaining the commandment to "honor thy father and thy mother," she asked, "Is there a commandment that teaches us how to treat our brothers and sisters?"

Without missing a beat, one boy (the oldest of a family of seven) answered, "Thou shalt not kill."

◆ Two-year-old Stevie was thrilled to see the candles being lighted during the church service. In the midst of the silent prayer that followed, he stood up in his seat and sang, "Happy Birthday to you. . ."[1]

Here's a story Rusty tells:

> When I was two years old, my parents took me to my younger brother's christening service. Dad left me in the back of the church with my grandmother, giving her strict orders not to let me get away. When it came time for John to be christened, my parents gave the baby boy to the pastor to hold. I assure you that I did not like that strange man messing with my little brother. I broke loose from my grandmother, sprinted up the aisle and tackled the preacher! (Fortunately he kept his footing.) Then I sat on the stage, facing the congregation, and kicked my heels against the wooden wall during the remainder of the christening!

Here's a story that Rusty's grandmother relates from one of her ministers:

◆ The minister taught a class of very young children and decided to see how well they had paid attention to his talks. He asked three boys what they remembered of the story of the crucifixion. One boy said, "Well, the cross was heavy—a man had to help." Another boy said, "It got dark as night and thundered." The third boy said, "Well, He came out the third day, saw His shadow and went back in, and they had six more weeks of winter."

—Virginia Bilderback

◆ Our small mountain church is located by a frequently traveled road. Sometimes during services, the church PA system picks up CB broadcasts from passing motorists. The CB'ers, of course, are unaware that their voices are being heard in a meeting. Once, the pastor began a prayer, saying, "O Lord, we beseech you to meet our various needs. . ." Suddenly he was interrupted by a loud voice that crackled over the PA, "I'll be right on down!"

◆ A small boy forgot his lines in the Sunday school presentation. His mother sat in the front row and tried to prompt him by gesturing and silently forming the words with her lips. It was no use. The boy's memory was blank.

Finally she leaned forward and whispered his cue: "I am the light of the world."

With a broad smile and beaming confidence the child said in a loud, clear voice,
"My mother is the light of the world."[2]

It is fun to see how kids look at God. . .and to laugh at
some of the real life situations we might encounter as we
consider God.

GOOD MEDICINE

The Old Testament book of Proverbs says, "A joyful heart
is good medicine, but a broken spirit dries up the bones."[3]
Pastor and professor Leslie B. Flynn wrote a book, *Serve
Him with Joy,* about the place of humor in the Christian life.
In his research, he combed the Bible for every reference that
included humor. He found humor in nearly sixty of the
sixty-six books of the Bible and filled one hundred pages of
notes on the verses.

Sometimes the Bible presents humor in ideas. The
book of Proverbs is especially full of these.

Go to the ant, O sluggard,
Observe her ways and be wise,
Which, having no chief,
Officer or ruler,
Prepares her food in the summer,
And gathers her provision in the harvest.
How long will you lie down, O sluggard?
When will you arise from your sleep?
"A little sleep, a little slumber,
A little folding of the hands to rest"—
And your poverty will come in like a vagabond,
And your need like an armed man.[4]

The idea of a big lazy oaf being admonished to learn from the tiny ant suggests a humor of contrasts. A similar contrast is presented in Proverbs 11:22:

As a ring of gold in a swine's snout,
So is a beautiful woman who lacks discretion.

Though Miss Piggy might take exception, the sight of a huge, fat sow with an exquisite gold ring in her snout seems comical. Similarly incongruous is the beautiful but indiscreet woman—her outer beauty is mocked by her lack of wisdom.

The perils of a quarrelsome marriage are alluded to in Proverbs 21:19 and 27:15:

It is better to live in a desert land,
Than with a contentious and vexing woman.

A constant dripping on a day of steady rain
And a contentious woman are alike.

Anyone who has ever suffered a leaky roof can laugh at the imagery. The constant source of irritation can eat away at one's patience. A contentious spouse (male or female) can do the same.

Sometimes the Bible uses understatement, a sort of tongue-in-cheek approach, to tickle the reader and get his attention. Acts 12 describes a miraculous jailbreak. The night before Peter was to face a hostile trial, an angel secretly removed him from prison. He negotiated chains that bound him between two guards, an additional set of guards and an iron gate, without the guards being even slightly aware of what was happening. Luke, the author of Acts, records, "Now when day came, there was no small disturbance among

the soldiers as to what could have become of Peter."[5]
Later he describes a two-hour riot in Ephesus as "no small
disturbance."[6]

The Bible also uses sarcasm. The prophet Elijah challenged the prophets of Baal to a contest on Mt. Carmel. He
and they would prepare sacrifices for burning, but neither
would light the flame. Each would call on his god to start
the fire. The prophets of Baal went first, but after calling on
Baal all morning they got no answer. " 'You'll have to
shout louder than that,'[Elijah] scoffed, 'to catch the attention of your god! Perhaps he is talking to someone. . . , or
maybe he is away on a trip, or is asleep and needs to be
awakened!' "[7] Try as they could, the prophets of Baal could
not call down fire.

Then Elijah built an altar of stones, piled on wood and
a slain ox, and thoroughly soaked everything with twelve
barrels of water. He called on God, and a fire flashed down
from heaven and burned up everything—the ox, the wood,
the stones, the dust—and evaporated the water that had
filled the trench surrounding the altar.

YOU CAN'T FOOL ME!

The Bible contains other examples of sarcasm. In Numbers
22, the prophet Balaam is rebuked by his donkey. In 1
Samuel 15, King Saul disobeys God's command and keeps
livestock he gained in battle. Early in the morning, Saul
greets the prophet Samuel with the announcement, "I have
carried out the command of the Lord." Samuel is not fooled.
He inquires, "What then is this bleating of the sheep in my
ears, and the lowing of the oxen which I hear?"[8]

In Acts 12, after Peter escaped from prison, he hurried to
Mary's home, where many Christians were gathered. When

he knocked at the gate, the servant girl was so excited to see him that she rushed into the home with the good news and left Peter still knocking at the gate!

THE MASTER AT WORK

Jesus provides some choice examples of humor in the Bible. He used humor in an atmosphere of strong antagonism and conflict. He had a wide following among the elite and the common people, including the prostitutes and unscrupulous tax collectors. Would multitudes come from miles around to sit in the hot sun and listen to a speaker who never sprinkled in humor? Would children have responded so positively to someone who lacked a warm and fun-loving manner?

It was Jesus' somewhat relaxed attitude that drew criticism from the rigid, legalistic religious leaders of His day, the Pharisees. In fact, at one point Jesus used humor to show the hypocrisy of their criticism. He compared them to fickle children who criticize others for whatever they do when it doesn't conform to their wishes. He says,

> To what then shall I compare the men of this generation, and what are they like?

> They are like children who sit in the market place and call to one another. . . "We played the flute for you, and you did not dance; we sang a dirge, and you did not weep."

> For John the Baptist has come eating no bread and drinking no wine; and you say, "He has a demon!"

> The Son of Man has come eating and drinking;

213

and you say, "Behold, a gluttonous man, and a drunkard, a friend of tax-gathers and sinners!"

Yet wisdom is vindicated by all her children.[9]

Elsewhere He warned:

Do not judge lest you be judged yourselves.

For in the way you judge, you will be judged; and by your standard of measure, it shall be measured to you.

And why do you look at the speck in your brother's eye, but do not notice the log that is in your own eye?

Or how can you say to your brother, "Let me take the speck out of your eye," and behold, the log is in your own eye?

You hypocrite, first take the log out of your own eye, and then you will see clearly enough to take the speck out of your brother's eye.[10]

Imagine someone walking around with a huge log in his eye and not noticing it! The image borders on slapstick. Now imagine that person walking up to someone else and saying, "Pardon me, friend. I notice that you have a small speck in your eye. Here, let me help you remove it. As you must know, I'm an expert at these things!" Jesus' audience probably had a good belly laugh over that one. We all have faults; how tempting it is to judge those same faults in others. Yet it is better that we deal with our own shortcomings.

214

Jesus criticized the Pharisees for being so hyperdevoted to the extreme letter of the traditions that they had concocted to interpret the law, while neglecting the proper concern for people and God. "You blind guides," He called them, "who strain out a gnat and swallow a camel!"[11] Imagine someone filtering some juice or water before drinking it, working very carefully to ensure that not even a tiny gnat remains in the liquid. Then he proceeds to drink something with a huge lump of impure substance in it, even something as large as . . .a huge, hairy, long-necked camel! The exaggeration amuses and delights us.

In the very next verse he criticizes the Pharisees for masking inward uncleanness with outward self-righteousness:

> Woe to you, scribes and Pharisees, hypocrites!
> For you clean the outside of the cup and of
> the dish, but inside you are full of robbery
> and self-indulgence. You blind Pharisee, first
> clean the inside of the cup and of the dish,
> so that the outside of it may become clean
> also,[12]

In our family we agree that, while Linda is the better cook, Rusty is the better dishwasher. But neither of us would meticulously scrub the outside of a cup or bowl and leave the inside filthy. It would be ridiculous! That is the effect Jesus sought when pointing out the Pharisees' hypocrisy.

DO YOU SMELL SOMETHING BURNING?

Jesus taught His followers to spread the light that God had given to them:

And He was saying to them, "A lamp is not
brought to be put under a peck-measure, is it,
or under a bed? Is it not brought to be put on
the lamptstand?"[13]

A lamp is supposed to cast light to help people see, so
it makes little sense to light one and hide it under a basket.
It makes even less sense to hide an open flame lamp under
a bed. Not only does the bed smother the light, but the flame
causes the mattress to smolder, making for most unpleasant
consequences. No, don't hide the light that God has given
you, Jesus taught. Instead, "Let your light shine before men
in such a way that they may see your good works, and glo-
rify your Father who is in heaven."[14]

For more insight into Jesus' use of humor, read *The
Humor of Christ* by Elton Trueblood.[15] Trueblood shows
that not only did Jesus use humor frequently, but several of
His statements and parables make sense only if understood
as being intended in a humorous vein.

Some who oppose humor point to a statement Jesus
made about "idle" or "careless" speech: "And I say to you,
that every careless word that men shall speak, they shall
render account for it in the day of judgement."[16] Professor
Leslie B. Flynn explains, however, that *idle* or *careless* is
not synonymous with humorous.

Words may be humorous without being idle, for
certain humor has its profitable place. The condemnation of idle words by Jesus therefore does not
necessarily refer to humor. The Greek word, "idle"
is composed of two parts, the noun "work" with a
negative prefix. An idle word is one which is not
working. The reason the Lord uttered the warning
was that the Pharisees had just uttered an idle state-

216

ment. When it was reported to the Pharisees that Jesus had healed a demon-possessed man who was blind and dumb, they had to react with some comment. In their jealousy of Jesus they blurted out, without thinking it through or working it over in their minds, that Jesus did the miracle through the power of Satan. This accusation easily backfired, for Jesus showed that if he cast out demons by Satan then the house of Satan was divided against itself. The Pharisees had cast out their accusation idly. It was then, after a few intervening words on the danger of attributing the works of the Holy Spirit to the devil, that Jesus warned against idle words. An idle word is a careless word, not a humorous word, though some humor may fall into the "idle" category. We are to beware of humor which is the reckless output of a vacant mind. "For as the crackling of thorns under a pot, so is the laughter of the fool"(Ecclesiastes 7:6).[17]

Others cite the apostle Paul in an apparent condemnation of humor:

But do not let immorality or any impurity or greed even be named among you, as is proper among saints; and there must be no filthiness and silly talk, or coarse jesting, which are not fitting, but rather giving of thanks.[18]

Once again, Professor Flynn illuminates us with grammatical and historical background:

The word "jesting" means "versatility" or "aptness in turning." It implies nimbleness of wit in turning

217

conversation into another channel and mixing in double meanings. It is our modern word "suggestiveness." But it is suggestiveness along certain lines. The context makes it clear that jesting along immoral lines is forbidden. Paul warns against impurity of life in verse 3, then in verse 4 against impurity of speech. Quick innuendo, smart repartee, and hidden inferences in which improprieties are implied are the targets of the apostle's censure . . .[He] does not mean to condemn all play of humor, which is a divine gift and which in moderation can refresh a spirit.

The city of Ephesus, to which Paul's letter was written, was famous for its shameless lust. On every hand street conversation would be twisted into double-meaning suggestiveness. Hidden sensual meaning would pollute much talk. Thus, this command would be well understood. Not jesting *per se,* but jesting that is vulgar draws the apostle's fire.[19]

Far from condemning humor, the Bible supports humor that is tasteful and appropriate. Perhaps the best rule of thumb is that whatever humor we use should be sprinkled generously with grace. "Let your speech always be with grace, seasoned, as it were, with salt, so that you may know how you should respond to each person."[20] (*Grace* here refers to an inner understanding and compassion for others.) Then our humor can help accomplish God's purposes of refreshing the spirit, communicating important truths or dissolving interpersonal barriers.

CHAPTER 14

~~~~~~

HOW'S YOUR
LOVE LIFE?

~~~~~~

WE'VE LOOKED AT HUMOR—what it is and how to use it successfully. The remainder of this book is packed with anecdotes, quips and jokes on a variety of topics. In this chapter, we'll look at the humorous side of love, dating and marriage.

LOVE

◆ Love has been described as a three-ring circus:
   first comes the engagement ring, then the
   wedding ring, and after that the suffering.[1]

◆ Joe: "Do you believe in love at first sight?"
   Bill: "I'll say one thing, it saves a lot of time."[2]

◆ Eve: "Oh, Adam, do you love me?"
   Adam: "Who else?"[3]

DATING

◆ Laura: "Tom do you love me with all your
   heart?"
   Tom: "Uh-huh."

Laura: "And do you think I'm the most beautiful woman in the world?"

Tom: "Uh-huh."

Laura: "Do you think my lips are as soft as rose petals?"

Tom: "Uh-huh."

Laura: "Oh, Tom, you say the most beautiful things."[4]

◆ Definition of a blind date: You expect to meet a vision, but she (he) turns out to be a sight.[5]

◆ Teenage girl answering telephone: "Mary isn't in right now. This is her 110-pound, five-foot-two, blond, blue-eyed sister."[6]

◆ We have a strange and wonderful relationship. You're strange and I'm wonderful.[7]

◆ The young woman looked back and smiled sweetly to the line of people waiting behind her at the telephone booth. "I won't be very long at all—I just want to hang up on him."[8]

◆ She's just like an appendix. You can take her out, but once is enough!

◆ The young man looked at the prices on the menu, then turned to his date and said, "And what will you have, my plump little doll?"[9]

◆ A shy country boy had his first college date with a young lady who seemed to take things a little faster than he did. After a fun evening of dinner and a show, he walked her up to the door of her sorority house. She obviously was expecting a goodnight kiss. As he was about to leave, she closed her eyes and puckered her lips. He said, "Good night," and leaned down and kissed her on the forehead. "A little lower, please," she responded. So he said (with a deeper voice) "Good night!"

—T. J. Diamond

◆ "The other night I had a date with a girl who said she doesn't kiss on the first date. . .so I asked her if she kisses on the last date!"

—T. J. Diamond

◆ Bill: "Last week I had a date with a pair of Siamese twins."
Phil: "Did you have a good time?"
Bill: "Yes and no."

—T. J. Diamond

◆ Q.: What's the difference between kissing your sweetheart and kissing your sister?
A.: About thirty seconds.[10]

◆ I never kissed my wife until the day we were married. . .However, I did kiss my fiancée. (She became my wife the day we were married.)

◆ One family had a parrot whose entire vocabulary consisted of the words, "Let's neck."

A pastor had a parrot whose only words were "Let's pray." The pastor suggested that the family cage their bird with his.

When the birds were put together, the family's bird, as usual, said, "Let's neck." The pastor's parrot replied, "My prayers have been answered!"[11]

◆ Uncle George was sadly disappointed in a volume he brought home from a second-hand bookstore. The book was titled HOW TO HUG. When he got home, he found it was part of an old set of encyclopedias.

◆ Bill and Vonette remember their first kiss with great fondness. They had dated for quite a while (about a week) when Bill, gentleman that he was, decided to ask her permission for a goodnight kiss. After a pleasant evening at dinner and a concert, he drove her back to her home. As he pulled up to her house, he stopped the car under an old oak tree. The light of the full moon filtered through the leaves and glimmered in her eyes. The moment was prime. Bill turned off the ignition, shifted in his seat and placed his right arm up across the back of the seat. Vonette could sense what was about to happen, and she snuggled over a bit closer. . . toward the door.

"Vonette," Bill said, "I've really enjoyed spending time with you and I'd like to kiss you. May I kiss you good night?"

Vonette just stared ahead in total silence.

"Vonette," Bill said, a bit nervous, "I asked if I could kiss you."

Silence.

"Vonette, are you deaf?"

"Bill, are you paralyzed?"

PROPOSALS

◆ Hope: "You finally asked my father for my hand
in marriage. What did he say?

Bruce: "Not a word. He just fell on my shoulder
and sobbed."[12]

◆ Every night, Barbara prays, "Dear Lord, I'm not
asking a thing for myself. I just want you to
send my parents a son-in-law."[13]

◆ Sue: "Has anyone ever asked you to get married?"

Sally: "Sure, lots of times."

Sue: "Oh, really? Who asked you?"

Sally: "Mother and Father."[14]

◆ Bob: "Why won't you marry me? Is there anyone
else?"

Betty: "There must be."[15]

◆ One bitterly cold winter night a young man plod-
ded through knee-high snow to the home of
his steady. During the evening, he asked her
to marry him. Being very practical, the young
woman replied, "When you have several thousand dollars, I will seriously consider it."

Six months later, the two strolled hand in
hand through a park alongside the river. He

223

stopped to kiss her and asked, "When are we going to get married?"

"Well, how much money have you saved?" the lady inquired.

"Exactly $75," he responded boldly.

"Oh well," she sighed as she smiled. "I guess that's enough."[16]

ENGAGEMENT

◆ Definition of engagement: "An urge on the verge of a merge."[17]

◆ Definition of an engagement ring: "It's a tourniquet applied to the third finger of a woman's left hand to stop circulation."[18]

◆ Lucy: "What happened when you showed your new engagement ring to the women in the office? Did they admire it?"
Lois: "Better than that—four of them recognized it!"[19]

◆ Esther: "So Tony and you are getting married? Why, I thought it was just a mere flirtation."
Edith: "So did Tony."[20]

MARRIAGE

◆ Marriage is a kind of graduation ceremony in which a fellow loses his bachelor's degree without acquiring a master's.

◆ Marriage is like deep-sea fishing. You never know what you've got until you get it in the boat.[21]

◆ A famous author sat in a department store autographing copies of his new book. He was especially pleased when one man brought up not only his new book, but reprints of his previous two novels as well.

"My wife really likes your writing," the man explained, "so I've decided to give her these autographed copies for her birthday."

"Oh, a surprise, eh?" the author guessed.

"I'll say," the customer agreed. "She's expecting a Cadillac."[22]

◆ A magazine article discussed the marriage of Kansas Senator Bob Dole and his wife Elizabeth, former President Ronald Reagan's Secretary of Transportation. The spread contained a photo of the Senator helping his wife make their bed. One incensed male reader wrote Dole "an irate letter complaining that I should never allow a picture to be taken of a man doing such things around the house."

Senator Dole says, "I wrote him back: 'Buddy, you don't know the half of it. The only reason she was helping me was that the photographer was there.'"[23]

◆ The wife of a university theater director was asked by one of her clients what her plans were for an upcoming weekend. She said, "I think I'll watch my husband's play."

"Oh, really," the client said. "How many do you have?"[24]

♦ A husband went to buy a birthday gift for his wife. Some friends had been invited over that night to celebrate her fortieth, and he wanted to get something special. At the store he spotted some cute little music boxes. One blue one was playing "Happy Birthday." Thinking they were all the same, he chose a red one and had it gift-wrapped. Later, at dinner, he gave it to his wife and asked her to open it. When she lifted the lid, out came the tune to "The Old Gray Mare, She Ain't What She Used to Be!"[25]

♦ The husband sat in the living room with his hand on the television knob. "Hey, Beverly," he shouted to his wife in the kitchen, "Is there anything you want to say before football season starts?"[26]

♦ Neighbors were complaining to Mrs. Brown about the racket her husband was making. "He always goes around cackling like a chicken," they told her.

"I know," Mrs. Brown said, "We get tired of it, too. Sometimes we think he's not in his right mind."

"But can't you do something for him? Can't he be cured?"

"Oh, I suppose a doctor could do something," she answered, "but we need the eggs."

◆ An old New England gentleman and his wife
  wanted to take a ride in a private plane,
  but they said the ten dollar charge was too
  much. The pilot offered them a deal. He
  would take them for a free ride if they
  promised not to say a single word during
  the trip. If they spoke, they would have to
  pay the ten dollars.

    The trip passed without a word spoken.
  Back on the ground, the pilot said he didn't
  think they could do it.

    "Well," the old man replied, "you almost
  won—I sure felt like hollerin' when mama
  fell out."[27]

CHILDBIRTH

◆ The attendant on desk duty in the maternity
  ward answered the phone. An excited
  voice at the other end said, "This is Tom
  Rogers and I'm bringing in my wife right
  now. . .she's about to have a baby!"

    "Try to keep calm," the attendant replied.
  "Is this her first baby?"

    "No," the voice replied, "this is her
  husband."[28]

MARITAL HARMONY?

◆ Two things cause unhappy marriages: men and
  women.[29]

◆ Bill: "My wife treats me like an idol."
Ralph: "Why do you say that?"
Bill: "She feeds me burnt offerings at meal-
time."[30]

◆ With some cooks, the call is "Come and get it!"
With her, it's "Try and eat it."

◆ When Bob was in the army, he was lined up
with the rest of his platoon at drill one morning. His commanding officer drew a line in
the dirt in front of the platoon. "OK," the
officer barked, "I want every man who is
henpecked by his wife to step over the line."
The entire platoon stepped over the line, with
the exception of Bob.

The commanding officer walked up to
Bob, looked him in the eye and said, "Soldier,
why didn't you step forward?"

Bob replied, "My wife told me not to."

◆ One husband reports: "Our argument was well
under way as my wife and I left the party.
Once we were in the car, words were flying.
The area we were driving through was not
the best, so we stopped long enough to lock
the doors. Then we started again.

"My wife had really worked up a storm,
and after a few choice words from me, she
shouted, 'Stop the car and let me out!'

"I pulled over to the curb. She unlocked
the door and got out, but then looked around
and got back in again, saying, 'Take me to
a better neighborhood.'

"That broke us both up—and the argument, too."[31]

◆ An interviewer asked W.C. Fields, "Do you believe in clubs for women?"

The comic replied, "Only when all other means of persuasion fail."[32]

◆ In our marriage, we decided never to go to bed mad. We've gone without sleep for four weeks.[33]

◆ "Say, how long have you been married?" a man asked his friend.

"We've been happily married for eight years," he replied. "Eight out of fifteen ain't bad."[34]

◆ Before the marriage, he talks and she listens. During their honeymoon, she talks and he listens. Later, they both talk and the neighbors listen.[35]

◆ In a secluded corner of their country club dining room, the sophisticated tycoon was being berated by his nagging wife. "You lousy skunk," the lady announced. "Of all the low-down snakes, I think you're the worst."

The husband noticed that a group of their friends had just taken a table within earshot. He quickly interjected, "Quite right, darling. And what else did you say to him?"[36]

229

◆ Someone approached the grieving widow at the funeral and said, "I'm sorry, my dear. Tell me, what were his last words?"

"You don't scare me with that shot-gun, Martha. You couldn't hit the side of a barn!"

◆ Actress Jane Wyman relates her most embarrassing moment, which happened when she was entertaining some very special guests. After making sure the entire house was in order, she put a note on the guest towels that said, "If you use these I will murder you." It was intended for her husband. In the haste of the preparations, she forgot to remove the note. When the guests had departed, she found the towels—and the note—exactly as she had left them.[37]

◆ One newly-married husband was concerned about his tight financial situation. His wife frequently made long-distance calls to her mother, even though he explained his concern to her. One evening he heard the familiar dialing. "Honey," he asked uneasily, "who are you calling?"

"Just checking on the time," she responded. Then, after a pause, he heard her say, "Hello, Mother? What time is it?"[38]

◆ The lady told her neighbor, "My husband's a do-it-yourself man. Whenever I ask him to do anything, he says, 'Do it yourself.' "[39]

◆ Shortly after the honeymoon, the new bride

started to complain about family finances. "When we were courting," she nagged, "you led me to believe you were well off."

"Oh, I was," the husband sighed. "I was."[40]

◆ Two newlyweds got along famously for months and then had their first serious argument late one evening. After contemplation, the wife decided that she couldn't stand to share the same bed with her husband that night.

Teary-eyed, she took a pillow from the linen closet, trudged into the darkened den and plopped down onto the sofa— on top of her husband.[41]

◆ "You're in incredibly fine condition," the doctor concluded after finishing a thorough physical. "How old did you say you were, sir?"

"Seventy-eight."

"Seventy-eight! Why, you have the health of a sixty-year-old. What's your secret?"

"I guess, Doc, it's due to a pact the wife and I made when we got married. She promised that if she was ever about to lose her temper, she'd stay in the kitchen 'till she cooled off. And I pledged that when I got angry I'd keep quiet, too, and go outside until I calmed down."

"I don't understand," the doctor said. "How could that help you stay so fit?"

"Well," the patient explained, "I guess you could say I've lived an outdoor life."[42]

◆ If you see a married couple walking down the sidewalk, the one who's three or four steps ahead is the one who is angry.[43]

◆ A divorce judge tried to reconcile the feuding couple that stood before his bench, but finally decided it was impossible. Each partner was too stubborn. "O.K.," the judge said, "I'll grant your divorce, but realize that all that you possess must be divided equally."

"What do we do about the three children?" the wife asked.

"You'll have to figure that one out yourselves," the judge replied.

The wife seized her husband by the collar and started to drag him away. "C'mon home, you no-good, lazy meathead." As they exited, she glanced back and called to the judge. "Your Honor, we'll be back in a year with four kids."[44]

◆ "You haven't taken proper care of your good wife," the divorce court judge ruled. "I'm going to give her $350 a month."

"Why that's mighty nice of you, Your Honor," beamed the defendant. "I'll give her a few dollars from time to time myself."[45]

◆ One woman married four times: first to a millionaire, next to an actor, then to a minister and finally to an undertaker.

One for the money; two for the show, three to get ready; and four to go.[46]

◆ It was quite late when the married couple arrived home from a party. The wife prepared for bed while the husband dashed into the kitchen and brought back a glass of water and two aspirin. When he handed the tablets to his wife, she asked with a puzzled look, "What's this?"

"Aspirin," the husband replied.

"But I don't have a headache," she explained.

"Aha!" the husband roared gleefully. "Gotcha!"[47]

CHAPTER 15

~~~~~~~~~~

HEAVENLY HUMOR

~~~~~~~~~~

ONE DAY BILL was hunting in the woods. It had been a slow day and he had yet to shoot any game. Suddenly, he heard a noise behind him. He whirled around and saw a ferocious mountain lion only twenty-five yards away. Bill quickly raised his rifle to his shoulder, took aim and pulled the trigger. Click. The rifle didn't fire. Click. . . click. . .click. Again, nothing—the gun was malfunctioning. By this time, the mountain lion had started toward Bill. In desperation, he threw down his rifle and ran.

Faster and faster he ran, with the mountain lion chasing him. The faster Bill ran, the more the mountain lion gained on him. Finally, Bill came to the edge of a cliff. There was nowhere to go, so he dropped to his knees and began to pray. "O Lord, I pray that this mountain lion is a Christian!"

As Bill looked up, he was surprised to see the mountain lion kneeling just a few feet away, praying, "Dear Lord, I pray that you'll bless this food that I'm about to partake to the nourishment of my body. . ."

A minister found three boys playing hooky
from Bible school. He asked them, "Don't
you want to go to heaven?"

"Not me," one said.

The minister was shocked. "You don't
want to go to heaven when you die?"

"When I die? Oh, sure!" the boy replied.
"I thought you were getting up a group to go
right now!"

—Virginia Bilderback

Special note: We have included in this book jokes
about dying and going to heaven. Some play off the popular notion that entrance into heaven is determined by
one's good and bad deeds (i.e., whether or not one
plays hooky from Bible school, etc.). As previously discussed, however, no amount of good works is sufficient
to gain eternal life. Only the substitutionary death of
Christ, individually accepted by the believer, will do it.
Eternal life is a free gift. Church membership won't earn
it, for. . .

Going to church doesn't make you a Christian
any more than walking into a garage makes
you an automobile.

Nor will any other deeds prevent one from gaining eternal life.

The other day a fellow asked me, "Can I
smoke and still get to heaven?" I told him.
"Sure, and if you smoke, you might get there
a lot sooner."

With that understanding, we have taken the liberty to scatter a few more "heaven" stories throughout this chapter. They are intended to amuse, rather than to instruct in doctrine or to offend. We hope you enjoy them.

> Once a country parson bought a horse. The dealer assured him he had made a perfect selection. "This horse was raised in a religious atmosphere," the dealer said. "You can't say 'Giddyap' to make him start. He won't respond. You've got to say 'Praise the Lord.' And instead of saying 'Whoa' to make him stop, you need to say, 'Amen.' "
>
> The parson paid for the horse, mounted him and said, "Praise the Lord." The horse cantered off toward the parson's parish. After a couple of miles, though, a jack rabbit darted into the road and spooked the horse. The horse took off at a gallop across an open field, directly toward a bluff that bordered a huge river two hundred feet below. In panic, the parson forgot his instructions. "Whoa!" he yelled several times as he pulled on the reins, but the horse kept galloping. Finally, at the last moment, the preacher remembered. "Amen!" he shouted, stopping the horse at the very brink of the chasm.
>
> "Whew," the grateful pastor said. "Praise the Lord!"[1]

BLESSED BLOOPERS

◆ The pastor happily told his congregation about the church's new public address system. He explained that the microphone and wiring were paid for with church funds. Then he added, "The loudspeaker was donated by a member of our congregation in memory of his wife."[2]

◆ A British clergyman struggled along with a small congregation in a poor neighborhood. A commercial firm offered to supply free hymn books, provided they could insert a bit of discreet advertising into the hymnals. The pastor was reluctant but finally agreed.

When the hymnals arrived, he eagerly examined them and was delighted to find no brash advertisements on or inside the covers. The next Sunday, his flock began to sing from the hymnals. All went well until the third song, in which the congregation lifted their voices in unison to the melodious notes of:

Hark the herald angels sing,
Hanson's pills are just the thing;
Peace on earth and mercy mild,
Two for man and one for child.[3]

◆ In the bulletin of the Zion Evangelical Lutheran Church in South Milwaukee: "The eighth-graders will present Shakespeare's *Hamlet* in the church basement on Friday at 7 P.M. The congregation is invited to attend this tragedy."[4]

◆ When a little church stopped buying from the local stationer, he called the deacon to ask why. The deacon explained, "Remember those pencils we ordered from you so that visitors could register?"

"Sure," the stationer replied, "didn't you get them?"

"Yes, but you sent us pencils from the country club that said, 'Play Golf Next Sunday.' "

◆ Bill: "I type on my typewriter by the biblical system."
Bob: "What's that?"
Bill: "Seek and ye shall find."[5]

◆ A mother didn't feel well one Sunday so she sent her little girl to church and told her to be sure to remember the text of the sermon. When she came home, the little girl said, "The minister said, 'Don't be scared, you'll get your quilt.' " The mother was perplexed. Finally she phoned the preacher. He explained that his text was, "Fear not, thy comforter will come."

◆ The three children usually were able to persuade their dad to buy them ice cream right after church. One Sunday he protested, "Where does it say that you should always get something to eat and drink after church?"

A quick-thinking daughter replied, "In the Bible it says, 'Blessed are those who hunger and thirst after righteousness.' "[6]

◆ The Sunday school teacher told the class about Lot being told to take his wife and flee out of the city. "Lot got away, but his wife disobeyed divine orders by looking back and was turned into a pillar of salt," the teacher explained. One little boy asked, "What happened to the flea?"

—Virginia Bilderback

◆ Little Jimmy was one of the best students in his Sunday school class. One day the teacher asked her students to draw and color a picture of something about the baby Jesus. Jimmy worked and worked and came up with a picture of a modern jet airplane with four people inside. The teacher couldn't quite figure it out. She thought perhaps it had something to do with how Christianity relates to modern times. So she asked him, "Jimmy, that's a nice picture, but what is it?"

"Why that's Joseph, Mary and baby Jesus on the flight into Egypt," Jimmy answered.

"Oh!. . .but Jimmy, there are *four* people in there. Who is the fourth one?"

"Why, that's Pontius, the pilot!"

◆ Q: What was the name of Pontius Pilate's great-aunt's straw-bonnet maker?
A: Nobody knows.[7]

◆ Reverend Haggerty, a respected church leader, arrived in a large city to deliver a series of speeches. At a banquet the first evening, he noticed some reporters in the audience.

Because he wanted to use some of the stories he told that night in his speeches the next day, he asked the reporters to omit them from their articles. One article that came out the next day, written by a cub reporter, concluded with this line: "Reverend Haggerty also told a number of stories that cannot be printed."[8]

◆ Two men with the same name lived near one another in the same subdivision. One was a pastor; the other was a salesman. The pastor died and, at about the same time, the salesman took a business trip to Florida. When he arrived, he sent a telegram to his wife to let her know he had gotten there safely. By mistake, the message was delivered to the wife of the deceased pastor. The telegram read:

    "ARRIVED SAFELY;
    HEAT HERE AWFUL."[9]

◆ Nine-year-old Joey was asked by his mother what he had learned in Sunday school. "Well, Mom, our teacher told us how God sent Moses behind enemy lines on a rescue mission to lead the Israelites out of Egypt. When he got to the Red Sea, he had his engineers build a pontoon bridge and all the people walked across safely. Then he used his walkie-talkie to radio headquarters for reinforcements. They sent bombers to blow up the bridge and all the Israelites were saved."

    "Now, Joey, is that really what your teacher taught you?" his mother asked.

"Well, no, Mom. But if I told it the way the teacher did, you'd *never* believe it![10]

◆ Two university professors were arguing about the Bible, each claiming to know more than the other. "Why, I'll bet you don't even know the Lord's Prayer," huffed one.

"Everybody knows that," the other snapped. "It's 'Now I lay me down to sleep. . .' "

"Wow," the first professor said admiringly. "I didn't realize you knew so much about the Bible."

◆ A minister was baptizing some new church members. As the first woman came up out of the water, she joyously exclaimed to the congregation, "Bless the Lord, O my soul."

The next new member said, "The Lord is my shepherd."

A third quoted, "I can do all things through Christ, who strengthens me."

The fourth to be baptized was a fellow with little knowledge of the Bible. He also was timid in front of a group. As he came up out of the water, he gave a wide grin to the congregation and exclaimed, "Merry Christmas, everyone!"[11]

◆ A nine-year-old boy was the son of the Commander of the Nantucket American Legion Post. His father, a seasoned military man, frequently told him vivid stories of the valor of combat.

One day in Sunday School, the teacher related a graphic account of the crucifixion and Christ being nailed to the cross. The boy listened in wide-eyed astonishment.

During a pause, the excited lad shouted with flushed face and clenched fists, "Well, what I want to know is, where were the Marines?"[12]

◆ A mother was trying to comfort her little daughter upon the death of her pet kitten. "But Mommy," the girl asked, "what in the world would God want with a dead cat?"

—Virginia Bilderback

◆ From the pulpit one Sunday, a preacher asked anyone who had never sinned to please stand. One man stood up in the back row. The preacher asked him, "Haven't you ever sinned?"

The man said, "Oh, yes, *I* have. I'm standing up for someone else—my wife's first husband."

◆ A Smogarian was filling out a form for college. One question asked him to state his church preference. His response: "red brick."

◆ The county's champion horse thief was converted at a camp meeting. The preacher called upon him to tell the group what the Lord had done for him.

The reformed thief stood up and said, "It looks like the Lord done ruined me."[13]

THE CLERGY

◆ Four clergymen from the same town were talking one evening over coffee. The subject was their personal failings, and each agreed that he had one.

"That's right," the first said, "Take me, for instance. I like to hit the bottle every once in a while. I know my congregation doesn't approve, and I even preach against it from time to time. But somehow I can't resist a couple of shots to brace me now and then."

"Gambling is my snag," the second pastor admitted. "I do OK around here, but when I get out of town, I can't seem to resist. In fact, I lost a bundle on my last trip two weeks ago."

"Drinking and gambling don't cause me problems," the third said. "But I do cheat a bit on my income tax each year. It's tempting to keep quiet about some income I get on the side, but I figure I need the money. I know it's wrong, but I can't resist."

The fourth clergyman had been silent up to this point, so the others asked him what his greatest struggle was. "Well, I appreciate you fellows being so honest, so I guess I will be, too. Drinking and gambling have never appealed to me and I don't cheat on my income tax, but I do have one serious vice: I just love to gossip, and right now I can hardly wait to leave here."[14]

◆ A small boy sat with his mother in church, listening to a sermon titled, "What is a Christian?" The minister punctuated his talk at several key intervals by asking, "What is a Christian?" Each time, he pounded his fist on the pulpit for emphasis.

At one point, the lad whispered to his mother, "Mama, do you know? Do you know what a Christian is?"

"Yes, dear," the mother replied. "Now try to sit still and listen."

As the minister was wrapping up the sermon, once again he thundered, "What is a Christian?" and pounded especially hard on the pulpit. At that, the boy jumped up and cried, *"Tell him, Mama, tell him!"*[15]

◆ A new preacher came to deliver his first sermon in a prairie parish, but no one showed up except one cowhand. The preacher wondered aloud whether to proceed with the services. The man replied, "I can't tell you what to do, I'm just a cowhand. But if I came to feed my cows and only one showed up, I'd be darned if I wouldn't feed her."

The preacher thanked him and gave the prepared hour-long sermon, which stretched to an hour and a half. When he finished, he asked the man if he had liked it.

"Well," the man replied, "I don't know much about sermons; I'm just a cowhand. But if I came to feed my cattle and only one showed up, I'd be darned if I'd give her the whole load."

◆ The minister, who had forty minutes worth of sermon and only twenty-five minutes in which to deliver it, said, "I feel like the Egyptian mummy—pressed for time."

◆ "Daddy," the little boy asked, "what does it mean when Pastor Thompson takes off his watch and puts it on the pulpit in front of him when he starts his sermons?"

"Absolutely nothing," the father sighed. "Absolutely nothing."

◆ One minister says that it doesn't bother him at all if his members look at their watches during his sermons. It does affect him, however, when someone not only looks at his watch, but also holds it up to his ear to see if it's still running.[16]

◆ Minister's prayer: "May the members of my congregation be as free with their money as they are with their advice, and may their minds be as open as their mouths."

◆ One old preacher rode the circuit on his horse, preaching in churches and camp meetings. His only source of support was voluntary contributions from the congregations to which he spoke. One night, after preaching earnestly in a small town, he passed his hat among the packed benches. After it had made the rounds, the hat was returned to the pulpit. The preacher gazed into it and saw that it was empty. Not even a penny was in it. At that, he raised his hands to the heavens and said, "Brethren, let us thank the Lord that this hat got back safely out of this audience."[17]

◆ "Be grateful for all that the good Lord had done for you," the minister told his flock. "Surely each of us should give one-tenth of all we earn to the Lord."

"Amen!" shouted a particularly fervent church member. "I say let's raise it to one-twentieth."[18]

◆ A minister who told his congregation there are one hundred different sins, already has received forty-six requests for copies of the list.

MISCELLANEOUS MIRTH

◆ A man named Jones was in his home when a flood came. He refused to evacuate, but climbed up on the roof where the water eventually reached his ankles. Soon a neighbor paddled by in a canoe and shouted, "Can I give you a ride to higher ground?"

"No, thanks," answered Jones. "I have faith in the Lord. I know He will save me."

A bit later, the water was up to his waist. A man in a rowboat pulled up and hollered, "Hey! Can I give you a lift out of danger?"

"No, thanks," Jones answered. "I have faith in the Lord. I know He will save me."

Eventually, Jones was standing on tiptoe

with water up to his neck. A helicopter flew in and dropped a rope. "Grab on," the pilot yelled, "I'll pull you up."

"No, thanks," Jones answered. "I have faith in the Lord. I know He will save me."

But after hours of trying to tread water and stay afloat, poor Jones drowned and went to meet his Maker. In heaven, he complained to the Lord. "Tell me, Lord, what happened? I had such great faith in You that You would save me. I don't understand. What went wrong?"

The Lord replied, "I can't understand it either. I sent two boats and a helicopter!"[19]

◆ (This one is good to tell on someone who introduces you at a meeting. We'll call him George Walsh.)

Last night I dreamt that I died and went to heaven. As I looked across the plains of glory, I saw scattered about what appeared to be millions of parking meters. Actually they looked like parking meters—they were on vertical standards—but the faces were like clocks, with one hand that could rotate all the way around the dial. Each had a nameplate attached to the base.

I flagged down a passing angel and asked what they were. The angel explained that these were not parking meters, but sin meters. They registered the sins a person currently was committing on earth. For each sin, the hand clicked forward one notch.

I began to look around for my friends' sin

meters. I found my spouse's. It was clicking right along (you see, we have three young children). I found my pastor's. It looked as if it were broken. It *never* moved! It had cobwebs on it.

But I couldn't find George Walsh's sin meter. I looked everywhere. Finally, I flagged down another angel to ask where it was. The angel laughed and said, "George Walsh's sin meter is a bit of a joke up here in heaven. You'll find it over in St. Peter's office. He uses it for a fan."

—Dave Swingley

◆ An admiral and a bishop arrived simultaneously at the Pearly Gates. The admiral received a spectacular welcome: angelic trumpets, choirs singing the "Hallelujah" chorus. . .the red carpet treatment. The bishop was told to wait outside. He became a bit perturbed as he waited while the admiral got all the attention.

Eventually the gates were opened and the bishop was ushered in. There was no fanfare— no choirs or trumpets or hoopla—just a few angels to say hello and that was it. The bishop was puzzled and asked why the admiral had received such a gala reception while his had been so modest. "Oh, don't let that bother you," the angels said. "You see, we get plenty of bishops up here, but this is the first admiral we've ever had."[20]

◆ Three people died at the same time and were met at the heavenly gate by Saint Peter. The first was a lawyer from California. "I'd like to enter, please," he told the saint.

"Very well, all in good time," Peter replied. "First you must pass one small test. You must spell 'God.' "

"That's a snap. *G-o-d*."

"Excellent," Saint Peter said. "You may enter."

The second was an oilman from Texas. "I'd sure like to enter," he said.

"Very well, all in good time. But first you must pass one test. Simply spell 'God.' "

"A cinch," the Texan said. "*G-o-d*."

"Excellent. You may enter."

The third person, an attractive female stockbroker from New York, approached Saint Peter.

"I'd like to enter, please," the woman said.

"Very well, all in good time. But first you must pass one small test—"

"Oh come on, Saint," the woman inter-jected. "I've had it tough all my life. I've had to fight for every promotion I've ever had just because I'm a woman. I've had to settle for lower pay for the same positions as my male co-workers. I've continually been hassled by a boss who is a male chauvinist pig. So now what? Are you going to give me a hard time, too?"

"But it's only a little test," Peter explained. "Spell 'Czechoslovakia.' "[21]

◆ Eighteen club women died in a bus crash. Saint Peter phoned the Devil and told him heaven

250

was overcrowded, and he asked if he would take the eighteen women. The Devil agreed to take them for a short time.

A week later the Devil called Saint Peter and said, "You've got to take these women! They've had rummage sales and bake sales and raffles, and pretty soon they'll have enough money to air condition this place!"

—Virginia Bilderback

◆ As a minister took his seat on a jet airplane, he noticed that the woman beside him had her Bible open and seemed to be reading it and praying fervently. As the plane taxied out to the runway, she appeared to become anxious. As the plane took off and gained altitude, she became more tense and grabbed the armrests tightly as sweat poured down her face. It was obvious that the higher the plane climbed, the more distressed the woman became.

Finally the pastor turned to comfort her. "There, there," he soothed, "you needn't be afraid. After all, remember that Jesus said, 'I am with you always.' "

"That's not what He said," the woman replied. "He said, '*LOW*, I am with you always.' "

CHAPTER 16

~~~~~~~~~~

MORE GOOD
JOKES AND STORIES

~~~~~~~~~~

WHAT FOLLOWS IS a potpourri of anecdotes, jokes and stories on a wide variety of subjects, from animals to the workplace.

ANIMALS

◆ The lion was proud of his mastery of the animal kingdom. One day he decided to make sure all the other animals knew he was king of the jungle. He was so confident that he bypassed the smaller animals and went straight to the bear. "Who is the king of the jungle?" the lion asked. "Why, of course, *you* are," the bear replied. The lion gave a mighty roar of approval.

Next he asked the tiger, "Who is the king of the jungle?" The tiger quickly responded, "Everyone knows that *you* are, oh mighty lion."

Next on the list was the elephant. "Who is the king of the jungle?" the lion asked. The elephant immediately grabbed the lion with his trunk, whirled him around in the air five or six times and slammed him into a tree.

Then he pounded him onto the ground several times, dunked him under water in a nearby lake and finally dumped him out on the shore.

The lion—beaten, bruised and battered—struggled to his feet. "Look," he told the e lephant, "just because you don't know the answer is no reason to get upset."[1]

◆ A woman opened her Westinghouse refrigerator to find a live white rabbit seated on the top shelf. "What in the world are you doing here?" the surprised woman asked.

"Well," the rabbit replied, "this is a Westinghouse, and I'm just westing."[2]

◆ Will Rogers said we should live in such a way that we would not be ashamed to sell our family parrot. . .to the town gossip.[3]

◆ Revised quote: Hickory, dickory dock, the mice ran up the clock. The clock struck one—all others escaped without injury.

◆ A seeing eye dog boarded a crowded streetcar and led his master to the only available space—a small gap on the seat that ran the length of the car. The space was too small for an adult, but the dog began nudging with his nose the people on either side. They moved farther apart, and their neighbors squeezed against one another until the empty space was large enough for two people. The dog then nudged his master, signaling him to be seated. The passengers broke into laughter as the dog climbed up into the space beside the blind man and relaxed with his head on his master's lap.[4]

BLOOPERS

◆ Sign in a laundry:
WE DON'T TEAR YOUR LAUNDRY IN OUR MACHINES. WE DO IT BY HAND.[5]

◆ Notice in a New York paper: William Anderson was released yesterday from the hospital where his right leg was placed in a cast following a fracture of his left ankle.[6]

◆ In an Ohio newspaper: Arthur Edwards left Park Street Hospital Wednesday, still recovering from a head injury and shock caused by coming into contact with a live wife.[7]

◆ Headline in a California paper: "TWO CONVICTS EVADE NOOSE, JURY HUNG."[8]

◆ Radio announcement: "This portion of 'Woman on the Run' is brought to you by Phillips' Milk of Magnesia."[9]

◆ Former President Gerald Ford: "Whenever I can I always watch the Detroit Tigers on radio."[10]

◆ In 1962, German President Heinrich Lubke was welcoming the president of India at an airport and wanted to greet him in English. Lubke struggled with English, however, and when he intended to ask, "How are you?" instead said, "Who are you?" His guest answered responsibly, "I am the president of India."[11]

CAMPUS COMEDY

◆ The college student grabbed a coin, flipped it in the air and said, "Heads, I'll go to sleep; tails, I'll stay up. If it stands on edge, I'll study."[12]

◆ A professor at the University of Pennsylvania was known for giving boring, cliché-ridden lectures. At the beginning of one semester, an innovative class breathed new life into the course by assigning baseball plays to each hackneyed phrase. For example, when the professor said, "On the other hand," that counted as a base hit. "By the same token" was a strike out; "and so on" counted as a stolen base. Divided into two teams by the center aisle of the lecture hall, the students played inning after inning of silent but vigorous baseball.

On the last day of class, the impossible happened—the score was tied and bases were loaded. Then the batter hit a home run! The winning team stood and cheered wildly. Though deeply appreciative, the professor later was quoted as wondering why only half of the students had been enthusiastic about his lectures.[13]

◆ "If any morons are in this class, I'd like them to stand up," the professor announced.

   After a long pause, a lone freshman stood up.

   "Young man," the prof asked, "do you consider yourself a moron?"

   "Well, not really, sir," the student answered. "But I hated to see you standing up there all alone."[14]

◆ Student: "Sir, I have a complaint. I don't believe I deserve a zero on this exam."

Professor: "Neither do I, but it's the lowest grade I can give."

◆ Letter home from college student: "Urgent! Please send Care packages with food. All they serve here is breakfast, lunch and dinner."

◆ When forty-six hundred Virginia Tech graduates gathered in the football stadium for commencement exercises in 1981, the exuberance of the occasion led to chants. The engineering students rose en masse, enthusiastically shouting, "We've got jobs! We've got jobs!" To which the graduates of the business college cheerfully responded, "Working for us! Working for us!"[15]

◆ A schoolteacher was ticketed for running a stop light and told to appear in traffic court the next Monday. She went to the court immediately and appealed to the judge to handle her

257

case right then, explaining that she had to teach on Monday.

"A schoolteacher, eh?" the magistrate said. "Your presence in my courtroom fulfills a lifetime ambition of mine. I want you to sit down at this table and write 500 times, 'I ran a red light.' "[16]

◆ Graffiti found at Clemson University: Underneath the question, "Where will you spend eternity?" someone scrawled, "The way things look now, in German 201."[17]

◆ The college student who worked so hard to graduate in three years later wonders what the hurry was.

◆ A professor is one who talks in someone else's sleep.[18]

◆ Education: A process by which information is transferred from the notes of a professor to the notes of a student without passing through the brains of either.

◆ "In college I majored in psychology and minored in psycho-ceramics."
"Psycho-ceramics? What's that?"
"The study of cracked pots."

◆ A Harvard professor was conducting a class in decision-making. In his first drill, he picked a student from Georgia.
"Now, son," he said, "I want you to tell

me the decision you'd make in this situation. You're driving a fully-loaded semi-truck down a mountain road at seventy miles an hour. Just as you get close to an oncoming truck two cars pull out from behind him to pass. You hit the brakes and your brakes go out. On your right side is a five-hundred-foot cliff; on your left side is a one-thousand-foot precipice. Now, son, you have three seconds. What would you do?"

"Well," the boy drawled, "I reckon I'd wake up Leroy."

"Leroy!" the professor exclaimed. "Who's Leroy?"

"Leroy's my relief driver, sir. You see, he's from a small country town and I'd want to wake him up 'cause he ain't *never* seen an accident like this before."

◆ My friend Roger recently got back from visiting Texas A&M University—home of the Aggies. I noticed his lips were all swollen, so I said, "What happened, Rog?" He replied, "I went to a party with a bunch of Aggies and we wound up bobbing for french fries."

◆ Q: Why did the Aggie write "T.G.I.F." on his tennis shoes?
A: Toes Go In First.

◆ Q: Why don't Aggies eat M&M's?
A: They say it takes too long to peel them.

(Note: the preppie, like the Aggie, is often the target of humor. Rusty is an official preppie, and together we enjoy poking light-hearted fun at the preppie mystique.)

◆ Q: What does a preppie do when he tears his Izod shirt?
   A: He sends it out for Gatorade.

◆ Q: Why are there so few divorces among preppies?
   A: Prohibitive costs. It is too expensive to change the monograms on everything.

◆ Q: How many letters are in the preppie alphabet?
   A: One. The letter "I."

◆ Q: What is the central theme of preppie theology?
   A: There is no God but Mammon.[19]

DEFINITIONS, APHORISMS

◆ MINIMUM: a small English mother.

◆ Many men smoke but Fu Man Chu.

◆ Did you hear about the two red corpuscles that loved in vein?

FOOD, AND SUCH

◆ A man was wakened in the middle of the night by a telephone call from a worried friend. "I've got *real* trouble," the friend said. "Come as quick as you can. Oh, and bring chocolate candy."

The puzzled fellow bought a box of chocolates and dashed across town to his friend's house. "What's the emergency?" he asked on arrival.

"I'm out of chocolate," the friend replied.[20]

◆ A friend of mine had a nightmare. He dreamt that all he could eat were marshmallows. In his dream he became so obsessed with marshmallows that he ate more and more and finally began to cram them into his mouth. When he woke up, his pillow was gone.

◆ Q: How can you improve the taste of salt?
A: Sprinkle a little on a steak.[21]

◆ Ethel Merman was lunching at an outdoor cafe in New York. Her dog begged for food, but the singer was eating salad and had nothing for her pet. When the man at the next table left, she saw a whole lamb chop still on his plate. Ethel snatched the chop and gave it to the excited pooch. The dog was finishing off the bone when the man returned to his lunch. He had left to take a telephone call.[22]

HEALTH, DIET, WEIGHT

◆ Remedy for baldness: Mix cashew juice with dill pickle juice and rub it on your head every day for a month. It doesn't make your hair grow,

261

but it makes your head shrink to fit what
you've got!

◆ A balding man's hair is like the ocean. The only
    trouble is, the tide has gone out.

◆ Fitness buff Jack LaLanne says he may never die:
    "It would wreck my image. I cannot even
    afford to have a fat dog."[23]

◆ A guy went to the doctor. The doctor said,
    "Mister, you're sick!" The patient responded,
    "I think I'd like a second opinion."
        "O.K., you're ugly, too!"

                                              —Dave Beitler

◆ He's so thin that when he stands sideways and
    sticks out his tongue, he looks like a zipper.

◆ He's so thin that when he wears a fur coat, he
    looks like a pipe cleaner.

◆ He weighs a hundred and plenty.[24]

◆ During Easter week, a woman proudly announced
    a personal victory at her Weight-Watchers
    meeting. She said this was the first year her
    kids realized that chocolate Easter bunnies
    came with ears.[25]

◆ The boarding school dietician told a worried
    mother, "There's not a thing to worry about.
    Here we serve perfectly balanced meals."
        "Oh," the mother asked, "balanced

between meat, vegetables and fruit?"

"No, everyone who dines here has a fifty-fifty chance of survival."[26]

◆ Epitaph on a hypochondriac's tombstone: "I told you I was sick!"[27]

◆ You know it's time to diet when you step on a pay scale and the message reads, "ONE AT A TIME, PLEASE!"

◆ Dunlop's disease: When your stomach done-laps over your belt.

MILITARY

◆ An army private was given guard duty at 2 A.M. He tried to stay awake, but succumbed to sleep at about 4 A.M. When he awoke, his officer was standing beside him. The private kept his head bowed another moment, then looked up and reverently said, "A-a-a-men!"[28]

◆ Voice on the telephone: "Hello. We need ten jeeps at the officers' mess immediately. Two of them must be covered."
Reply: "I'll bet the covered jeeps are to haul those fat-slob generals around in."
Voice: "Soldier, do you know who is speaking to you?"
Reply: "No, who?"
Voice: "This is General Boynton."
Reply: "Do you know who this is, sir?"

263

Voice: "No, I don't."
Reply: "See ya later, fatso!"

◆ The instructor had just finished a lecture to the new paratroop recruits on the packing of a parachute. He concluded with, "And remember, if it doesn't open, that's what's known as jumping to a conclusion!"

◆ A sign on a Pentagon desk: "The secrecy of my job does not permit me to know what I am doing."[29]

MISCELLANEOUS

◆ The chairman of a meeting interrupted debate on an issue to announce that a minibus was blocking the driveway and to ask that it be moved. A voice in the audience called out, "I move the minibus." Another voice said, "I second it." The chairman banged his gavel. "The minibus has been moved and seconded. Proceed!"[30]

◆ "What kind of flower is that?" a fellow asked his neighbor who was tending his garden.

"Why that's a chrysanthemum," the neighbor answered.

"Sure looks like a rose to me."

"No, it's a chrysanthemum."

"Spell it," the fellow challenged.

"Khry. . .Kris. . .Cris. . .Golly, you're right. It *is* a rose."[31]

◆ Three contestants in a television quiz show were down to the last round. The master of ceremonies explained the final question. "I'm going to give you a phrase with a word missing at the end. Come up with the missing word and you'll win our grand prize—an all expenses paid two-week trip to Europe. Ready? The phrase is, 'Old MacDonald had a _____' And remember, you must not only name the missing word. You must spell it."

The first contestant answered: "Old MacDonald had a ranch—r-a-n-c-h."

The studio audience moaned.

The second contestant tried: "Old MacDonald had a barn—b-a-r-n."

More groaning.

The third contestant rose and said, "Old MacDonald had a farm."

The applause was deafening. After the audience calmed down, the emcee continued. "O.K., now for the super-deluxe, fabulous European trip, all you have to do is spell the magic word."

"That's easy," the contestant said. "E-I-E-I-O."[32]

◆ Clara: "When I get down in the dumps, I buy myself some new clothes."
Sara: "Oh, so that's where you get them."

◆ A tourist asked a hippie in downtown San Francisco what time it was.

"Twelve o'clock," the hippie answered.

"Oh, really?" the tourist said. "I'd have

265

thought it was later than that."

"Man, you see, it never gets later than that around here. I mean, like when it gets to be twelve o'clock, we start over again."[33]

◆ A small boy explained the broken window to a policeman: "You see, officer, I was cleaning my slingshot and it went off."[34]

◆ A man was drowning. "Help, I can't swim! I can't swim!" An old man, sitting on the river bank chewing tobacco, said, "Neither can I, but I'm not hollerin' about it."[35]

◆ An outlaw burst in the Dodge City saloon, guns blazing, yelling, "All you dirty skunks—get out of here—pronto!"

The saloon emptied in a hail of bullets. A lone Englishman remained at the bar, calmly finishing his drink. "Well?" blurted the desperado, waving his smoking gun.

"Well," the Brit replied, "there certainly were a lot of them, weren't there!"[36]

◆ A customer in a Mexican restaurant was unfamiliar with Spanish. When he headed for the rest-room, he walked through the door marked "Senoritas." Realizing his error almost at once, he dashed for the door and exited just as a woman was entering. Startled as she saw him, she turned on her heels and charged into the other door. . .the one labeled "Senores."[37]

◆ The famous comic actor Lou Costello once lived across the street from comedian George Gobel. Every December, Costello had an elaborate Christmas display in his yard that was the envy of all Hollywood.

Sight-seers came from miles around to see the Costello display. One year, George Gobel's front yard had a lone sign that read, "See our display across the street."[38]

◆ Two kings each had a castle on the top of a mountain. Every day they gathered their knights together and rode down into the valley to fight. Finally, one side had suffered so many casualties that they were down to seven knights, a dog and a cook. That night when the group was sitting around the bare supper table, the cook stepped forward and volunteered for the fight. He said, "I'll saddle up that dog and ride him down to battle tomorrow." The king turned to him and said, "Naw, I wouldn't send a knight out on a dog like this."

◆ A king, who lived in a priceless all-glass house deep in the jungles of Africa, had an unusual hobby. He spent a fortune sending emissaries around the world to collect unique thrones. His wife caused him much grief and cautioned against his collecting so many thrones, for they were everywhere. . .the kitchen, the bedrooms, the attic. . .all over the house. She feared that the weight of all those thrones would be greater than the glass house could bear. Finally, one day as the men put another throne in the attic, the glass house collapsed. The moral of the story: People who live in glass houses shouldn't stow thrones.

◆ There once was a famous king whose castle and vast lands were surrounded by an invading army. His only chance for survival was to get someone to cross the river and get help from another nearby king. However, each day as one of his men rode down into the valley and got to the bridge to cross the river, a giant yellow hand came out of the sky, swooped up the soldier and killed him. Finally, the king was desperate. Nearly all of his men had been killed. As the king was just about to give up, a pageboy stepped forward and said, "Oh king, I will go for you." The king watched with fear in his heart as the little page ran toward the bridge to cross the river. The giant hand came out of the sky to grab the page, but the boy slipped through his fingers and got safely across the bridge. The moral of the story: Let your pages do the walking through the yellow fingers.

◆ Did you hear about the terrorist revolutionary who was told to blow up a bus? He burned his lips on the exhaust pipe!

◆ A sampling of unusual laws of the universe, taken from Arthur Bloch's *Murphy's Law—and Other Reasons Why Things go Wrong:*[39]

1. MURPHY'S LAW
    If anything can go wrong, it will.

2. O'TOOL'S COMMENTARY ON MURPHY'S LAW
    Murphy was an optimist.

3. THE UNSPEAKABLE LAW
    As soon as you mention something . . .
    . . .if it's good, it goes away.
    . . .if it's bad, it happens.

4. NONRECIPROCAL LAWS OF EXPECTATIONS
    Negative expectations yield negative results.
    Positive expectations yield negative results.

5. HOWE'S LAW
    Every man has a scheme that will not work.

6. ZYMURGY'S FIRST LAW OF EVOLVING SYSTEMS DYNAMICS
    Once you open a can of worms, the only way to recan them is to use a larger can.

7. ETORRE'S OBSERVATION
    The other line moves faster.

8. SKINNER'S CONSTANT (FLANNAGAN'S FINAGLING FACTOR)
    That quantity which, when multiplied by, divided by, added to, or subtracted from the answer you get, gives you the answer you should have gotten.

9. LAW OF SELECTIVE GRAVITY

   An object will fall so as to do the most damage.

9a. JENNING'S COROLLARY

   The chance of the bread falling with the buttered side down is directly proportional to the cost of the carpet.

10. GORDON'S FIRST LAW

   If a research project is not worth doing at all, it is not worth doing well.

11. MAIER'S LAW

   If the facts do not conform to the theory, they must be disposed of.

12. HOARE'S LAW OF LARGE PROBLEMS

   Inside every large problem is a small problem struggling to get out.

13. BOREN'S FIRST LAW

   When in doubt, mumble.

14. THE GOLDEN RULE OF ARTS AND SCIENCES

   Whoever has the gold make the rules.

15. BARTH'S DISTINCTION

   There are two types of people: those who divide people into two types, and those who don't.

16. SEGAL'S LAW

A man with one watch knows what time it
is. A man with two watches is never sure.

17. NINETY-NINETY RULE OF PROJECT
SCHEDULES

The first 90 percent of the task takes 90 percent of the time, and the last 10 percent
takes the other 90 percent.

18. FARBER'S FOURTH LAW

Necessity is the mother of strange
bedfellows.

More unusual laws from Bloch's *Murphy's Law, Book
Two: More Reasons Why Things Go Wrong:*[10]

1. O'REILLY'S LAW OF THE KITCHEN

Cleanliness is next to impossible.

2. LIEBERMAN'S LAW

Everybody lies; but it doesn't matter, since
nobody listens.

3. GOLD'S LAW

If the shoe fits, it's ugly.

4. HANDY GUIDE TO MODERN SCIENCE

If it's green or it wriggles, it's biology.
If it stinks, it's chemistry.
If it doesn't work, it's physics.

5. CONWAY'S LAW

In any organization there will always be one

person who knows what is going on. This person must be fired.

6. GREEN'S LAW OF DEBATE
Anything is possible if you don't know what you're talking about.

7. STEWART'S LAW OF RETROACTION
It is easier to get forgiveness than permission.

8. FIRST RULE OF HISTORY
History doesn't repeat itself—historians merely repeat each other.

9. FINSTER'S LAW
A closed mouth gather no feet.

10. OLIVER'S LAW OF LOCATION
No matter where you go, there you are.

11. LYNCH'S LAW
When the going gets tough, everyone leaves.

12. GLYME'S FORMULA FOR SUCCESS
The secret of success is sincerity. Once you can fake that, you've got it made.

13. THE SAUSAGE PRINCIPLE
People who love sausage and respect the law should never watch either one being made.

14. **HARRISON'S POSTULATE**

For every action, there is an equal and opposite criticism.

15. **HANLON'S RAZOR**

Never attribute to malice that which is adequately explained by stupidity.

16. **MUIR'S LAW**

When we try to pick out anything by itself, we find it hitched to everything else in the universe.

◆ Q: How many Californians does it take to change a lightbulb?
A: Four. One to screw in the bulb and three to share the experience.

—Greg Loomis

◆ Q: How many psychologists does it take to change a lightbulb?
A: Just one, but the lightbulb has to really want to change.

◆ The Water Closet

A little old English lady was looking for a room in Switzerland. She asked the local village schoolmaster to help her. A place that suited her was finally found, and the woman returned to London for her luggage. Then she remembered that she had not noticed a bathroom, or as she called it, a water closet. So she wrote to the schoolmaster. He was puzzled by the initials "W.C.," never dreaming that she was inquiring about a bathroom. He finally asked the parish priest, who decided that W.C. stood for Wesleyan Church. The schoolmaster then replied:

Dear Madam,

The W.C. is situated nine miles from the house in the center of a beautiful grove of trees. It is capable of holding three hundred fifty people at a time and is open each Tuesday, Thursday and Sunday. A large number of folks attend during the summer, so it is suggested you go early, although there is plenty of standing room. Some people like to take their lunches and make a day of it, especially on Thursday, when there is organ accompaniment. The acoustics are very good and everyone can hear the slightest sound.

You may be interested to know that my daughter met her husband and was married in our W.C.

We hope you will be here in time for our upcoming bazaar. The proceeds will go toward the purchase of plush seats, which the folks agree are a long-felt need, as the present seats all have holes in them.

My wife is rather delicate, therefore she cannot attend regularly. It has been six months since the last time she went. Naturally, it pains her very much not to be able to go more often.

I shall close now with the desire to accommodate you in every way possible. I will be happy to save you a seat down front or near the door, whichever you prefer.

Schoolmaster

—Submitted by Danny Newell

MONEY, FINANCES

◆ Confucius say: "Man who miss air conditioner payments lose his cool."

◆ The Scotsman, trying to save some money, put a picture of a piece of cheese into the mousetrap one night. The next morning, when he looked at the mousetrap, he found nothing but a picture of a mouse.

◆ Epitaph in a Scottish cemetery (or so the story goes): "Here lies Hamish McTavish, whose deeply sorrowing widow continues to carry on his flourishing green-grocery business at 11 High Street—open daily until 8:00."[41]

◆ A gentlemen lost a dog and placed a newspaper ad offering a $1,000 reward. There were no replies. He stopped by the newspaper office and asked for the advertising manager.

"He's not in." the office boy replied.

"What about the assistant manager?"

"He's out, too."

"Good grief! Is everyone out?"

"Yes, sir. They're all looking for your dog."[42]

275

◆ A man subscribed to an investment advisory service of questionable value. He wrote to tell them he had followed their advice to the letter and that he had lost all his money. His letter continued with, "You repeatedly told me to contact you if problems arose so that you could instruct me how to act. I am now broke. How should I act? Please wire."

Three days later a telegram came from the service. It read, "ACT BROKE."[43]

◆ Q: What's the best way to prevent water from coming into your house?
A: Don't pay the water bill.[44]

◆ An elderly woman received $1,500 from an insurance company to compensate her for the loss of some jewelry. Several weeks later she found the jewelry in a cupboard and wrote the insurance company. "I didn't think it fair to keep the money and the jewels," she wrote, "so I thought it would please you to learn that I have sent the $1,500 to the Red Cross."[45]

◆ An old miser on his deathbed called in his doctor, lawyer and minister. "Gentlemen," he said, "I'm going to disprove the myth that 'you can't take it with you.' Under my mattress are three envelopes, each containing $30,000. I want you each to take one now, and then throw it in the grave just before they shovel in the dirt."

At the funeral, each threw his envelope into

the grave. As they left the cemetery, the minister said, "I don't feel right about this. . . I've got something to confess. I needed $10,000 very badly for our church building program, so I kept $10,000 and threw in only $20,000."

Then the doctor confessed. "I needed money for a new wing for the hospital. I'm sorry to say that I kept $20,000 and threw in $10,000."

The lawyer replied, "Why I'm shocked and ashamed of you both. How could you withhold that money! Why, I threw in a personal check for the full amount."[46]

◆ Rose Sachs, a Palm Beach, Florida socialite, commented on the pastimes of her fellow residents, "We have this terrible image that we play all the time. I went to three balls last week, and all of them were for charity."[47]

◆ A Kansas man received a computerized bill from a store showing that he owed "$00.00." He discarded it.

The next month he received another bill stating, "This account is now past due." He circled the zeros and returned it.

A few days later came a scorching computer letter exhorting him to pay his debt of $00.00. The man finally mailed a check in the amount of $00.00. He received no further pleas from the store.[48]

◆ The vanishing American: one who pays cash for everything he buys.

◆ The farmer had been taken so many times by the local car dealer that when the dealer wanted to buy a cow, the farmer priced it to him like this: Basic cow, $200; two-tone exterior, $45; extra stomach, $75; product storage compartment, $60; dispensing device, four spigots at $10 each, $40. Genuine cowhide upholstery, $125; dual horns, $15; automatic fly swatter, $35. Total, $595.

◆ When your outgo exceeds your income, your upkeep becomes your downfall.[49]

◆ A millionaire was asked the secret of his success. "I give full credit to my wife," he replied.
   "Oh, really? How did she help?"
   "Well," the millionaire replied, "I wanted to see if there was any income that she couldn't live beyond."[50]

◆ Some people are so poor they can't pay attention.

◆ A fellow from Texas stepped into a Los Angeles phone booth to call Disneyland. The operator told him to deposit thirty-five cents.
   "Thirty-five cents?!!" the man exclaimed. "Why, in Texas you can call hell and back for a dime."
   "Yes, sir," the operator answered, "but there it's a local call."

◆ An Indian asked a bank in Oklahoma for a $500 loan. "What security do you have?" the banker inquired.

"Got 200 horses."

That seemed satisfactory, so the banker granted the loan.

Two months later, the Indian returned to the bank, took out a fat roll of bills, counted out $500 plus interest and turned to leave.

"Say," the banker remarked, "you've got quite a bit of cash there. Why don't you let us take care of the rest of that for you?"

The Indian replied, "How many horses you got?"[51]

◆ A Washington state firm could not get Mr. Adams to pay his bill. Finally they wrote, "Dear Mr. Adams: What would your neighbors think if we came and repossessed your car?"

One week later the firm received their letter back. Scrawled across the bottom was: "Dear Sirs: I checked with my neighbors and they think it would be a lousy trick. Sincerely, Herbert Adams."[52]

NONSENSE

◆ Do you walk to work or carry your lunch?

◆ Is it farther to Chicago or by bus?

◆ I'm so glad you got to meet me.

◆ Keep in touch with yourself.

◆ If you need us, we'll call you.

◆ The future isn't what it used to be.

◆ What you don't mean won't hurt you.

◆ How can you be in two places at once when you're not anywhere at all?

CHAPTER 17

STILL MORE GOOD JOKES AND STORIES

PARENT/CHILD/FAMILY

◆ A young married couple took their four-month-old daughter to the movies with them. As they entered, an usher informed them that they'd be asked to leave if the baby cried, but their money would be refunded.

Forty minutes into the film, the wife turned to her husband.

"Well, what do you think of it?" she asked.

"Terrible. Worst movie I've ever seen!"

"That's what I say," she agreed. "Pinch little Debbie."[1]

◆ A mother saw her two-year-old boy swallow a nickel. Immediately she picked him up, turned him upside down and sharply hit his back. The child coughed up two dimes. Beside herself, she called outside to her husband, "Little Billy just swallowed a nickel and then coughed up two dimes. What do I do?"

The father yelled back, "Keep feeding him nickels!"[2]

◆ A little boy had a bad habit of sucking his thumb. His mother tried in vain to break him of the habit. Finally, she pointed out a very fat man and told her son the man had such a fat stomach because he sucked his thumb.

The next day, the boy spotted a very pregnant woman in the supermarket. He stared and stared in amazement at her obviously oversize belly. Finally the woman became annoyed and told him, "Stop looking at me like that. You don't even know me."

"No," the boy replied, "but I know what you've been doing."[3]

◆ A six-year-old girl told her dad, "I want a magic wand for my birthday. And I want one that works."[4]

◆ The entire text of a post card received by the parents of an eight-year-old camper: "Dear Folks, I knew all along that something awful was going to happen. Well, last night it did. Love, Jimmy."[5]

◆ A modern child asked, "Mother, where did I come from?" She received the traditional answer, "God sent you."

"And how about you, Mother, did God send you, too?" she asked.

"Yes, honey."

"And Grandma?"

"Yes."

"And Great Grandma, too?"

"Yes, dear."

"Mother, do you mean to tell me that there have been no sexual relations in this family for more than two hundred years?"[6]

◆ A kid came home with five "*F*'s" on his report card and said, "What do you think it is, Dad, heredity or environment?"

—Lewis Timberlake

◆ A father concerning his teenage daughter: "Her room is such a mess, why I wouldn't go in there without a tetanus shot."[7]

◆ To ensure the education of their teenagers, parents need to unplug a few wires: TV, telephone and ignition.

◆ How to communicate with a teenage girl: make a noise like a telephone dial tone before you speak.

◆ "How do you let your daughter's boyfriends know it's time to go home?" one salesman asked another.

"I usually walk through the room with a box of breakfast cereal."

POLITICS, GOVERNMENT, GOVERNMENT RELATIONS

◆ In Chicago, Illinois, Governor James Thompson was introduced once as "the Mayor of Illinois." Thompson says that was a step down

283

from the time he was presented as "the Governor of the United States."[8]

◆ President Calvin Coolidge was well-known for his brevity of speech. Some considered it a challenge to get him to talk. At a White House dinner, one Washington woman smiled and said, "Mr. President, I've made a bet that I can get you to say at least three words."

"You lose," Coolidge replied.[9]

◆ Thomas E. Dewey lost a close race for the U.S. Presidency in 1948. Dewey said that the day after the upset, he felt like the mourner at a funeral who passed out from too much drinking. Some friends laid him in a spare coffin to sleep it off. When he awoke and saw where he was, he said to himself, "If I'm alive, why am I in this coffin? And if I'm dead, why do I have to go to the bathroom?"[10]

◆ Television moderator to his guest: "We only have a few minutes left, Senator. I wonder if you could briefly give us an idea of what you've been talking about for the last half-hour?"[11]

◆ A state representative entertained a fifth grade class visiting the state capitol. Later he received a letter from one of the students thanking him for his hospitality. At the bottom of the letter: "P.S. You have been exposed to chicken pox."[12]

◆ Government authorities use metal strips to band certain birds. The strips are inscribed: Notify Fish and Wild Life Service, Washington, D.C." In former times, the strips read, "Wash. Biol. Surv.," an abbreviation for "Washington Biological Survey." The inscription was changed after an Alberta farmer complained to the U.S. Government. His letter read, "Dear Sirs: I shot one of your pet crows the other day and followed instructions attached to it. I washed it and boiled it and surved it. It was terrible. You should stop trying to fool the people with things like this. . ."[13]

◆ A standard joke in government is that before you throw away any paperwork, photocopy it so you'll have a copy.[14]

QUIPS

◆ (Concerning something impractical) "That's about as practical as a screen door in a submarine."

◆ (Concerning an endeavor that is bound to backfire) "That's like taking a drink of water from a fire hydrant." Or. . .

◆ "That's like trying to tee off a golf ball in the shower."

—Roe Brooks

A few other quips, used to express certainty (source unknown):

◆ "Does a fat baby burp?"

◆ "Does a bear sleep in the woods?"

◆ "Does a cat have climbin' gear?"

RIDDLES, QUESTIONS AND ANSWERS

◆ Q: What does a two-thousand-pound canary say?
   A: CHIRRRRP! (deep, loud voice)

◆ Q: If an athlete get athlete's foot, what does an astronaut get?
   A: Missile-toe

◆ Q: What animal has two humps and can be found in Alaska?
   A: A lost camel.[15]

◆ Q: What's a Grecian urn?
   A: That depends on the kind of work he does.

◆ Q: What's the greatest invention in the world?
   A: Venetian blinds. If it wasn't for them, it would be curtains for all of us.

◆ Q: What happened when the canary backed into the fan?
   A: Out came shredded tweet.

◆ Q: What goes "Ha, ha! Thump"?
A: A man laughing his head off.

◆ Q: What goes "Zzub, zzub"?
A: A bee flying backward.

◆ Q: What does a tiger get by walking across the road?
A: Sandy claws.

◆ Q: Why do bees hum?
A: Because they don't know the lyrics.

◆ Q: How long is a minute?
A: That depends on which side of the bathroom door you happen to be on.

◆ Q: What do you get when you cross a praying mantis with a termite?
A: A bug that says grace before it eats your house.

SMALL TOWNS

◆ That town is so small that the "Entering" and "Leaving" signs are back to back.

◆ That town is so small. . .when you're driving through you can blink twice and miss it.

◆ That town wasn't backward at all—it used to have a car wash. Then the man with the car moved away.

We went out at 10 P.M., did the town, and went
home at 10:15.

SPEAKERS
Speaking Before a Group—by Erma Bombeck

Have you any idea what fear was rated No. 1 in a recent survey among adults?

Speaking before a group.

That's right, the anxiety of standing before an audience
beat out fear of death, fear of failing, fear of heights, and
fear of alienation. (Come to think of it, they all mean the
same thing).

It occurred to me that this year a virtual army of amateur speakers will, for the first time, take to the podiums
to conduct club meetings, volunteer seminars and instruc-
tional classes.

How do the professionals handle it?

- Demand a podium capable of supporting a dead
   body (yours) up to 187 pounds. Throw yourself over it, being sure to hook your arm over
   the microphone so you won't slip away.
- Adhere to the old wives' tale, "Feed a cold
   crowd, starve a speaker." It cuts down on
   spitting up.
- Insist on a table near the restroom. For some un-
   explained reason, speakers have a kidney wish.
- Never read a speech. Use note cards which
   serve a double purpose. You can rearrange
   them to fit your audience and in the event the
   person who introduces you uses the jokes on
   your first eight cards, use the sharp cutting
   edges on your wrists.[16]

◆ Popular speaker Leighton Ford is the brother-in-law of Billy Graham, having married Billy's sister, Jean. This relationship has led to some rather humorous introductions. Leighton's biographer, Norman B. Rohrer, describes one such incident when a distinguished pastor and educator presented Leighton to students in a college chapel.

"We are happy to have Leighton Ford as our speaker this morning," he began. "Perhaps some of you don't know that Leighton is married to Billy Graham's brother."

The crowd tittered and this venerable gentleman, nonplussed by the reaction, was so thrown off his usual impeccable stride that he concluded, "That makes Leighton Billy Graham's son-in-law."

Now the audience was doubling over with laughter. The speaker, startled and not realizing what he had said, plunged on to total disaster:

"So. . .now I present to you, Leighton Ford's brother-in-law, Billy Graham!"[17]

◆ The emcee at a large dinner rose to begin the program. "Ladies and gentlemen," he began, "the job of toastmaster is to be so terribly dull that the speakers who follow will appear brilliant by contrast."

The succeeding speakers, seated at the head table, chuckled in self-indulgence.

"Well," the toastmaster continued, "I've looked over the list of speakers, and I don't think I can do it."

The speakers' chuckling ceased and the audience roared.[18]

◆ One clever toastmaster introduced the distinguished speaker at a Thanksgiving banquet saying, "Ladies and gentlemen, you have been focusing your attention on turkey stuffed with sage. Now it's my privilege to introduce to you a sage stuffed with turkey."[19]

◆ He has a mind like lightning: one quick flash of light and then total darkness.

◆ Emcee: "This is the man about whom former President Ronald Reagan said, 'Who?'"

◆ Emcee: "Now here is a person who needs no introduction. . .because nobody wants to meet him!"

◆ Emcee: "Rumor has it that tonight's speaker made straight *A's* through out his college career. Rumor has it that he was captain of the football team, the basketball team and the track team for three years in a row. Rumor has it that he has a waiting list of women who have called asking to take him out. Rumor has it that he's able to leap tall buildings with a single bound. And now, I'd like you to meet the man who started all these rumors. . ."

◆ I'd rather hear Steve speak than eat. . .and I've heard him do both.

◆ (After being introduced) "Bob, our emcee, is really a great guy. He told me so himself."

◆ A journalist once listened patiently as his friend told a seemingly interminable story. After quite some time, the friend began to conclude, "So to make a long story short. . ." "Too late!" the journalist cried.[20]

Quick comebacks after a slip of the tongue:

◆ I have a speed impeachament.

◆ I got my merds wixed.

◆ I just washed my tongue and can't do a thing with it.

◆ I just got my nose fixed and now my mouth won't work.

SPORTS

◆ Did you hear about the Smogarian who entered the Indianapolis 500? He made nine pit stops: four for fuel and tire changes and five to ask directions.

A woman, while touring a small American country, was shown a bullfight. The guide told her, "This is our number one sport."

The horrified woman said, "Isn't that revolting?"

"No," the guide replied, "that's our number two sport."

◆ The football team was heading home on the bus after being shellacked 64-0. The team was down; the coach, bitter. "It's no use, men," he said as he stood at the front of the bus. "We'll have to start over at the beginning." He took a football in his hands. "This," he said distinctly, "is a football."

From the back of the bus, one player interjected, "Wait a minute—not so fast, Coach."

◆ Three baseball umpires were asked how they distinguished between balls and strikes. The first one said, "Well, some pitches are balls and some are strikes. I call them as I see them." The second answered, "Some are balls and some are strikes. I call them as they are." The third said, "Some are balls and some are strikes, but they ain't nothin' 'til I call them."

◆ Hurry-Up Yost, the one-time Michigan football coach, once gave such an inspiration-filled half-time talk to his players that he got carried away and at the final exhortation led his team on the run through the wrong locker-room into the swimming pool.[21]

◆ Lowell Thomas related the story of an explorer who brought gifts to an Indian maharajah. The items could not be obtained in Asia. The potentate was extremely grateful and wanted to reciprocate, but the explorer felt no need. Finally he said, "Oh well, if in your travels around England you happen to find any golf clubs, buy a few for me."

Later the maharajah contacted the explorer. "I've bought two golf clubs for you. Both have 18 holes, and one even has a swimming pool. But I have a disappointment for you. St. Andrews refuses to sell."[22]

◆ A young tiger hunter was advised by a veteran hunter: "Hunt at night, because then you can see the tiger's eyes shining in the dark. Shoot between the eyes."

The novice returned after the hunt without a kill. The veteran asked if he hunted at night, and if he had seen the tiger's eyes and aimed between them.

"Yes," the novice replied, "but the tigers are getting smarter. They walk in pairs now, and each keeps one eye closed."

♣ The old Milwaukee Braves once had a pitcher named Mel Faimey. One hot July afternoon he was pitching brilliantly. Then he began to have a beer or two in the dugout each time his team left the field. Soon his pitching became more and more erratic. He walked players right and left.

Finally, in the ninth inning, he loaded the bases on walks and then walked in the winning run.

As two players on the opposing team trotted to their dugout, one of them spotted the empty beer cans that littered the floor of the Braves' dugout. "Look," he told his buddy, "there's the beer that made Mel Faimey walk us."

◆ A horse-racing fan was telling his pal about his latest day at the track. "I went out to the track. . .it was on the eleventh day of the eleventh month. I got there exactly at 11 A.M. My daughter was eleven years old that day and the eleventh race had eleven horses. I put all the money I had on the eleventh horse on the card."

"And that horse won?" the pal asked.

"No," the racing fan replied. "He came in eleventh."[23]

◆ A duck hunter, proud of his marksmanship, took a friend one morning to witness his skill. After some time, a lone duck flew by. "Watch this," the hunter whispered, as he took careful aim and fired. The duck flew serenely on. "My boy," the hunter said, "you are witnessing a great miracle. There flies a dead duck."

◆ Rainer, a friend from Germany, once spent several months with us in the United States. One day we were watching a baseball game on television. Rainer had never seen a baseball game. At one point a batter on the home team hit the ball out of the park for a home run. The fans went wild. Rainer turned to us with a puzzled look and asked, "Why are they cheering? They've lost the ball!"

TRAVEL, TRANSPORTATION

◆ Cartoon caption on a professor's door at Kansas State University: "The first prize in our contest is a free, all expenses paid, one-week vacation in Kansas. Second prize. . .a free, all expenses paid, two-week vacation in Kansas."

◆ Conrad Hilton, of the famous Hilton hotel chain, was once asked on national television if he had one vitally important message he would like to share with Americans. Turning to the cameras, Hilton said, "Please. . .place the shower curtain on the *inside* of the tub."[24]

◆ Ah, yes, the jet age. Breakfast in London, dinner in Tokyo, luggage in Milwaukee.[25]

◆ Pilot to passengers: "Good afternoon, ladies and gentlemen. We hope you're enjoying your flight. I have some good news and some bad news. The bad news is that we're flying at thirty-six thousand feet in a dense cloud formation, hopelessly lost. The good news is that we're twenty minutes ahead of schedule."

◆ Did you hear about the guy who was about to take a plane trip but was deathly afraid of flying? He call up odds-maker, Jimmy the Greek, in Las Vegas.

"Hey, Jimmy, what are the odds on there being a bomb on a plane?"

"A bomb on a plane?" the Greek said. "Oh, about a million to one."

The fellow thanked him and hung up. A few minutes later he called again. "Say, I was wondering. What are the odds on there being two bombs on the plane?"

295

"*Two* bombs on the plane? Why, the odds are thirty million to one against it!"

Whereupon, the man, being an astute mathematician, bought a bomb and carried it on the plane with him, knowing that he was increasing his chances from one million to one, to thirty million to one!

◆ A New York businessman boarded a train in Albany on his way to Buffalo. As it was a night train, he took a sleeper car and gave the porter strict instructions to waken him and put him off in Buffalo. "I'm a very heavy sleeper," the passenger said, "and I may give you a hard time. But whatever you do, be sure to put me off in Buffalo. . .even if you have to put me off in my pajamas."

The next morning, the man woke up to find himself in Cleveland. He located the porter and chewed him out with some very abusive language. After the man left, a bystander asked the porter how he could stand there and take that verbal abuse.

"That weren't nothin'," the porter replied. "You should've heard the guy I put off in Buffalo."[26]

◆ The captain of the luxury liner instructed a crew member on part of his job. "Your responsibility, sailor, in case of danger, is to yell, 'Man the life boats! Man the life boats!' " The sailor practiced it and had it down perfect.

Later, when the boat was shipwrecked, the sailor yelled, "Woman the life boats!

Woman the life boats!"

The captain was appalled. "What's going on?!" he demanded.

"Listen, Skipper," the sailor replied. "You fill your boats the way *you* want, and I'll fill my boats the way *I* want!"

◆ Garage mechanic giving estimate to car owner: "First, the good news—your glove compartment and sun visor are in excellent condition!"

◆ Dave was driving the wrong way on a one-way street. A guy on the sidewalk hollered, "Hey, buddy, can't you read? This is a one-way street!"

Dave yelled back, "I'm only going one way!"

◆ The Smogarian was driving to Minneapolis when he saw a sign on the freeway that said, "Minneapolis left." So he turned around and headed home.

◆ The Smogarian was driving along the highway and approached a service station that had a sign reading "Clean Restrooms." So he did.

◆ Joe was driving through Arizona and, when night came, found he was near an Indian reservation. Weary from his journey, he drove into the reservation and asked the chief if he could spend the night. The chief graciously invited Joe to stay in his special guest teepee. Before

Joe bedded down for the night, he went to the bathhouse to brush his teeth. The bathhouse was the only modern building on the entire reservation. It had a toilet, sink, shower and lighting fixtures. But when Joe flipped the light switch, nothing happened. The wires were not connected. Being an amateur electrician, and to show his gratitude to the chief, Joe got out his tools and flashlight, and wired the bathroom so the lights would work. He then brushed his teeth and turned in for the night. The next morning he drove on his way, having become the first person to wire a head for a reservation.

◆ Long, long ago an old Indian chief was about to die, so he called for Geronimo and Falling Rocks, the two bravest warriors in his tribe. The chief instructed each to go out and seek buffalo skins.

About a month later, Geronimo came back with two hundred pelts, but Falling Rocks never returned. Even today, as you drive throughout the West, you still see signs that say, "Watch for Falling Rocks."

WORK

◆ Careful planning is essential for success. Poor planning can be disastrous, as illustrated by a man who was injured at work. When the insurance company asked him to clarify a few points on his claim, he responded:

Dear Sir: I am writing in response to your request for additional information. In block 3 of the accident report form, I put "poor planning" as the cause of my accident. You said in your letter that I should explain more fully, and I trust that the following details will be sufficient.

I am a bricklayer by trade. On the day of the accident, I was working alone on the roof of a new six-story building. When I completed my work, I discovered that I had about five hundred pounds of brick left over. Rather than carry the bricks down by hand, I decided to lower them in a barrel by using a pulley which, fortunately, was attached to the side of the building, at the sixth floor.

Securing the rope at ground level I went up to the roof, swung the barrel and loaded the brick into it. Then I went back to the ground and untied the rope, holding it tightly to ensure a slow descent of the five hundred pounds of brick.

You will notice in block 11 of the accident report form that I weigh 135 pounds.

Due to my surprise at being jerked off the ground so suddenly, I lost my presence of mind and forgot to let go of the rope. Needless to say, I proceeded at a rather rapid rate up the side of the building.

In the vicinity of the third floor, I met the barrel coming down. This explains the fractured skull and broken collarbone.

Slowed only slightly, I continued my rapid ascent, not stopping until the fingers of my right hand were too deep in the pulley.

Fortunately, by this time, I had regained my presence of mind and was able to hold tightly to the rope in spite of my pain.

At approximately the same time, however, the barrel of bricks hit the ground, and the bottom fell out of the barrel. Devoid the weight of the bricks, the barrel now weighed approximately fifty pounds.

I refer you again to my weight in block 11. As you might imagine, I began a rapid descent down the side of the building.

In the vicinity of the third floor, I met the barrel coming up. This accounts for the two fractured ankles and the lacerations of my lower body and legs.

The encounter with the barrel slowed me enough to lessen my injuries when I fell onto the pile of bricks and, fortunately, only three vertebrae were cracked.

I'm sorry to report, however, that as I lay there on the bricks, in pain, unable to stand and watching the empty barrel six stories above me, I again lost my presence of mind. . .I let go of the rope![27]

—Submitted by John Mansfield

◆ Some people say he's a self-made man. That shows you the horrors of unskilled labor.

◆ Two telephone company crews were putting up telephone poles. At the end of the first day, the company foreman asked the first crew how many poles they had put in the ground. "Fifteen" was the answer.

"Fifteen, eh," the foreman replied. "Not bad; not bad at all." He asked the second crew how many telephone poles they had put in.

"Four," came the answer.

"Four?" the foreman exclaimed. "The other crew did fifteen and you only did *four*?"

"Yes," replied the leader of group number two. "But look at how much they left sticking up out of the ground."[28]

◆ A wealthy developer enjoyed knowing as much as he could about the employees who worked for his huge company. One day he encountered a new employee, a young man, who was expertly counting a large amount of company cash into individual pay envelopes.

"Where did you receive your training in finance, young man?" the developer inquired.

"Yale," the employee answered.

"Oh, good, good!" said the developer, who was a great advocate of higher education. "And what is your name?"

"Yackson."[29]

◆ Q: What do you call a lion trainer who puts his right arm down a lion's throat?
A: Lefty.[30]

◆ An employer was interviewing a job applicant. After broaching the subject of wages, the

301

employer said, "Young man, you are asking for some high wages for a man with no experience."

"Well, you see, sir," the applicant replied, "the work is a lot harder when you don't know anything about it."[31]

◆ His folks are in the iron and steel business. His mother irons and his father steals.

◆ One office has a telephone answering/recording device that instructs callers to leave their name and address and to spell any difficult words.

Early one Monday morning, when the receptionist was reviewing the weekend messages, she heard an enthusiastic young woman recite her name and address and then confidently offer, "My difficult word is reconciliation. *R-E-C-O-N-C-I-L-I-A-T-I-O-N*."[32]

◆ The salesclerk said, "This little machine will do half your work for you."

"Sounds great," the customer replied. "I'll take two."[33]

◆ An assembly line worker at Chrysler was picked for jury duty, but asked the judge to excuse him. "This is a very busy time at the plant, Your Honor, and I need to be there."

"Oh, I see," the judge said. "You're one of those folks who think you're indispensable, that Chrysler can't get along without you."

"No, sir, not at all," the worker replied. "I

know they can do just fine without me, but I don't want them to find that out."

"Excused," the judge said.[34]

◆ A man was out of work, but finally got a job in a circus, playing the part of a gorilla. Every day he soared over the circus on the trapeze, twisting, turning and chanting to the delight of the crowd.

One day he slipped and fell into the lion's cage directly below. Though unhurt by the short fall, he was frightened by the lion and began to scream. "Help! Help! Get me out of here!" The lion came up to him and said, "Be quiet, you fool, or we'll both lose our jobs."

◆ Definition of an expert: an ordinary person away from home.

—Bill Bright

◆ A car in New York City carries a warning sign: "Don't hit me. My daughter's a lawyer."[35]

◆ Two house painters lived and worked together in a tiny little town. Business was difficult, as jobs were scarce and paint was expensive. Then one of the painters came up with an idea of how to decrease costs and increase business. They could water down all of the paint. This would give them more paint for their money; it would make it easier to spread the paint; and it would decrease the expected life of a job, so business naturally would increase over time.

The painter convinced his partner to go along with the idea. Soon they were thinning out paint and spreading it on houses. Business increased and profits rolled in.

Several times the second painter approached the first with misgivings. "I can't do this anymore. It's wrong; it's cheating the customer and I feel guilty." Each time, the first painter reminded him of all the money they were making and convinced him to keep on watering down the paint.

As his guilt feelings mounted, the second painter started to have bad dreams. Night after night they got worse and worse until one night, in the middle of his worst nightmare of all, the light on his ceiling flashed on. He woke up with a bolt and sat straight up in bed. Then he heard a deep booming voice thundering from above, "REPAINT, YOU THINNER! REPAINT."

—Karl H. Mülle

The following is adapted from a notice on our office bulletin board (source unknown):

NEW SICK LEAVE POLICY

SICKNESS: No excuse. We no longer will accept your doctor's statement; if you are able to go to the doctor, you are able to come to work.

LEAVE OF ABSENCE (for an operation): We no longer will allow this practice. We wish to discourage any thoughts that you may need an operation. As long as you are employed here, you will need all of whatever you have and should not consider having anything removed. We hired you as you are, and to have anything removed certainly would make you less than we bargained for.

Additionally, too much time is being spent in the restroom. In the future, we will go to the restroom in alphabetical order. For instance, those whose names begin with "A" will go from 8 A.M. to 8:05 A.M., "B" will go from 8:05 to 8:10 A.M., and so on. If you are unable to go at your time, you will need to wait until the day when your turn comes again.

DEATH (other than your own): This is no excuse. You can do nothing for them, and we are sure that someone else in a lesser position can attend to the arrangements. If the funeral can be held in late afternoon, however, we will be glad to let you off one hour early, provided that your share of work is ahead enough to keep the job going in your absence.

DEATH (your own): This will be accepted as an excuse, but we would like a two-week notice, as we feel it is your duty to teach someone else your job.

NOTES

Chapter 1
You Can Use
Humor Successfully!

1. John C. Pollock, *A Foreign Devil in China* (Minneapolis: World Wide Publications, 1971), p. 51.

Chapter 2
Why We All Need Humor

1. Prov. 17:22.
2. Leslie B. Flynn, *Serve Him With Joy* (Wheaton, Ill.: Key Publishers, 1960), p. 43
3. Ibid.
4. Ibid., p.55, a.
5. *How's Your Sense of Humor?* (New York: Good Reading Rack Service Division, Koster-Dana Corp., 1962), p. 5.
6. Albert Rapp, *The Origins of Wit and Humor* (New York: E.P. Dutton & Co., 1951), p. 168.
7. Ibid.
8. J. J. Walsh, *Laughter and Health* (New York and London: Appleton, 1928), p. 58; in Rapp, Origins of Wit, p. 170.
9. Bob Phillips, *A Humorous Look at Love and Marriage* (Eugene, Ore.: Harvest House, 1981), p. 93, a.
10. Ibid., pp. 86-87, a.

11. Bob Phillips, *The Last of the Good Clean Joke Books* (Eugene, Ore.: Harvest House, 1981), pp. 33-34, a.
12. Bob Phillips, *More Good Clean Jokes* (Irvine, Calif.: Harvest House, 1974), p. 47, a.
13. Contributed by Shirley Read to *Reader's Digest*, June 1982, p. 79, a.
14. James F. Engel, Ph.D., *Contemporary Christian Communications* (Nashville, Tenn.: Thomas Nelson Publishers, 1979).
15. *Pulpit Digest;* in *Reader's Digest*, August 1981, p. 88, a.
16. *Dixie Yarns;* in *Reader's Digest*, July 1981, p. 114, a.
17. *Tulsa World; in Reader's Digest*, January 1982, p. 83, a.
18. Phillips, *Last of Good Clean Joke Books,* p. 43, a.
19. Bob Phillips, *The World's Greatest Collection of Clean Jokes* (Santa Ana, Calif.: Vision House Publishers, 1974), pp. 150-51, a.
20. Flynn, *Serve Him*, p. 52.

Chapter 3
Some Keys to Natural One-on-One Humor

1. Diane Kanner, "Interview: Jonathan Winters," *PSA Magazine,* December 1983, p. 76.
2. Prov. 25:20, TLB.
3. Rom. 12:15.
4. Prov. 31:25.
5. Linda Raney Wright, *Staying on Top When Things Go Wrong* (Wheaton, Ill.: Tyndale House Publishers, 1983), a.

6. Kanner, "Interview: Jonathan Winters," p. 75.
7. Gary Hanauer, "The Joke's on Them," *Continental Magazine,* November/ December 1983, p. 44.

Chapter 4
Spontaneity in Humor

1. Dr. Laurence J. Peter and Bill Dana, "Humor in Power—How to Become a Person of Wit," *New Woman,* September 1983, p. 94.
2. Ibid.
3. Ibid., pp. 94, 98.
4. Contributed by A.P. to *Reader's Digest*, January 1984, p. 111, a.
5. Contributed by Rosa A. Gil to *Reader's Digest*, March 1984, p. 88, a.
6. Linda Rancy Wright, *Staying on Top When Things Go Wrong* (Wheaton, Ill.: Tyndale House Publishers, 1983).

Chapter 5
Why Funny Stories Are Funny

1. Leslie B. Flynn, *Serve Him with Joy* (Wheaton, Ill.: Key Publishers, 1960), p. 15.
2. "Peterborough" in *The Daily Telegraph* (London); in *Reader's Digest*, January 1982, p. 135, a.
3. *Reader's Digest*, May 1982, p. 79, a.
4. Ralph L. Woods, *The Modern Handbook of Humor* (New York: McGraw-Hill, 1967), p. 364, a.

5. Flynn, *Serve Him,* p. 26, a.
6. Martin Grotjahn, MD, FAPA, *Beyond Laughter* (New York: McGraw-Hill, 1957), pp. 255-56.
7. *How's Your Sense of Humor?* (New York: Good Reading Rack Service Division, Koster-Dana Corp., 1962), p. 7.
8. Ibid., p. 10.
9. Isaac Asimov, *Isaac Asimov's Treasury of Humor* (Boston: Houghton Mifflin Co., 1971), p. 68.
10. Steve Allen, *More Funny People* (Briarcliffe Manor, N.Y.: Stein and Day Publishers, 1982), p. 307.
11. Tal D. Bonham, *The Treasury of Clean Jokes* (Nashville, Tenn.: Broadman Press, 1981), p. 22, a.
12. Bennett Cerf, *Laugh Day* (Doubleday); in *Reader's Digest,* April 1982, p. 123, a.
13. Woods, *Modern Handbook,* p. 82, a.
14. Maurice Zolotow, "Here's Steve Martin . . . Maybe," *Reader's Digest,* October 1981, p. 149.
15. Steve Benson in *Fun Fare* (Pleasantville, N.Y.: The Reader's Digest Association, 1949), p. 276, a.
16. Asimov, *Treasury of Humor,* p. 2.
17. Bonham, *Treasury of Clean Jokes,* p. 154, a.
18. Bernie Allen, quoted by Norton Mockridge, United Feature Syndicate; in *Reader's Digest,* January 1983, pp. 77-78.
19. Bob Phillips, *The Last of the Good Clean Joke Books* (Eugene, Ore.: Harvest House, 1981), p. 65, a.
20. Jim Whitehead, quoted by Seymour Rosenberg in Spartanburg, S.C., *Herald;* in *Reader's Digest,* May 1982, p. 79, a.
21. Phillips, *Last of Good Clean Joke Books,* p. 51, a.
22. Bob Phillips, *The All American Joke Book* (Irvine,

Calif.: Harvest House, 1976), p. 111, a.

23. Allen, *More Funny People,* pp. 68, 77.

Chapter 6
Finding Good Material

1. Steve Allen, *More Funny People* (Briarcliffe Manor, N.Y.: Stein and Day Publishers, 1982), p. 172.
2. Steve Allen, *Funny People* (Briarcliffe Manor, N.Y.: Stein and Day Publishers, 1982), p. 2.
3. Ibid., a.
4. Ibid.
5. Herman Silas, quoted by Neil Morgan in San Diego *Tribune;* in *Reader's Digest,* December 1983, p. 140, a.
6. Irving Wallace, David Wallechinsky, Amy Wallace, Sylvia Wallace, *The Book of Lists 2* (New York: Bantam Books, 1981), p. 494, a.
7. Ibid., p. 496.
8. Ibid., p. 495.
9. Contributed by Mrs. G. Tubb to *Reader's Digest,* January 1983, p. 20, a.
10. David L. Bradley (Keene, NY) in *Reader's Digest,* June 1983, p. 82, a.
11. Wallace, et al., *Books of Lists,* p. 316, a.
12. Ibid., p. 317, a.
13. Barbara Seuling, *You Can't Eat Peanuts in Church and Other Little-Known Laws* (Garden City, N.Y.: Doubleday, 1975), a.

Chapter 7
More Good Sources of Humor

1. "Trivia Topics: 2080 AD," *Saturday Evening Post,* May/June 1980, p. 22, a.

2. "American," *Time*, 5 April 1982, p. 27.

3. Eugene Carlson in *The Wall Street Journal;* in *Reader's Digest,* July 1983, p. 17.

4. The five previous ads taken from Louis Untermeyer, ed., *A Treasury of Laughter* (New York.: Simon & Schuster, 1946), pp. 601-604.

5. The four previous ads taken from Ralph L. Woods, *The Modern Handbook of Humor* (New York: McGraw-Hill, 1967), p. 65.

6. The four previous boners taken from Untermeyer, *Treasury of Laughter,* pp. 601-604.

7. The three previous boners taken from Woods, *Modern Handbook,* pp. 264-65.

8. Edward Moser, *Globe and Mail* (Toronto); in *Have a Good Day* (Wheaton, Ill.: Tyndale House Publishers, July 1983).

9. The three previous items taken from Untermeyer, *Treasury of Laughter,* pp. 601-604, a.

10. Isaac Asimov, *Isaac Asimov's Treasury of Humor* (Boston: Houghton Mifflin Co., 1971), p. 150.

11. George Plimpton, "How to Make a Speech," *Time,* 14 September 1981, pp. 92-93.

Chapter 8
Knowing Your Audience

1. Ralph L. Woods, *The Modern Handbook of Humor* (New York: McGraw-Hill, 1967), p. 410, a.
2. "How's Your Sense of Humor?" (New York: Good Reading Rack Service Division, Koster-Dana Corp., 1962), p. 13.
3. John Pollock, *Billy Graham: The Authorized Biography* (Grand Rapids, Mich.: Zondervan, 1966) p. 122.
4. Woods, *Modern Handbook,* p. 517, a.
5. Ibid., p. 521, a.
6. Winston K. Pendleton, *Complete Speaker's Galaxy of Funny Stories, Jokes and Anecdotes* (Parker); in *Reader's Digest,* February 1983, p. 70, a.
7. Steve Allen, *More Funny People* (Briarcliffe Manor, N.Y.: Stein and Day Publishers, 1982), p. 159.
8. Wendell Trogdon in *Indianapolis News*; in *Reader's Digest,* April 1981, p. 137, a.
9. Bill Farmer in St. Paul *Dispatch*; in *Reader's Digest,* April 1981, p. 137.
10. Art Buchwald in Los Angeles *Times*; in *Reader's Digest,* April 1982, p. 74.
11. T. J. McInerney in GLOBE; in *Reader's Digest,* February 1982, p. 79, a.
12. Woods, *Modern Handbook,* p. 103, a.
13. Ibid., p. 104, a.
14. Steve Allen, *Funny People* (Briarcliffe Manor, N.Y.: Stein and Day Publishers, 1981), p. 211.
15. Allen, *More Funny People,* pp. 35-36.
16. Isaac Asimov, *Isaac Asimov's Treasury of Humor*

(Boston: Houghton Mifflin Co., 1971), p. 192.

17. Allen, *More Funny People,* p. 33.

Chapter 9
Delivering Your Story With a Punch

1. Ralph L. Woods, *The Modern Handbook of Humor* (New York: McGraw-Hill, 1967), p. 461, a.

2. Ibid., p. 69, a.

3. Steve Allen, *More Funny People* (Briarcliffe Manor, N.Y.: Stein and Day Publishers, 1982), p. 159.

4. Gerald Clarke, "Barbs for the Queen (and Others)," *Time,* 11 April 1983, p. 85.

5. Fun Fare (Pleasantville, N.Y.: The Reader's Digest Association, 1949), p. 211, a.

6. Allen, *More Funny People,* p. 165.

7. Ibid.

8. Alex F. Osborn in *Fun Fare*, p. 76, a.

9. Contributed by Steve Deardorff to *Reader's Digest*, November 1982, p. 281, a.

10. Bob Phillips, *The All American Joke Book* (Irvine, Calif.: Harvest House, 1976), p. 105, a.

11. Allen, *More Funny People,* pp. 80-81.

12. Woods, Modern Handbook, p. 483, a.

13. George Plimpton, "How to Make a Speech," TIME, 14 September, 1981, pp. 92-93, a.

14. Woods, *Modern Handbook,* p. 455, a.

15. Ibid., a.

16. Ibid., p. 240, a.

17. Leslie B. Flynn, *Serve Him With Joy* (Wheaton, Ill.: Key Publishers, 1960), pp. 53-54, a.

Chapter 10
What To Do When It Bombs

1. Ralph L. Woods, *The Modern Handbook of Humor* (New York: McGraw-Hill, 1967), p. 215, a.
2. Ibid., p. 442, a.
3. Ibid., p. 425, a.
4. David Wallechinsky, Irving Wallace, Amy Wallace, *The Book of Lists* (New York: Bantam Books, 1978), pp. 469-70.
5. Woods, *Modern Handbook,* p. 451, a.
6. George Plimpton, "How to Make a Speech, *Time,* 14 September, 1981, pp. 92-92.

Chapter 11
Our Self Concept:
How To Live With Yourself and Like It

Special Note: The subtitle for this chapter, "How to Live With Yourself and Like It," is borrowed from our good friend Dick Purnell, who uses it as the title of one of his very successful campus talks on self-concept.

1. Ralph L. Woods, *The Modern Handbook of Humor* (New York: McGraw-Hill, 1967), p. 183, a.
2. Steve Allen, *More Funny People* (Briarcliffe Manor, N.Y.: Stein and Day Publishers, 1982), p. 214.
3. Steve Allen, *Funny People* (Briarcliffe Manor, N.Y.: Stein and Day Publishers, 1982), p. 214.
4. Gerald Clarke, "Cuddly Dudley, The Wee Wonder," *Time,* 21 February 1983, p. 70.

5. Ibid.
6. Ibid.
7. Ibid.
8. Illustration adapted from Zig Ziglar, *See You at the Top* (Gretna, La.: Pelican Publishing Co., 1979), p. 46, a.
9. Robert Schuller, mailing dated July 27, 1982, reporting on the Gallup Poll that he commissioned.
10. Henry Charles Sutter in *Fun Fare* (Pleasantville, N.Y.: The Reader's Digest Association, 1949), p. 60, a.
11. O. H. Howrer, "Sin, the Lesser of Two Evils," quoted in Henry R. Brandt, Ph.D., *The Struggle for Peace* (Wheaton, Ill.: Scripture Press, 1965).
12. William Glasser, M.D., *Reality Therapy* (New York: Harper and Row, 1965), p. 7.
13. James C. Coleman, *Abnormal Psychology and Modern Life,* Glenview, Ill.: Scott, Foresman and Co., 1964), p. 72.
14. Ibid., p. 160.
15. "A Scientific Report on What Hope Does for Man" (New York: New York State Heart Assembly); in S. I. McMillen, M.D., *None of These Diseases* (Old Tappan, N.J.: Fleming H. Revell Co., 1968), p. 110.
16. "Billoc of St. Petersburg," quoted by Dick Bothwell in St. Petersburg *Times*; in *Reader's Digest,* April 1981, p. 77, a.
17. Bob Phillips, *The World's Greatest Collection of Clean Jokes* (Santa Ana, Calif.: Vision House Publishers, 1974), p. 78, a.
18. Allen, *Funny People,* p. 147.
19. Gene Fowler, *Schnozzola, The Story of Jimmy Durante;* quoted in Allen, *Funny People,* pp. 147-48.

20. Contributed by Lorraine Henley to *Reader's Digest,* February 1983, pp. 17, 19, a.
21. Woods, *Modern Handbook,* p. 196, a.
22. Gerald Clarke, "Barbs for the Queen (and Others)," *Time,* 11 April , 1983, p. 88.
23. Allen, *Funny People,* p. 231.
24. Ibid., p. 211.
25. Leo Rosten, "I Remember Groucho," *Reader's Digest,* November 1982, pp. 105-106.
26. Allen, *More Funny People,* p. 281.
27. Richard Schnickel, "Sellers Strikes Again," *Time,* 3 March 1980, pp. 66-67.
28. *Reader's Digest,* June 1982, p. 120.
29. David Gelman with George Hackett, "Making Fun for Profit," *Newsweek,* 25 April 1983, p. 70.
30. Prov. 14:13.
31. Eccles. 2:2.

Chapter 12
Mirror, Mirror . . .

1. Bob Phillips, *The World's Greatest Collection of Clean Jokes* (Santa Ana, Calif.: Vision House, 1974), p. 7, a.
2. *This Week Magazine,* quoted in *Fun Fare* (Pleasant-ville, N.Y.: The Reader's Digest Association, 1949), p. 262.
3. Contributed by Dan Bell to *Reader's Digest,* December 1983, p. 82, a.
4. Kenneth Pelletier, "Mind as Healer, Mind as Slayer," *Psychology Today,* February 1977, p. 40.
5. Linda Raney Wright, *Staying on Top When Things Go*

Wrong (Wheaton, Ill.: Tyndale House Publishers, 1983).

6. John 3:16.

7. John 10:10b.

8. Josh McDowell, *More Than a Carpenter* (Wheaton, Ill.: Tyndale House, 1977). *Evidence That Demands a Verdict* (San Bernardino, Calif.: Campus Crusade for Christ, 1972).

9. Louis Untermeyer, ed. *A Treasury of Laughter* (New York: Simon & Schuster, 1946), p. 84, a.

10. Rom. 3:23.

11. Rom. 6:23.

12. Rom. 5:8.

13. 2 Cor. 5:21, TLB.

14. See Eph. 2:8,9.

15. Rev. 3:20.

16. Ps. 103:12.

17. See Heb. 10:17.

18. 1 John 5:11-13.

19. Phil. 4:19.

20. Matt. 6:31,33.

21. Rom. 8:38,39.

22. Matt. 24:30.

23. 2 Cor. 5:20.

24. Heb. 13:5.

25. Matt. 28:20.

26. 1 John 1:9.

27. Eph. 5:18.

28. 1 John 5:14,15.

Chapter 13
Divine Antidotes

1. Dick Van Dyke, *Faith, Hope and Hilarity* (New York: Doubleday, 1970).
2. Bob Phillips, *The World's Greatest Collection of Clean Jokes* (Santa Ana, Calif.: Vision House Publishers, 1974), pp. 46-47, a.
3. Prov. 17:22.
4. Prov. 6:6-11.
5. Acts 12:18.
6. Acts 19:23.
7. 1 Kings 18:27, TLB.
8. 1 Sam. 15:13,14.
9. Luke 7:31-35.
10. Matt. 7:1-5.
11. Matt. 23.24.
12. Matt. 23:25,26.
13. Mark 4:21.
14. Matt. 5:16.
15. Elton Trueblood, *The Humor of Christ* (New York: Harper & Row, 1964).
16. Matt. 12:36.
17. Leslie B. Flynn, *Serve Him with Joy* (Wheaton, Ill.: Key Publishers, 1960), pp. 66-67.
18. Eph. 5:3,4.
19. Flynn, *Serve Him,* p. 59.
20. Col. 4:6.

Chapter 14
How's Your Love Life?

1. Bob Phillips, *A Humorous Look at Love and Marriage* (Eugene, Ore.: Harvest House, 1981), p. 37, a.
2. Ibid., p. 38, a.
3. Bob Phillips, *The World's Greatest Collection of Heavenly Humor,* Eugene, Ore.: Harvest House, 1982, p. 4, a.
4. Phillips, *Love and Marriage,* pp. 11-12, a.
5. Ibid., p. 111, a.
6. Kirk Stiles in *Colliers*; in *Fun Fare* (Pleasantville, N.Y.: The Reader's Digest Association, 1949), p. 260, a.
7. Bob Phillips, *More Good Clean Jokes* (Irvine, Calif.: Harvest House, 1974), p. 124, a.
8. Phillips, *Love and Marriage,* p. 28, a.
9. Ralph L. Woods, *The Modern Handbook of Humor* (New York: McGraw-Hill, 1967), p. 275, a.
10. Bob Phillips, *Lots O' Laughs* (Old Tappan, N.J.: Fleming H. Revell Co., 1976), p. 59, a.
11. Tal D. Bonham, *The Treasury of Clean Jokes* (Nashville, Tenn.: Broadman Press, 1981), p. 156, a.
12. Phillips, *Love and Marriage,* p. 15, a.
13. Ibid., p. 12, a.
14. Ibid., a.
15. Ibid., p. 26, a.
16. Woods, *Modern Handbook,* p. 283, a.
17. Ibid., a.
18. Phillips, *Love and Marriage,* p. 112, a.
19. Ibid., p. 11, a.

20. Ibid., p. 14, a.
21. Dick Bothwell in St. Petersburg *Times*; in *Reader's Digest,* January 1983, p. 14.
22. Bennett Cerf, *Anything for a Laugh* (Grosset & Dunlap) in *Fun Fare*, p. 141, a.
23. Michael Small in *People*; in *Reader's Digest,* September 1983, p. 104.
24. Contributed by Robert M. Putnam to *Reader's Digest,* September 1983, p. 118, a.
25. Contributed by Mrs. Earl Davenport to *Reader's Digest*, February 1982, p. 126, a.
26. Mary Callahan in *Globe*; in *Reader's Digest*, September 1982, p. 110, a.
27. Woods, *Modern Handbook,* p. 362, a.
28. Bob Phillips, *The All American Joke Book,* (Irvine, Calif.: Harvest House, 1976), p. 79, a.
29. Phillips, *Love and Marriage,* p. 51, a.
30. Phillips, *More Good Clean Jokes,* p. 53, a.
31. Contributed by William F. Merten to *Reader's Digest,* October 1983, p. 97.
32. Woods, *Modern Handbook,* p. 242, a.
33. Bob Phillips, *The Last of the Good Clean Joke Books* (Eugene, Ore.: Harvest House, 1981), p. 88, a.
34. Phillips, *Love and Marriage,* p. 104, a.
35. Ibid., p. 139, a.
36. Montreal *Star* in *Fun Fare*, pp. 268-69, a.
37. *Woman's Home Companion in Fun Fare,* p. 28, a.
38. Contributed by Peggy Doonehoo to *Reader's Digest*, April 1983, p. 175, a.
39. Phillips, *Last of Good Clean Joke Books,* p. 101, a.
40. Lane Olinghouse in Reader's Digest, April 1981, p. 93, a.

41. Contributed by Wilna Botha to *Reader's Digest*, March 1982, p. 242, a.
42. Woods, *Modern Handbook,* p. 169, a.
43. Helen Rowland in Ibid., p. 287, a.
44. Woods, *Modern Handbook,* p. 301, a.
45. AP in *Fun Fare*, p. 111, a.
46. Louis Untermeyer, ed., *A Treasury of Laughter* (New York: Simon and Schuster, 1946), p. 254, a.
47. St. Louis *Globe-Democrat*; in *Reader's Digest*, October 1982, p. 111, a

Chapter 15
Heavenly Humor

1. Bob Phillips, *The World's Greatest Collection of Clean Jokes* (Santa Ana, Calif.: Vision House Publishers, 1974), pp. 31-32, a.
2. Ralph L. Woods, *The Modern Handbook of Humor* (New York: McGraw-Hill, 1967), p. 420, a.
3. Ibid., p. 421, a.
4. *Reader's Digest,* November 1983, p. 48, a.
5. Bob Phillips, *The Last of the Good Clean Joke* Books (Eugene, Ore.: Harvest House, 1981), p. 11, a.
6. Contributed by Bob Bonebrake to *Reader's Digest*, June 1982, p. 77, a.
7. Bob Phillips, *Lots O' Laughs* (Old Tappan, N.J.: Fleming H. Revell Co., 1976), p. 38, a.
8. "The Sign" in *Fun Fare* (Pleasantville, N.Y.: The Reader's Digest Association, 1949), p. 303, a.
9. Woods, *Modern Handbook,* p. 422, a.

10. Tal D. Bonham,*The Treasury of Clean Jokes* (Nashville,Tenn.: Broadman Press, 1981), pp. 140-41, a.
11. Ibid., p. 96, a.
12. Dr. Joseph L. Cochrane in *Fun Fare*, p. 75, a.
13. Woods, Modern Handbook, p. 444, a.
14. Ibid., p. 421, a.
15. *The Clergy Journal* in *Reader's Digest,* April 1981, pp. 92-93, a.
16. Woods, *Modern Handbook,* p. 410, a.
17. Ibid., p. 424, a.
18. Ibid., a.
19. Contributed by Brad Lohr and Helen Lorber to *Reader's Digest*, October 1983, p. 116, a.
20. Woods, *Modern Handbook,* p. 442, a.
21. Contributed by W.N.P. to *Reader's Digest,* October 1982, p. 110, a.

Chapter 16
More Good Clean Jokes and Stories

1. Ralph L. Woods, *The Modern Handbook of Humor* (New York: McGraw-Hill, 1967), p. 484, a.
2. Ibid., p. 486, a.
3. Ibid., p. 240, a.
4. *Fun Fare* (Plcasantville, N.Y.: The Reader's Digest Association, 1949), p. 88, a.
5. Woods, *Modern Handbook,* p. 65, a.
6. Ibid., p. 265, a.
7. Ibid., a.
8. Ibid., p. 266.

9. Roger Rosenblatt, "Oops! How's That Again?," *Time*, 30 March 1981, p. 85.
10. Ibid.
11. Ibid., a.
12. Bob Phillips, *The World's Greatest Collection of Clean Jokes* (Santa Ana, Calif.: Vision House Publishers, 1974), p. 82, a.
13. Louis De V. Day, Jr., *Pennomena;* in *Reader's Digest*, April 1981, p. 49, a.
14. Phillips, *Collection of Clean Jokes,* pp.82-83, a.
15. Contributed by Cindy Massie to *Reader's Digest*, June 1982, p. 17, a.
16. *Fun Fare,* p. 29, a.
17. *News from Clemson University;* in *Reader's Digest*, February 1977, p. 172, a.
18. W. H. Auden in Woods, *Modern Handbook,* p. 195.
19. The four previous jokes are from D. J. Arneson, *The Original Preppy Joke Book* (New York: Dell, 1981), a.
20. Scott Beach, quoted by Herb Caen in San Francisco *Chronicle*; in *Reader's Digest*, January 1982, p. 33, a.
21. Bob Phillips, *Lots O' Laughs* (Old Tappan, N.J.; Fleming H. Revell Co., 1976), p. 64, a.
22. *Everywoman's Magazine;* in *Fan Fare,* p. 28, a.
23. On the Record, *Time,* 14 July 1980, p. 67.
24. Phillips, *Collection of Clean Jokes,* p. 98, a.
25. Contributed by Debra Schneider to *Reader's Digest*, April 1983, p. 10, a.
26. Arneson, *Original Preppy Jokebook,* p. 27, a.
27. Tal D. Bonham, *The Treasury of Clean Jokes* (Nashville, Tenn.: Broadman Press, 1981), p. 157, a.

28. Bob Phillips, *The World's Greatest Collection of Heavenly Humor* (Eugene, Ore.: Harvest House, 1982), p. 14, a.

29. Woods, *Modern Handbook,* p. 444.

30. *Brief Cases,* March 1973, a.

31. Winston K. Pendleton, *2121 Funny Stories and How to Tell Them* (Bethany); in *Reader's Digest,* August 1982, p. 65, a.

32. Vyto Kapocius, quoted by Alex Thien in Milwaukee *Sentinel*; in *Reader's Digest,* September 1982, p. 111, a.

33. *Anecdotes For All Occasions* (Pleasantville, N.Y.: The Reader's Digest Association, 1972), pp. 27-28, a.

34. Gene Carr cartoon in *The Saturday Evening Post*; in *Fun Fare,* p. 207, a.

35. Church newsletter, a.

36. "Tit Bits," in *Fun Fare,* p. 307, a.

37. Contributed by Jean M. Chmurski to *Reader's Digest,* July 1983, p. 14, a.

38. Steve Allen, *More Funny People* (Briarcliffe Manor, N.Y.: Stein and Day Publishers, 1982), p. 15, a.

39. Arthur Bloch, *Murphy's Law—and Other Reasons Why Things Go Wrong* (Los Angeles: Price/Stern/Sloan Publishers, 1977); in David Wallechinsky, Irving Wallace, Amy Wallace, *The Book of Lists* (New York: Bantam Books, 1978), pp. 480-81.

40. Arthur Bloch, *Murphy's Law, Book Two: More Reasons Why Things Go Wrong*; in Irving Wallace, David Wallechinsky, Amy Wallace, Sylvia Wallace, *The Book of Lists 2* (New York: Bantam Books, 1981), pp. 489-90.

41. P. C. R. Hampshire, quoted in *Evening Standard*

(London); in *Reader's Digest*, November 1983, p. 104.

42. *Anecdotes For All Occasions*, p. 8, a.
43. Woods, *Modern Handbook*, p. 58, a.
44. Phillips, *Lots O' Laughs*, p. 38, a.
45. *Fun Fare*, p. 5, a.
46. Phillips, *Collection of Clean Jokes*, p. 141, a.
47. On the Record, *Time,* 19 April 1982, p. 57.
48. Tal D. Bonham, The Treasury of Clean Jokes (Nashville, Tenn.: Broadman Press, 1981), p. 27, a.
49. Woods, *Modern Handbook*, p. 55, a.
50. Ibid., p. 28, a.
51. Ibid., p. 385, a.
52. Fred R. Fritch in *Fun Fare*, p. 263, a.

Chapter 17
Still More Good Jokes and Stories

1. Dick Niehoff, quoted by Alex Thien in Milwaukee *Sentinel*; in *Reader's Digest*, January 1982, p. 82, a.
2. Contributed by John Galbreath to *Reader's Digest*, August 1982, p. 65, a.
3. Ralph L. Woods, *The Modern Handbook of Humor* (New York: McGraw-Hill, 1967), p. 317, a.
4. Lenny Anderson in Seattle *Times*; in *Reader's Digest*, November 1982, p. 138, a.
5. *Reader's Nutshell*, in *Reader's Digest*, August 1983, p. 118.
6. MaryWareDennett in *Fun Fare* (Pleasantville, N.Y.: The Reader's Digest Association, 1949), p. 207, a.
7. John Adams in Bellevill, Wis., *Recorder*; quoted by

Jay Scriba in Milwaukee *Journal;* in *Reader's Digest*, April 1981, p. 77, a.

8. Roger Rosenblatt, "Oops! How's That Again?", *Time*, 30 March 1981, p. 85, a.

9. Louis Untermeyer, ed., *A Treasury of Laughter* (New York: Simon & Schuster, 1946), p. 85, a.

10. *Quote Magazine*; in *Reader's Digest*, November 1982, p. 131.

11. Lichty and Wagner, Field Newspaper Syndicate; in *Reader's Digest*, March 1983, p. 32, a.

12. Contributed by Marian Newton to *Reader's Digest*, November 1983, p. 44, a.

13. Hugh Newton in *Liberty*; in *Fun Fare,* p. 84, a.

14. Andrew A. Rooney, *A Few Minutes with Andy Rooney* (New York: Warner Books, 1982), p. 196, a.

15. Bob Phillips, *Lots O' Laughs* (Old Tappan, N.J.: Fleming H. Revell Co., 1976), p. 36, a.

16. Erma Bombeck, *At Wit's End* (Field Enterprises, Inc.); in A. Duane Liftin, *Public Speaking for Christians* (Grand Rapids, Mich.: Baker Book House, 1982).

17. Norman B. Rohrer, *Leighton Ford, A Life Surprised* (Wheaton, Ill.: Tyndale House Publishers, 1981), p. 11.

18. Woods, *Modern Handbook*, p. 449, a.

19. Ibid., p. 447, a.

20. Howard Teichmann, *George S. Kaufman* (Althencum); in *Reader's Digest*, February 1983, p. 26, a.

21. George Plimpton, "How to Make a Speech," *Time*, 14 September 1981, pp. 92-93. Advertisement copyright 1981, International Paper Company.

22. Leonard Lyons in *Fun Fare*, p. 230.

23. *Grit*; in *Reader's Digest*, January 1982, p. 83, a.

24. George F. Will in *Newsweek*; in *Reader's Digest*, December 1983, p. 119, a.

25. Shelby Friedman in *Reader's Digest*, May 1981, p. 93, a.

26. Woods, *Modern Handbook*, p. 362, a.

27. *PDQ*, 1 April 1981, a.

28. Contributed by Michael A. Colucci to *Reader's Digest*, November 1983, p. 60, a.

29. Tal D. Bonham, *The Treasury of Clean Jokes* (Nashville, Tenn.: Broadman Press, 1981), p. 34, a.

30. Phillips, *Lots O' Laughs*, p. 65, a.

31. Willow Grove, Penn., *Guide*; in *Fun Fare*, p. 62, a.

32. Contributed by Connie Green to *Reader's Digest*, November 1982, p. 38, a.

33. *Parts Pups*; in *Reader's Digest*, April 1982, p. 79, a.

34. Woods, *Modern Handbook*, p. 10, a.

35. Evelyn Mocbeichel in New York *Sunday News Magazine*; in *Reader's Digest*, April 1983, p. 69, a.

ABOUT THE AUTHORS

Rusty Wright is an author and traveling speaker. He was born in Miami, Florida, and educated at the Choate School, Wallingford, Connecticut. He has a bachelor of science degree in psychology from Duke University and a master of arts degree from the International School of Theology. A popular speaker, he lectures each year to thousands of students, faculty and laypersons in major universities and cities across the nation. He has spoken on over 170 campuses in the United States, Canada and Europe and has also lectured in Asia, Africa, Australia and South America. He is a member of two national honor societies and the Lambda Chi Alpha fraternity. His articles have appeared in numerous periodicals and he has coauthored four books, including *How to Unlock the Secrets of Love, Sex and Marriage*.

Linda Raney Wright was born in San Diego, California, and has an A.B. degree in rhetoric from the University of California at Berkeley. In addition to lecturing in various campuses and cities across the United States and on six continents, she is also a writer. Her articles have appeared in *Ladies' Home Journal*, *Decision* and many other magazines and newspapers. Her eight books include *Good Days, Bad Days*; *A Cord of Three Strands*; *Raising Children*; and *Staying on Top When Things Go Wrong*. Linda was featured as one of twenty leading women in the book, *Why Doesn't Somebody Do Something?*, by Daisy Hepburn (Victor).

The Wrights have been frequent guests on television talk shows in cities around the nation.

ACKNOWLEDGMENTS

Any major project involves the contribution of numerous individuals. This one is no exception. We wish to thank:

Several friends and co-workers who contributed jokes and stories. Their names are listed after the material they supplied.

The thousand of jokesters, professional and amateur, who have tickled our ribs and passed down stories over the years. Though we faithfully tried to give credit where due, this was often difficult, and we apologize if we missed anyone. Frequently, jokes and stories become part of folklore, and no one knows who first told them. Some material, however, can be documented from books and magazines. In those cases, we have listed sources in the notes at the end of the book. Adapted material is identified by the letter a at the end of the appropriate note.

Carol Puckett, Brenda Read and Cheryl Henderson for typing the manuscript and revisions.

Tim Downs, Bob Horner and Tim Timmons for their valuable critiques.

Our present and former staff, David Docter, Bruce Hedrick, Hope Hedrick, and Carole Olson, for their faithful help in running our operations and freeing us to write.

LIKE BIBLE TRIVIA?

Then check out these great books from Barbour Publishing!

The Bible Detective by Carol Smith
Solve mysteries posed by a mixed-up story using biblical characters, places, and quotations.
ISBN 1-57748-838-5/Paperback/224 pages/$2.97

My Final Answer by Paul Kent
Thirty separate quizzes feature twelve multiple-choice questions each—and the questions get progressively harder!
ISBN 1-58660-030-3/Paperback/256 pages/$2.97

Bible IQ by Rayburn Ray
One hundred sections of ten questions each—and a systematic scoring system to tell you just how well you did.
ISBN 1-57748-837-7/Paperback/256 pages/$2.97

Test Your Bible Knowledge by Carl Shoup
Over 1,400 multiple-choice questions to test your mettle, tickle your funny bone, and tantalize your intellect.
ISBN 1-55748-541-0/Paperback/224 pages/$2.97

Fun Facts About the Bible by Robyn Martins
Challenging and intriguing Bible trivia—expect some of the answers to surprise you!
ISBN 1-55748-897-5/Paperback/256 pages/$2.97
